Windows Server 2016 Administration Fundamentals

Deploy, set up, and deliver network services with Windows Server while preparing for the MTA 98-365 exam and pass it with ease

Bekim Dauti

BIRMINGHAM - MUMBAI

Windows Server 2016 Administration Fundamentals

First published: December 2017

Production reference: 1051217

Published by Packt Publishing Ltd.
Livery Place
35 Livery Street
Birmingham
B3 2PB, UK.

ISBN 978-1-78862-656-9

www.packtpub.com

Credits

Author
Bekim Dauti

Reviewer
Ed Tittel

Commissioning Editor
Vijin Boricha

Acquisition Editor
Rahul Nair

Content Development Editor
Nikita Pawar

Technical Editor
Manish D Shanbhag

Copy Editor
Safis Editing

Project Coordinator
Judie Jose

Proofreader
Safis Editing

Indexer
Aishwarya Gangawane

Graphics
Tania Dutta

Production Coordinator
Aparna Bhagat

Foreword

Technology is powerful, but only if you know how to use it, and so is certification, it's the best way to show others what you know.

Windows Server 2016 has security built-in at the start; it's modern and ready for the cloud when you are and enables application innovation with little or no code changes, and this book ensures that you get the most out of it.

Microsoft Technology Associate Certification is a perfect start to build a solid career, as it will help you to prove your knowledge of fundamental techniques and, in this case, knowledge about Windows Server 2016.

As a Doctor of Philosophy (PhD) holder, a University lecturer, and a Microsoft Certified Trainer (MCT) for nearly two decades, I can happily recommend this book as it covers MTA 98-365 as it should be, from helping you understand every important detail. The book is not just designed to give you the theoretical knowledge, it also covers how you can implement this theory in practice, and it gives you tips on how to do so. I hold many Microsoft certifications, I read many books, and I can confidently say that this book has all the basics for you to not just understand and pass the exam objectives but also gain the knowledge you need for your future.

I wish I had a book that had this all in one place when I started my career many, many years ago.

Just one more recommendation before I finish my foreword to this book: even though this book is designed to help you understand all the concepts of the exam easily, it still does not have a magic wand; you need to read, put your hands on the keyboard, and practice, as well as take many practice tests to pass the exam with flying colors.

Good luck on passing the exam.

Erdal Ozkaya

PhD, Chief Cybersecurity Advisor / MCT

Microsoft UAE

About the Author

Bekim Dauti works with computer technology, mainly with the administration of computer systems and networks, as well as vocational training in Cisco and Microsoft technologies. Bekim has a bachelor's degree from the University of Tirana and a master's from UMUC Europe, both in information technology. Additionally, he holds several IT certifications from vendors such as ECDL, MOS, CompTIA, Cisco, Microsoft, and Sun Microsystems. Bekim has contributed to over 10 computer books and dozens of articles for PC World Albanian and CIO Albania. Currently, he works as a system administrator at Kosovo Telecom JSC.

About the Reviewer

Ed Tittel is an IT industry veteran with over 30 years as a developer, manager, technical evangelist, trainer, and more. A contributor to over 100 computing books, Ed is perhaps best known for creating the Exam Cram series of short, focused study guides in 1997. Today, Ed blogs on IT certification and career topics for GoCertify.com, and oversees IT training and certification coverage for Tom's IT Pro. Ed also works as an occasional expert witness or consultant.

As always, I would like to thank my family—wife Dina and son Gregory—for putting up with my crazy and demanding writing schedule. I'd also like to thank my long-time business partner, project manager, and writer/editor extraordinaire, Kim Lindros, for keeping me on schedule and on target. Also, thanks finally to the folks at Packt and the author for inviting me along for the ride.

Customer Feedback

Thanks for purchasing this Packt book. At Packt, quality is at the heart of our editorial process. To help us improve, please leave us an honest review of this book's Amazon page at https://www.amazon.com/dp/1788626567/.

If you'd like to join our team of regular reviewers, you can e-mail us at customerreviews@packtpub.com. We award our regular reviewers with free eBooks and videos in exchange for their valuable feedback. Help us be relentless in improving our products!

www.PacktPub.com

For support files and downloads related to your book, please visit www.PacktPub.com.

Did you know that Packt offers eBook versions of every book published, with PDF and ePub files available? You can upgrade to the eBook version at www.PacktPub.com and as a print book customer, you are entitled to a discount on the eBook copy. Get in touch with us at service@packtpub.com for more details.

At www.PacktPub.com, you can also read a collection of free technical articles, sign up for a range of free newsletters and receive exclusive discounts and offers on Packt books and eBooks.

https://www.packtpub.com/mapt

Get the most in-demand software skills with Mapt. Mapt gives you full access to all Packt books and video courses, as well as industry-leading tools to help you plan your personal development and advance your career.

Why subscribe?

- Fully searchable across every book published by Packt
- Copy and paste, print, and bookmark content
- On-demand and accessible via a web browser

Table of Contents

Preface

Windows Server 2016 is the server operating system developed by Microsoft as part of the Windows NT family of operating systems, developed concurrently with Windows 10. This book is designed to get you started with Windows Server 2016, and it will prepare you for your MTA 98-365 exam. With step-by-step instructions driven by targeted, easy-to-understand graphics, you will be able to use the roles and features, functions, and quirks of Windows Server 2016.

This book begins with the basics of Windows Server 2016, which includes the installation process and basic configuration. It then moves on to roles and features, such as Active Directory, Hyper-V, Remote Access, storage, and printer. With the help of real-world examples, you will get to grips with the fundamentals of Windows Server 2016, which will help you solve difficult tasks in an easier way. Later, the book will also introduce you to maintenance and troubleshooting tasks, where with the help of best practices, you will be able to manage Windows Server 2016 with ease. Each chapter ends with a questionnaire, to ensure that you make full use of the content provided. By the end of this book, you will have enough knowledge to administer Windows Server environments.

If you feel that it is time to replace your existing way of learning with something refreshing, and entertaining at the same time, then this book is for you! It is an excellent collection of how-tos, tips and tricks, and easy ways of getting the job done in Windows Server 2016, while getting ready for your MTA 98-365 exam as well. Trust me, you will love it!

What this book covers

Chapter 1, *Introducing Windows Server*, provides you with an introduction to Windows Server 2016. Right at the beginning of this chapter, there is a recap of the most basic concepts of computer networks. So, this chapter is organized into two parts, where each part attempts to provide a concise yet complete description. Definitions such as hosts, nodes, peer-to-peer, and clients/servers are covered in the *Computer network overview* section.

Chapter 2, *Installing Windows Server*, provides you with detailed instructions for installing Windows Server 2016. The step-by-step instructions, driven by easy-to-understand graphics, show you how to master the installation of Windows Server 2016. You will quickly learn how to perform the installation process without hitting any obstacles. It is an excellent collection of how-to tips and provides information on getting the job done easily.

Chapter 3, *Post-Installation Tasks in Windows Server*, explains the steps to take in Windows Server post-installation, including managing devices and device drivers, checking the registry and the status of services, and taking care of the initial server configuration. As you may notice, this chapter is divided into three parts. Each topic is accompanied by step-by-step instructions driven by targeted, easy-to-understand graphics.

Chapter 4, *Directory Services in Windows Server*, shows you now that you have learned how to install Windows Server 2016 and run the initial server configuration, it is time to set up the very first services in your organization's IT infrastructure. With that in mind, this chapter explains directory services. Additionally, you will become familiar with **Organizational Units (OUs)**, default containers, user accounts, and groups so that you can organize the user and computer accounts in your domain.

Chapter 5, *Adding Roles to Windows Server*, provides a broader explanation of what a role is, as well as the importance of roles in determining the server's function when providing network services. You will also get to know all the roles and features that Windows Server 2016 supports. You will learn how to add roles to your server, as well as the requirements after you have added roles so that you can set up your server whenever it is required.

Chapter 6, *Virtualization with Windows Server*, teaches you about virtualization concepts, as well as getting you familiar with the Hyper-V software, which enables the virtualization of Windows-based servers. You will find out the steps it takes to add the Hyper-V role to your server, get familiar with Hyper-V Manager, and learn the steps it takes to create virtual machines. That way, you will be able to understand what virtualization is, and how you can enable the Hyper-V role and create virtual machines.

Chapter 7, *Group Policy in Windows Server*, helps you gain an understanding of **Group Policy (GP)** in Windows Server. You will learn about GP processing, become familiar with the GP Management Console, find out about both computer and user policies, and get to know about local policies for when your server is not part of a domain. At the same time, you will learn the steps involved in configuring computer and user policies in a domain-based network.

Chapter 8, *Storing Data in Windows Server*, explains storage technologies. Other than understanding storage technologies in general, you will learn about a variety of related topics. These include physical interfaces and disk controllers. We will also explore how data is stored in a medium, storage system types used in network environments, and various storage protocols. You will get to know the concepts and types of RAID.

Chapter 9, *Tuning and Maintaining Windows Server*, covers the best practices and considerations for server hardware. By understanding the importance of a server's role in a computer network, and learning about of each server component, we can be vigilant when selecting server hardware. In addition, this chapter teaches you server performance monitoring methodologies and procedures. Performance monitoring will help you identify the cause of server performance issues at an early stage.

Chapter 10, *Updating and Troubleshooting Windows Server*, outlines the server startup process; advanced boot options and Safe Mode; backup and restore; disaster recovery plan; and updating the OS, hardware, and software. Event Viewer is mentioned too, and it will help you monitor different logs in your system, thus helping you to troubleshoot and solve the problem. In this way, you will be able to minimize downtime, which from a business point of view is expressed in money loss.

Appendix A, *Studying and Passing the MTA 98-365 Exam*, provides you with the detailed objectives of the MTA 98-365 exam, as well as the chapter reference for each and every objective so you can find more information in this book on the respective objectives. Last but not least, learn and practice as much as you can with the technology in general, and Windows Server 2016 in particular, because only by doing so will you be able to gain the skills to administer Windows Server 2016 and pass the exam without difficulties.

Appendix B, *Examples of GPOs for Sysadmins*, provides you with some of the most used GPOs in Windows Server-based networks. There are thousands of policies in GP, who's the main purpose is to configure and manage Windows-based computers. Nonetheless, the other purpose of the examples is to show how the work is done with GPOs.

Appendix C, *Keyboard Shortcuts in Windows Server*, provides you with the majority of Windows key combinations in Windows Server 2016. In general in Windows OSes, besides working with the mouse, there is also the alternative to use a single key or keyboard keystrokes to do something that you would typically do with a mouse. You will notice that throughout this book keyboard shortcuts are used to perform certain actions in Windows Server 2016 without using a mouse.

Appendix D, *Answers to Chapter Questions*, provides you the answers to chapter questions. As you have noticed, each chapter is accompanied by a considerable number of questions to help you reinforce the concepts and definitions provided. In this appendix, you can find the answers to questions so you can compare your answers with the answers in the book.

What you need for this book

This book requires you to have either a testing computer where you can cleanly install Windows Server 2016 Evaluation, or use any other virtual platform, such as Hyper-V, Virtual Box, or VMware. In Chapter 1, *Introducing Windows Server,* you will find information about how to download Windows Server 2016 Evaluation from the TechNet Evaluation Center web portal. The same chapter lists the minimum requirements for the Windows Server 2016 Evaluation edition. In Chapter 2, *Installing Windows Server,* you will find an explanation of how to cleanly install Windows Server 2016 Evaluation.

Windows Server 2016 Evaluation can be installed either on bare metal or a virtual machine. However, this book requires that you have enough resources for the whole setup. The minimum hardware or virtual requirements are listed here:

- Processor: 1.4 GHz with 64-bit architecture
- RAM: 512 MB
- HDD: 32 GB
- Monitor: It must support Super VGA (1024 x 768) resolution and above
- Other hardware: Has support for optical disk drives such as DVDs and support for SSDs with USB, keyboard, and mouse
- Internet connection: Cable or DSL connection

Internet connectivity is required to activate Windows Server 2016 Evaluation and install Windows Updates.

Who this book is for

If you are a System administrator or an IT professional interested in configuring and deploying Windows Server 2016 then, this book is for you. This book will also help readers clear the MTA: Windows Server Administration Fundamentals: 98-365 exam.

Conventions

In this book, you will find a number of text styles that distinguish between different kinds of information. Here are some examples of these styles and an explanation of their meaning.

Code words in the text, database table names, folder names, filenames, file extensions, pathnames, dummy URLs, user input, and Twitter handles are shown as follows: "We can include other contexts through the use of the include directive."

A block of code is set as follows:

```
[default]
exten => s,1,Dial(Zap/1|30)
exten => s,2,Voicemail(u100)
exten => s,102,Voicemail(b100)
exten => i,1,Voicemail(s0)
```

When we wish to draw your attention to a particular part of a code block, the relevant lines or items are set in bold:

```
[default]
exten => s,1,Dial(Zap/1|30)
exten => s,2,Voicemail(u100)
exten => s,102,Voicemail(b100)
exten => i,1,Voicemail(s0)
```

Any command-line input or output is written as follows:

```
# cp /usr/src/asterisk-addons/configs/cdr_mysql.conf.sample
/etc/asterisk/cdr_mysql.conf
```

New terms and important words are shown in bold. Words that you see on the screen, for example, in menus or dialog boxes, appear in the text like this: "Clicking the **Next** button moves you to the next screen."

Warnings or important notes appear in a box like this.

Tips and tricks appear like this.

Reader feedback

Feedback from our readers is always welcome. Let us know what you think about this book—what you liked or disliked. Reader feedback is important for us as it helps us develop titles that you will really get the most out of.

To send us general feedback, simply e-mail `feedback@packtpub.com`, and mention the book's title on the subject of your message.

If there is a topic that you have expertise in and you are interested in either writing or contributing to a book, see our author guide at `www.packtpub.com/authors`.

Customer support

Now that you are the proud owner of a Packt book, we have a number of things to help you to get the most from your purchase.

Downloading the color images of this book

We also provide you with a PDF file that has color images of the screenshots/diagrams used in this book. The color images will help you better understand the changes in the output. You can download this file from `http://www.packtpub.com/sites/default/files/downloads/WindowsServer2016AdministrationFundamentals_ColorImages.pdf`.

Errata

Although we have taken every care to ensure the accuracy of our content, mistakes do happen. If you find a mistake in one of our books—maybe a mistake in the text or the code—we would be grateful if you could report this to us. By doing so, you can save other readers from frustration and help us improve subsequent versions of this book. If you find any errata, please report them by visiting `http://www.packtpub.com/submit-errata`, selecting your book, clicking on the Errata Submission Form link, and entering the details of your errata. Once your errata are verified, your submission will be accepted and the errata will be uploaded to our website or added to any list of existing errata under the Errata section of that title.

To view the previously submitted errata, go to `https://www.packtpub.com/books/content/support` and enter the name of the book in the search field. The required information will appear under the Errata section.

Piracy

Piracy of copyrighted material on the Internet is an ongoing problem across all media. At Packt, we take the protection of our copyright and licenses very seriously. If you come across any illegal copies of our works in any form on the internet, please provide us with the location address or website name immediately so that we can pursue a remedy.

Please contact us at copyright@packtpub.com with a link to the suspected pirated material.

We appreciate your help in protecting our authors and our ability to bring you valuable content.

Questions

If you have a problem with any aspect of this book, you can contact us at questions@packtpub.com, and we will do our best to address the problem.

1
Introducing Windows Server

This chapter is designed to provide you with an introduction to Windows Server in general, and Windows Server 2016 in particular. Windows Server 2016 is the server's operating system developed by Microsoft as part of the Windows NT family of operating systems and developed concurrently with Windows 10. Besides introducing Windows Server, right at the beginning of this chapter, there is a reminder of the very basic concepts of computer networks. So, this chapter is organized into two parts, where each part attempts to provide a concise yet complete description. Definitions such as hosts, nodes, peer-to-peer, and clients/servers are covered in the *Computer Network Overview* section. In contrast, the *Windows Server Overview* section uncovers the essentials of Windows Server in general and Windows Server 2016 in particular.

In this chapter, we will cover:

- Understanding hosts and nodes
- Understanding clients and servers
- Understanding network architectures
- Understanding IP addressing and subnetting
- Windows Server overview
- Identifying Windows Server 2016 editions
- Identifying minimum and recommended system requirements
- Downloading Windows Server 2016

Computer network overview

It all started as a need to *share resources*! Starting with the initial design of computers in the 1950s, the impetus to use computers to communicate was first realized in the 1960s as a number of university computers on different campuses were interconnected. Over time, the development and advancement of computer network technologies took place. Thus, the need to connect and interconnect more computers to computer networks and with it more geographical locations created a need for well-defined terms and concepts to describe computer networking. Because of this, types of computer networks, computer network topologies, computer network architectures, and computer network components were born. Certainly, computer networking represents one of the biggest inventions of mankind in the field of communications. Simply mention the *internet* and one will immediately understand how huge the benefit of computer networks is to humanity

Understanding hosts and nodes

Before offering the definition of a computer network, let us first look at the general definition of a network in order to then recognize the computer network definition. If you search for the word *network* in the Merriam-Webster dictionary, you will find the following definition: "*network is a group of people or organizations that are closely linked and that work with each other.*" In the same Merriam-Webster dictionary, the phrase *networking* means "*exchange of information or services among individuals, groups or institutions.*" Based on that, the *computer network* is a group of computers connected to each other in order to share resources. When talking about resources in a computer network, usually the *resources* can be data, network services, and peripheral devices.

Obviously, when talking about computer networks it is essential to mention *components* of a computer network because computer networks are ultimately composed of their constituent components. Usually, computers and peripheral devices are just some of the computer network components known to most people. However, there are also intermediary devices and network media.

When talking about hosts and nodes, although their first impression might drive us towards thinking that they are the same thing, in fact they are not! The difference between hosts and nodes is that, while all hosts can be nodes, not every node can act as a host. Because every host is assigned an **Internet Protocol (IP)** address (see the *IP addressing and subnets* section for more on IP addresses). There are some nodes such as hubs, bridges, switches, modems, and access points that have no IP address assigned, but are still used for communications. So, a *host* is any device that offers networking resources to any other node and user on the network. In contrast, a *node* is any device that can generate, receive, and transmit the networking resources on the computer network. Based on that, *Figure 1.1* represents a computer network with hosts (servers, printer, PC, laptop) and nodes (switch).

Understanding clients and servers

Since computer networks have been designed to share resources then it is very important to look at the way these resources are shared. Let us try to understand precisely, the computer network components that share resources and computer network components that request resources. For example, when accessing social networking portals on the internet, we know that our device is the network component that requests resources, while the devices where social networking applications are located are network components that provide resources. However, there are situations when these computer network components exchange roles, from requesting a resource to providing a resource and vice-versa, and that is going to be explained in the next section, *Understanding network architectures*.

Now, going back to the concepts of requesting a resource and providing a resource, actually, that is what is shaping the definition of clients and servers in the computer network. *Clients*, in most cases, are computers that request the resources in a computer network. Because they are components, the clients have an active role in the computer network. Furthermore, *servers* are a network component that provides resources to clients. Servers too have an active role. The following figure, *Figure 1.2*, presents the server with a shared printer in the role of resource provider, and the PC, laptop in the role of resource requesters.

 If you did not know, the origin of the word *servers* originates from the word serve. If you search for the word serve in the Merriam-Webster dictionary, among the results you will find one that says: *To provide services that benefit or help*. Thus, a server in a computer network means the computer that provides services to the clients. In this case, the server serves the clients.

Understanding network architectures

When talking about computer networks, actually we are talking about the essential and broader concept of the elements that make up a computer network. In this form of discussion, while the computer network types deal with the area coverage, the physical and logical topologies deal with the physical arrangement and logical structure of the computer network. Having said that, the *computer network architecture* represents the computer network design that allows the computer network components to communicate with one another. Usually, there are two types of architectures in a computer network:

- **Peer-to-peer networking (P2P)**: This is a computer network in which the participating computers do not play the predefined roles in the network, instead they change roles from client to server and vice-versa based on the actual activity on the network. For example, if computer A is accessing resources from computer B, then computer A acts as the client while computer B acts as the server. After some time, if computer B accesses resources from computer A, then computer B becomes a client and computer A becomes a server. As you may notice, they switch roles based on who is requesting and who is providing a resource on the network. *Figure 1.1* presents an example of peer-to-peer networking:

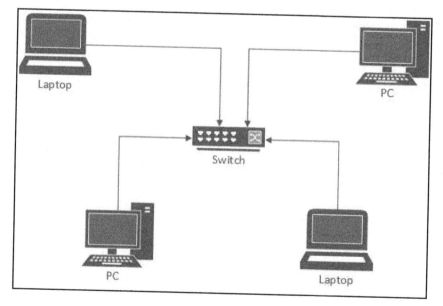

Figure 1.1. Peer-to-peer computer network

- **Client/server networking**: This is a computer network in which participating computers have a predefined role. That means that in this computer network architecture, computers that access resources act as clients, while computers that provide resources act as servers. In general, this is a computer network architecture with dedicated servers that provide resources on the network. Mid-sized and enterprise computer networks are the best example of the client/server computer network. *Figure 1.2* presents an example of client/server networking:

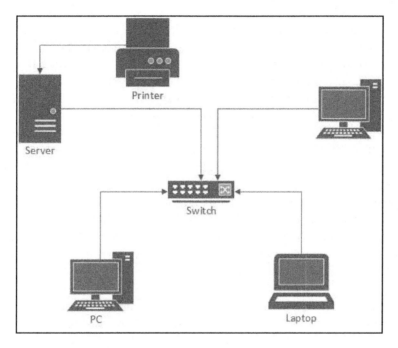

Figure 1.2. The clients/server computer network

 Another way to categorize computer networks is by their topology, or the way in which nodes are arranged and connected to one another, and how they communicate. The computer network mainly recognizes two types of topologies: physical and logical topologies.

Understanding IP addressing and subnetting

Nowadays, a lot of effort is being made to advance the development of IP addressing technologies. Specifically, IPv6 addressing is the best example of such an effort. Nevertheless, even though the IPv6 addressing technology is becoming more and more plausible, it still prefers the role of spectator in the great arena of the internet, where IPv4 addressing technology continues to be the norm.

- **IPv4 addressing technology** is the fourth version of IP addressing. In brief, an IPv4 address, or simply IP address, is a logical element that consists of 32 bits. It is organized into four (4) groups of eight (8) bits (octet) each divided by a decimal point. For the purpose of easier interpretation, it is represented in decimal format (for example, 192.168.1.1). Knowing that one (1) byte equals eight (8) bits, then an IP address is four (4) bytes. From that, the total number of IPv4 addresses is 2^{32}, or 4,294,967,296. When compared with the total world population, it is obvious that nearly 3 billion IP addresses are missing if we assign an IPv4 address to every individual.

- **IPv6 addressing technology** has been introduced to overcome IPv4 limitations. Similar to IPv4, IPv6 is a logical component of computer networks too. However, it consist of 128 bits organized into eight (8) groups of sixteen (16) bits (hextet) each divided by a colon. For the purpose of easier interpretation, it is represented in hexadecimal format (for example, 2001:0DB8:85A3:0000:0000:8A2E:0370:7334). From that, the total number of IPv6 addresses is 2^{128}, or 340,282,366,920,938,463,463,374,607,431,768,211,456. And that is more than enough IPv6 addresses!

- **IPv4 subnetting** helps implement multiple logical networks within existing IPv4 classes such as A, B, and C. In subnetting, a subnet mask plays an important role in determining the size of the network. So, by definition, a subnet mask is a 32-bit address used in combination with an IPv4 address to indicate the network and its computers. Each class has a default subnet mask. Table 1.1. shows the default subnet masks for each class of IPv4 addresses.

Table 1.1. Default subnet masks for each class of IPv4 addresses:

IPv4 class	Default subnet mask
A	255.0.0.0
B	255.255.0.0
C	255.255.255.0

Windows Server overview

In an attempt to combine the performance of Windows Server 2008 with the robustness and advanced security of Windows Server 2012, Microsoft created *Windows Server 2016*. Equipped with the best technologies of *both worlds* and the newest inventions in the Windows Server environment, Windows Server 2016 became the first server operating system designed specially for the cloud. That said, Windows Server 2016 is shaping the new era of computing, that of *cloud computing*.

Understanding Network Operating Systems (NOS)

A **Network Operating System (NOS)** is software that is capable of managing, maintaining, and providing resources in the network. Additionally, NOS is capable of sharing files and applications, providing web services, managing access to resources, administering users and computers, providing tools for configuration, the maintenance and provision of resources, as well as other functions related to network resources. With that in mind, a NOS is an important component when it comes to managing computer network resources. Nowadays, the operating systems offered on the market, such as Windows, Linux, and macOS, are known as NOS because they are capable of providing resources. Of course, if you want to take advantage of their resource provider potential then you should go with server versions of the aforementioned operating systems.

Figure 1.3 shows the most commonly used NOS today:

Figure 1.3. The most well-known Network Operating Systems (NOS)

Understanding server hardware and software (5.1)

In general, *computer hardware* is any physical component regardless of the material that it is made of, such as metal, plastic, or wood. On the other hand, *software* is the instruction or program that tells hardware what to do. It is a virtual component which we have no physical contact with and is represented by the OS, programs, utilities, and any other type of software. When talking about the server's hardware and software, the computer definition of hardware and software applies to servers as well. However, as already explained, because servers provide network services, more powerful hardware is required. At the same time, the software is different too. For example, Windows Server 2016 is different to Windows 10 although both are Microsoft's products.

Now that we have explained the concepts of hardware and software, the following points outline the hardware components that affect the overall performance of your servers, thus you should not make any compromises when you want to build or buy, and set up a server.

- **Processor**: A chip on a server's motherboard, often called the computer's *brain*, that does all the processing and calculations. Intel and AMD are the well-known processor manufacturers. The newest processors on the market are 64-bit architecture compared to the old ones of 32-bit.
- **RAM**: Stands for **Random Access Memory (RAM)**. It is a working memory used by your server's OS and applications. The more RAM you have in your servers, the more applications you can run simultaneously.
- **Disk:** This is where you store data on your servers. Usually servers have more than one disk known as a server's disk sub-system. The higher the read-and-write speed, the higher the performance of your disk system.
- **Network interface**: Provides a network connection in and out of your servers. Usually servers have more than one network interface. The higher the speed of your server's network connection, the faster the server can send and receive data over the network.

Concerning the size and form factors, servers come in three formats:

1. **Rack mountable servers:** These are traditional big servers that are mounted on a rack (see *Figure 1.6*).
2. **Blade servers**: These are usually small modules known as *blades* that are mounted on a server's chassis to save space.
3. **Tower servers**: These are single servers that stand upright.

 Running Windows Server 64-bit on 64-bit hardware means double the amount of data is being processed by the processor and sent between the processor and the RAM when compared to Windows Server 32-bit running on 32-bit hardware.

Understanding Windows Server

What is your answer if someone asks you, *What is Windows Server?* I am sure you will answer that it is Microsoft's NOS for servers. In general, when talking about servers, whether it is a server that runs on Windows, Linux, or macOS it still does not make any difference as it continues to be a server that provides network services. But, when talking about how to deploy a server, the user interface, managing resources, and maintaining a server, then the differences are obvious.

Introducing Windows Server 2016

After nearly two years of public testing through its **Technical Previews** one to five, Microsoft released Windows Server 2016 as the latest NOS for servers. The improvements made in server roles and features, virtualization, storage management, and security have made Windows Server 2016 more stable, robust, scalable, and secure. Additionally, the introduction of Nano Server as a new installation option, together with Windows Server containers, nested virtualization, shielded virtual machines, Storage Spaces Direct, and many other improved and new features, represents the tremendous potential that Windows Server 2016 adds to an organization's network infrastructure. Another interesting thing in Windows Server 2016 is the return of the Start Menu.

You can learn more about new features and improvements of Windows Server 2016 at: `https://www.microsoft.com/en-us/cloud-platform/windows-servers`.

Windows Server 2016 editions (1.3.1)

Planning before you start deploying Windows Server 2016 will save you time, reduce costs, and provide a platform for you or your business to set up and run the services on your network infrastructure. To do so, you need to know the available editions of Windows Server 2016. Windows Server 2016 comes in three editions:

- **Windows Server 2016 Datacenter:** This edition is designed for enterprises that own highly-virtualized data centers or act as cloud providers.
- **Windows Server 2016 Standard:** This edition is designed for medium-sized businesses that use servers on-premises to run their network services.
- **Windows Server 2016 Essentials:** This edition is designed for small businesses that run a single server in their IT infrastructure.

To learn more about the comparisons between Windows Server 2016 editions, navigate to the following site: `https://docs.microsoft.com/en-us/windows-servers/get-started/2016-edition-comparison`.

Minimum and recommended system requirements

As with the installation of previous versions of Windows Server, pay attention to the minimum hardware requirements. Windows Server 2016 has the same minimum hardware requirements as Windows Server 2012. Thus, it is required that you have the following or better hardware to install Windows Server 2016:

- **Processor:** 1.4 GHz with 64-bit architecture
- **RAM:** 512 MB
- **HDD:** 32 GB
- **Monitor:** It must support Super VGA (1024 x 768) resolution and above
- **Other hardware:** Has support for optical disk drives such as DVDs and support for SSDs with USB, keyboard, and mouse
- **Internet connection:** cable or DSL connection

However, if you want to avoid slow performance of your server then there are also recommended system requirements:

- **Processor:** 2.0 GHz or higher
- **RAM:** 32 GB or higher
- **HDD:** 1 TB
- **Monitor:** It must support Super VGA (1024 x 768) resolution and above
- **Other hardware:** Has support for optical disk drives such as DVDs, support for SSDs with USB, keyboard, and mouse
- **Internet connection:** cable or DSL connection
- **Network access:** at least one Gigabit Ethernet NIC

Downloading Windows Server 2016

As you might know, Windows Server 2016 is not free! So, whether you are using it for your own personal experience or to provide network services for your company, Windows Server 2016 is a NOS that you need to pay for. However, Microsoft, through the TechNet Evaluation Center (`https://www.microsoft.com/en-us/evalcenter`) web portal provides the option to download and explore all the new improvements of Windows Server 2016 as evaluation software as shown in *Figure 1.4*.

In case your server's hardware is the same as, or exceeds the minimum hardware requirements as described above, then you can download a Windows Server 2016 evaluation version. To do so, try completing the following steps:

1. Open up your browser and navigate to the following website: `www.microsoft.com/en-us/evalcenter/evaluate-windows-servers-2016`.

2. Click the **Sign in** button. On the next page, provide your Microsoft account credentials. If you do not have a Microsoft account then you can sign up for one.

3. Select the preferable file type (my recommendation is ISO), and then click **Register** to continue.

4. A form should be filled in for the download to begin. On the same form, if you would like to hear from Microsoft or Microsoft partners, then check the **My email address** checkbox.

5. Click the **Continue** button. Then, select the language for your Windows Server download. Shortly, the Windows Server 2016 download will begin. If not, you can go on and click the **Download** button.

6. Once your Windows Server 2016 download completes, then you should **burn the ISO file to a DVD**. If you do not know how, then follow the instructions from the following URL: `https://support.microsoft.com/en-us/help/15088/windows-create-installation-media`. When done, you are all set to move on with the installation of the Windows Server 2016 evaluation version:

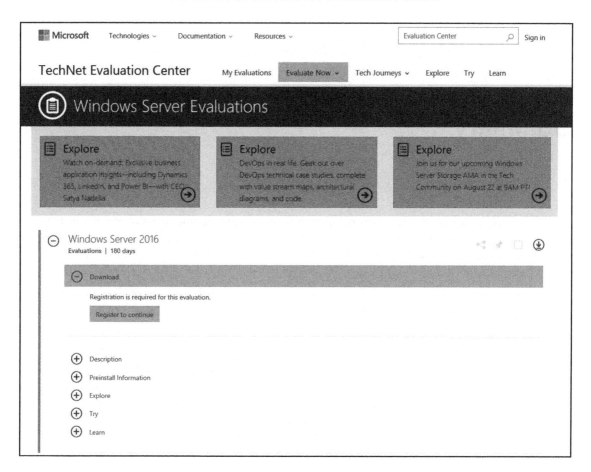

Figure 1.4. Microsoft's TechNet Evaluation Center web portal

References from Windows IT Pro Center

1. Get started with Windows Server 2016 (`https://docs.microsoft.com/en-us/windows-server/get-started/server-basics`)
2. What's new in Windows Server 2016 (`https://docs.microsoft.com/en-us/windows-server/get-started/whats-new-in-windows-server-2016`)
3. Important issues in Windows Server 2016 (`https://docs.microsoft.com/en-us/windows-server/get-started/windows-server-2016-ga-release-notes`)

Summary

We summarize the chapter with following points:

- A computer network is a group of computers connected to each other in order to share resources.
- The components of a computer network are the substance that constitutes the computer network.
- A host is any device that offers networking resources to any other nodes and users on the network.
- A node is any device that can generate, receive, and transmit the networking resources on the computer network.
- A client is a computer that requests the resources in a computer network.
- A server is a network component that provides resources to the clients.
- Peer-to-peer (P2P) networking is a computer network in which the participating computers do not have predefined roles in the network.
- Client/server networking is a computer network in which participating computers have predefined roles in the network.
- NOS is software that provides, manages, and maintains resources on the network.
- Computer hardware is any physical component regardless of the material that it is made of, such as metal, plastic, or wood.
- The software is an instruction or the program that tells the hardware what to do.

- A processor is a chip on a server's motherboard, often called the computer's *brain*, that does all the processing and calculations.
- RAM is the working memory used by your server's OS and applications.
- A disk is a storage where your servers are storing data.
- A network interface provides a network connection to and out of your servers.
- Rack-mountable servers are big servers that are mounted on a rack.
- Blade servers are small modules known as *blades* that are mounted on a server's chassis to save space.
- Tower servers are single servers that stand upright.
- The Start menu is returned in Windows Server 2016.
- The TechNet Evaluation Center is a web portal that provides the option to download and evaluate Microsoft's products free of cost.
- The Windows Server 2016 Datacenter is designed for enterprises that own highly virtualized data centers or act as cloud providers.
- Windows Server 2016 Standard is designed for medium-sized businesses that use servers on-premises to run their network services.
- Windows Server 2016 Essentials is designed for small businesses that run a single server in their IT infrastructure.

Questions

1. Windows Server 2016 is Apple's latest operating system for servers. (True | False)
2. The _____ is a group of computers connected to each other in order to share resources.
3. Which of the following are computer network components? (Choose two)
    1. computers
    2. servers
    3. Master Boot Record (MBR)
    4. Basic Input/Output System (BIOS)
4. Resources can be data, network services, and peripheral devices. (True | False)

5. Which of the following are Windows Server 2016 editions? (Choose three)
    1. Windows Server 2016 Essentials
    2. Windows Server 2016 Standard
    3. Windows Server 2016 Datacenter
    4. Windows Server 2016 Enterprise

6. _____ is a web portal that provides the option to download and evaluate Microsoft's products free of cost.

7. Which of the following are servers size and format factors? (Choose two)
    1. Blade servers
    2. Tower servers
    3. Network printer
    4. Network switch

8. The Start menu is returned in Windows Server 2016. (True | False)

9. _____ is any device that can generate, receive, and transmit the networking resources on the computer network.

10. Which of the following hardware components affect the performance of your servers? (Choose two)
    1. Processor
    2. RAM
    3. Printer
    4. Monitor

11. A server is a computer that requests resources in a computer network. (True | False)

12. _____ networking is a computer network in which the participating computers do not have predefined roles in the network.

2
Installing Windows Server

This chapter is designed to provide you with detailed instructions for installing Windows Server 2016. The step-by-step instructions, driven by easy-to-understand graphics, explain and show you how to master the installation of Windows Server 2016. With the guidance provided by this easy-to-follow chapter, you will quickly learn the installation process without obstacles. It is an excellent collection of how-to tips and an easy way of getting the job done. With that in mind, this chapter covers the following installation types:

- Clean installation
- Installation over a network using **Windows Deployment Service (WDS)**
- Unattended installation
- Upgrade and migration

In this chapter, we will cover:

- Understanding partition schemes
- Understanding boot options
- Understanding installation options
- Performing a clean installation
- Performing a network installation
- Performing an unattended installation
- Performing upgrade and migration

Understanding server installation (1)

Among a system administrator's day-to-day tasks, installing a new operating system quicken the pulse as few others can do. It is more than an installation, as it includes steps such as preparing for the installation, installing the OS, verifying the installation, and initial server configuration. Simply, everything starts from there! Although there might be rare situations when servers come with preloaded operating systems, in most cases it is a system administrator's responsibility to get the job done.

Understanding partition schemes (1.3.2)

The disk partition is a disk's logical division so that an operating system can manage data. In general, there are two partition schemes:

- **Master Boot Record (MBR)**: This is an old partition scheme known today as a legacy boot option. It operates on a 512-byte disk sector with a maximum of four primary partitions, or three primary partitions and one extended partition. An extended partition can have up to 26 logical partitions. The MBR uses **logical block addressing (LBA)** to support disks up to 2 TB. The MBR, in the past and currently, has proven to be a very useful partition scheme for multiboot platforms.
- **GUID Partition Table (GPT)**: This coexists with the MBR and is a new partition scheme that overcomes the limitations of the MBR. The **globally unique identifier (GUID)** in a GPT is a 128-bit number that Microsoft uses to identify resources. In a GPT, block sizes from 512 bytes and up are supported, where the most common default these days is 4K or 4,096 bytes, and the size of the partition entry is 128 bytes. The GPT is part of the **Unified Extensible Firmware Interface (UEFI)** standard that replaces the old **basic input/output system (BIOS)** to support modern hardware. By its nature, the GPT is fault tolerant and supports up to 18 EB disk storage, and up to 128 partitions on each disk.

Understanding boot options

Depending on the manufacturer, different keys on a keyboard can be used to access the BIOS. The most frequently used keys are *Del* and *F2*. Upon entering the BIOS, there are several boot options available:

- **Installation media**: In most cases, there may be a DVD disk. Prior to accessing the BIOS, make sure to insert the bootable DVD disk into the DVD drive. Specify the DVD as a first boot option, and then save the changes and exit the BIOS.
- **USB flash drive:** The capacity of a USB flash drive must be a minimum of 8 GB. Plug in your *bootable USB flash drive* before you access the BIOS. Specify the USB flash drive as a first boot option, and then save the changes and exit the BIOS.
- **Network boot**: This occurs when installing Windows Server 2016 over the network. First things first, enable booting from the **local area network (LAN)** and then specify booting from the network as a first boot option. Save the changes and exit the BIOS.

Regardless of which option you are using, soon your computer will restart and attempt to boot from the specified boot option. *Figure 2.1* shows the boot from a DVD disk:

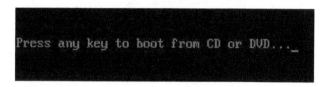

Figure 2.1. Booting from a DVD disk

 To make a bootable USB flash drive, you can use the Windows USB/DVD Download Tool. This can be downloaded from `https://www.microsoft.com/en-us/download/windows-usb-dvd-download-tool`.

Advanced startup options (1.3.3)

In Windows Server 2016, there is no *F8* option. Instead, you can use the **Advanced startup** options to recover your server's OS. That said, to access the **Advanced startup** options, complete the following steps:

1. Click the **Start** button.
2. Select **Settings** from the **Start** menu.
3. In **Windows, Settings** select **Update and security**.
4. Select **Recovery** from the navigation on the left side of the screen.
5. Click the **Restart now** button and then **Continue**, as shown in *Figure 2.2*:

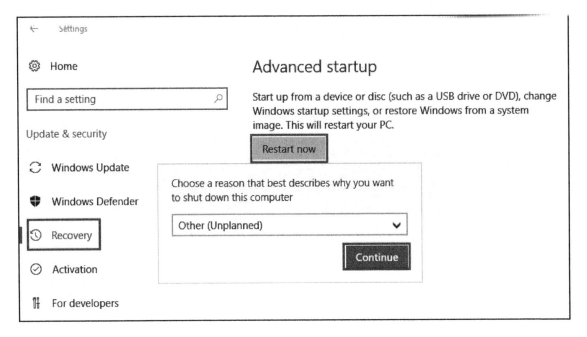

Figure 2.2. Accessing advanced startup options in Windows Server 2016

6. Shortly, options like **Continue**, **Troubleshoot**, and **Turn off your PC** will be displayed.
7. Click **Troubleshoot** to access **Advanced options**.

8. From the **Advanced options** screen select any of the available options, as shown in *Figure 2.3*:

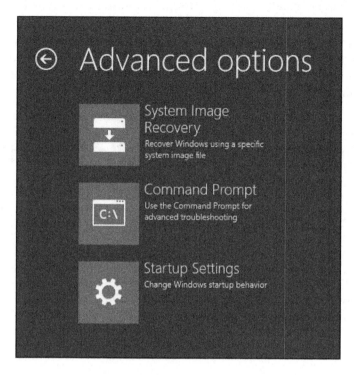

Figure 2.3. Advanced startup options in Windows Server 2016

Desktop Experience versus Server Core versus Nano Server installation options (1.3.4)

Windows Server 2016 offers three installation options. However, the selected installation option affects the availability of roles and features, and therefore one should take the planning very seriously before choosing the desired installation option:

- **Desktop Experience**: This is an installation option that contains everything from Windows Server 2016, choosing **Desktop Experience** means that you have installed everything on Windows Server 2016. However, your hardware needs to exceed the minimum requirements specification in order to benefit from the full-featured **Graphical User Interface (GUI)**.

- **Server Core**: This is an installation option recommended by Microsoft due to its minimal hardware resource consumption and higher security. The roles and features can be installed locally through Windows PowerShell, or remotely through Server Manager.
- **Nano Server**: This is a replacement for Server Core that takes up far fewer hardware resources, has fewer updates, and supports only 64-bit applications. It is administered remotely since it has no local login capabilities. In a few words, this installation option is best understood as *set it and forget it*.

Understanding server installation options (1.3)

When it comes to installing Windows Server, there are many methods. So, depending on the environment in which you will deploy Windows Server 2016, you can choose from the following:

- Clean installation
- Installation over a network using WDS
- Unattended installation
- Upgrade
- Migration

Performing a clean installation (1.3.5)

Whether you are installing Windows Server 2016 on a new hard disk or on an existing disk, the *clean installation* overwrites the existing operating system on a hard disk. Be aware, that the clean option requires user interactivity, although that might be more limited than the upgrade option. Turn on your computer, depending on the selected boot option, and wait for the boot prompt on the screen. The message on the screen requires user confirmation to boot the system from a DVD, USB flash drive, or network boot.

To perform the clean installation of Windows Server 2016, complete the following steps:

1. The installation files are loaded in RAM, as shown in *Figure 2.4*:

Figure 2.4. Loading installation files into RAM

2. Enter your language and other preferences, as shown in *Figure 2.5*. Click **Next** to continue:

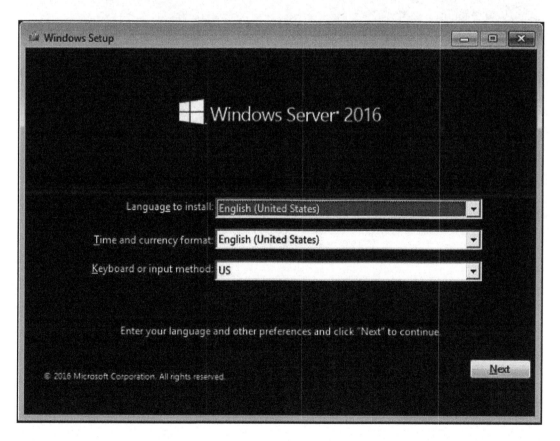

Figure 2.5. Windows Server's 2016 Windows Setup

3. Click **Install now** to start installing Windows Server 2016, as shown in *Figure 2.6*:

Figure 2.6. Windows Server 2016 is about to start

4. Select **Windows Server 2016 Standard Evaluation (Desktop Experience)** and then click **Next,** as shown in *Figure 2.7:*

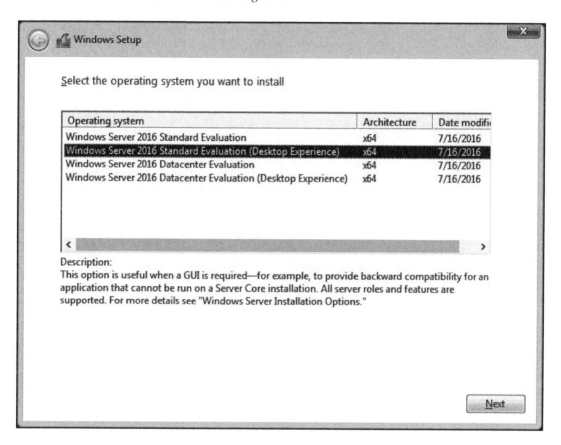

Figure 2.7. The available Windows Server 2016 OSs for the installation

5. Take your time to read the license terms. When done, check **I accept the license terms** and then click **Next,** as shown in *Figure 2.8*:

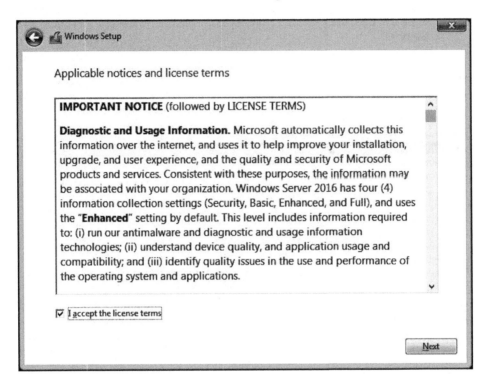

Figure 2.8. The Microsoft's Software License Terms

6. Select **Custom,** as shown in *Figure 2.9,* to run the clean installation:

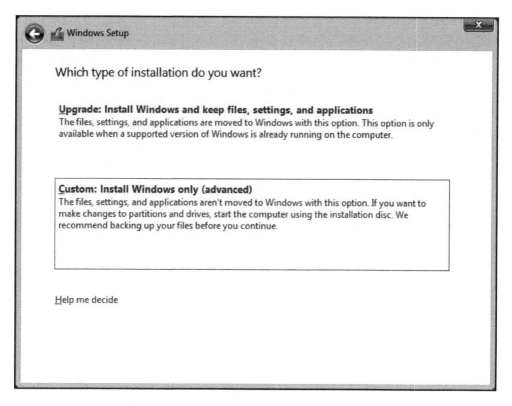

Figure 2.9. The available types of installation

7. After preparing the drive, select the partition where you want to install Windows Server 2016. Click **Next,** as shown in *Figure 2.10*:

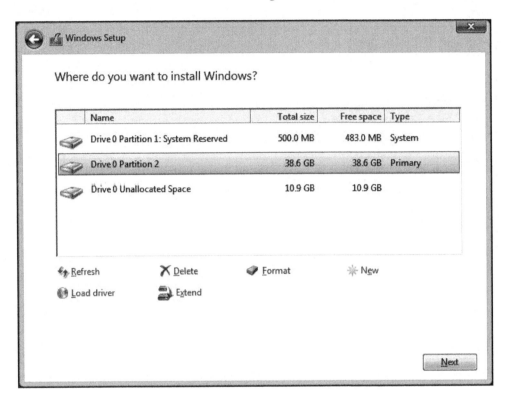

Figure 2.10. After formatting is complete the installation files on the RAM will begin installing OS on a disk

8. Windows Setup is installing Windows Server 2016, as shown in *Figure 2.11*. Sit back and relax:

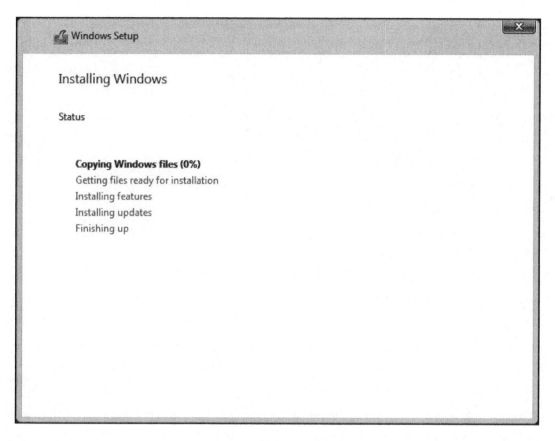

Figure 2.11. Several steps must be completed from the checklist before the Windows Server 2016 gets installed

9. After getting the devices ready and performing a few restarts, set up the administrator's password and click **Finish,** as in *Figure 2.12*:

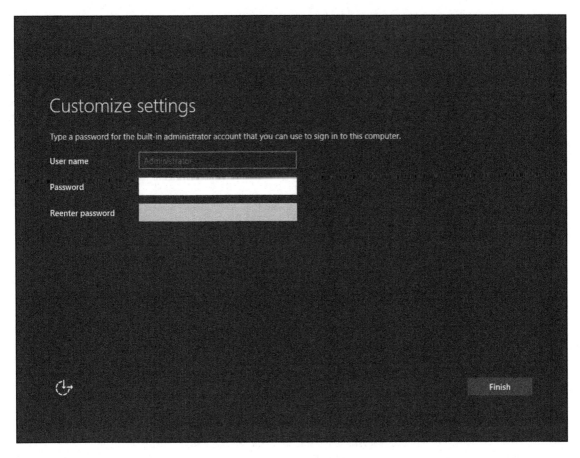

Figure 2.12. An administrator account in Windows Server 2016 is recommended to have a password

10. Congratulations, you have successfully installed Windows Server 2016. Press *Ctrl + Alt + Delete,* as in *Figure 2.13*, to unlock. Provide the administrator's password to make the first login to Windows Server 2016:

Figure 2.13. The famous key combination *Ctrl+Alt+Del* is available in Windows Server 2016 too

 If the competition has a single reason to compliment Microsoft, then that would without a doubt be regarding the Windows Installer. The Windows Installer is an **application programming interface** (**API**) used by Windows for software installation, maintenance, and uninstalls.

Performing installation over a network using WDS (1.3.7)

Often, organizations deploy hundreds of servers in their IT infrastructures, and they use WDS to enable installation over the network. Setting up WDS is fairly easy; it requires adding the WDS role to your server and then adding install and boot images. Additionally, an answer file is required to automate the deployment of an unattended installation. The unattended installation is explained in the next section: *Performing an unattended (automated) installation.*

To perform the network installation of Windows Server 2016 using WDS, complete the following steps:

1. The **Pre-Boot Execution Environment (PXE)** takes place and establishes a communication with the WDS server, as shown in *Figure 2.14*:

```
Hyper-V
PXE Network Boot 09.14.2011
(C) Copyright 2011 Microsoft Corporation, All Rights Reserved.


CLIENT MAC ADDR: 00 15 5D 02 87 08  GUID: B16774B3-B69E-4DF1-BCF8-80B04EE5CF1E
CLIENT IP: 192.168.0.114  MASK: 255.255.255.0  DHCP IP: 192.168.0.1
GATEWAY IP: 192.168.0.1

Downloaded WDSNBP from 192.168.0.105 WinSrv2012R2.PacktBiz.local

Architecture: x64
Contacting Server: 192.168.0.105.
TFTP Download: boot\x64\pxeboot.n12
```

Figure 2.14. Pre-Boot Execution Environment (PXE)

2. Load Windows Server 2016's installation files from the WDS server into the server's RAM, as shown in *Figure 2.15:*

Figure 2.15. Installation files are loaded from WDS server into the server's RAM

3. Choose the appropriate settings for the **Locale** and **Keyboard** or **input method** and click **Next,** as in *Figure 2.16*:

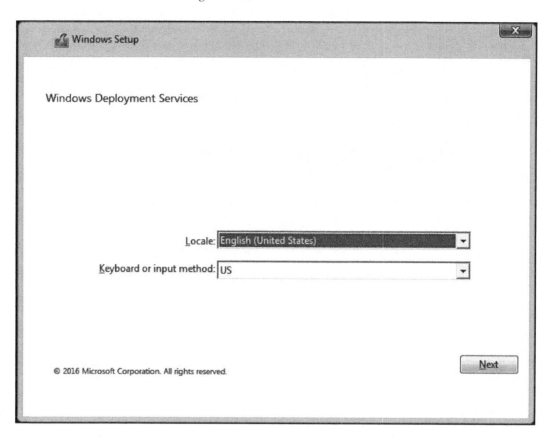

Figure 2.16. At this step the authentication with WDS server is required

4. After you provide the authenticated user's credentials, select the operating system you want to install and click **Next,** as in *Figure 2.17*:

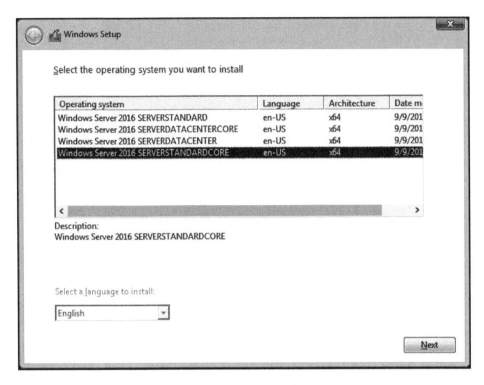

Figure 2.17. Installing Windows Server 2016 Server Core over network (WDS server)

5. After completing the rest of the steps that are similar to a clean installation, the *Windows Server 2016 Server Core* network installation is completed successfully. However, in Server Core there is no GUI, it has a CLI user interface, as shown in *Figure 2.18*:

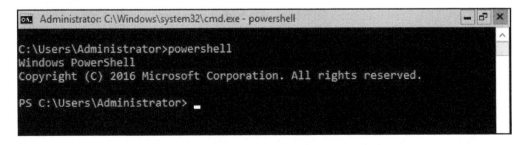

Figure 2.18. Windows Server's 2016 Server Core user interface

Performing an unattended installation (1.3.6)

In contrast to a clean installation, an *unattended* installation involves little interactivity during the installation. In conjunction with WDS, it is known as an *automated installation* and is used to deploy a large number of servers in enterprises. Part of the unattended installation is the *answer file*. This is an XML file that stores the answers for an installation prompt. You can use *Notepad* to create an answer file from scratch, or you can download sample answer files from the internet. Additionally, Microsoft provides several tools for automating the installation. Apart from WDS, explained in a previous section, tools like the **Windows Assessment and Deployment Kit (Windows ADK)** and the **Microsoft Deployment Toolkit (MDT)** provide the unique platform for automating desktop and server deployments. Both tools are available for download.

To perform an unattended installation of Windows Server 2016, complete the following steps:

1. Install the Windows ADK, as shown in *Figure 2.19*:

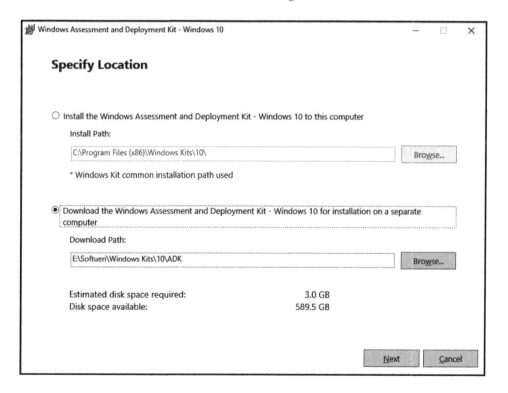

Figure 2.19. Installing Windows ADK

2. Install the MDT, as shown in *Figure 2.20*:

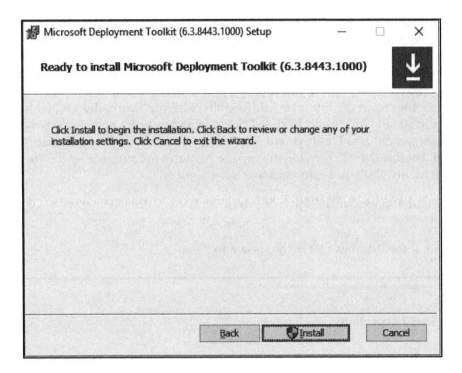

Figure 2.20. Installing MDT

3. After both the Windows ADK and MDT are installed, run the **Deployment Workbench** and select the **New Deployment Share Wizard,** as in *Figure 2.21*:

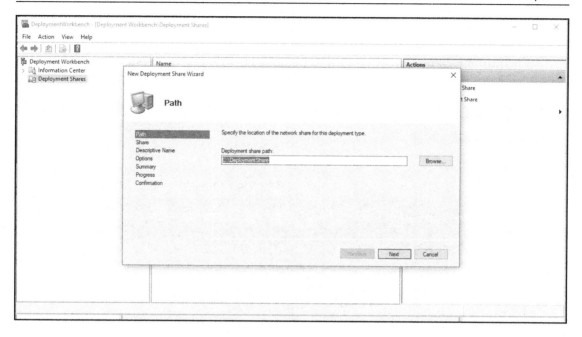

Figure 2.21. The New Deployment Share Wizard

4. After creating the deployment share, run **Import Operating System Wizard** to import Windows Server 2016 files.

5. Afterwards, run the **New Task Sequence Wizard** to create the answer file for an unattended installation.

6. Then, **Update Deployment Share** to **Create Boot-able PE image**.

7. Boot the new server with the **LiteTouchPE_x64** image, located in the `Boot` subfolder within the `Deployment Share` folder. After the successful boot, select **Run the Deployment Wizard to install a new Operating System,** as in *Figure 2.22*:

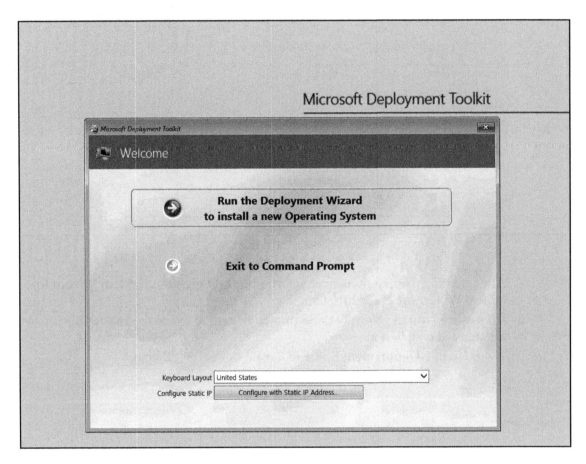

Figure 2.22. Deploying Windows Server 2016 over MDT

8. Provide credentials to access the `Deployment Share` folder. Ensure that the provided user has full control in the `Deployment Share` folder.

9. Select the `Task Sequence` (that is the answer file) created earlier with **Deployment Workbench**, and click **Next**.

10. After providing the **Computer Details**, **Locale,** and **Time**, specifying whether to capture the image and specifying the BitLocker configuration, you are ready to begin deploying Windows Server 2016.

11. Windows Server 2016 is being deployed through MDT.

12. After the installation progress step completes, the installation takes care of getting devices ready and the Windows Server 2016 Standard is deployed successfully, as shown in *Figure 2.23:*

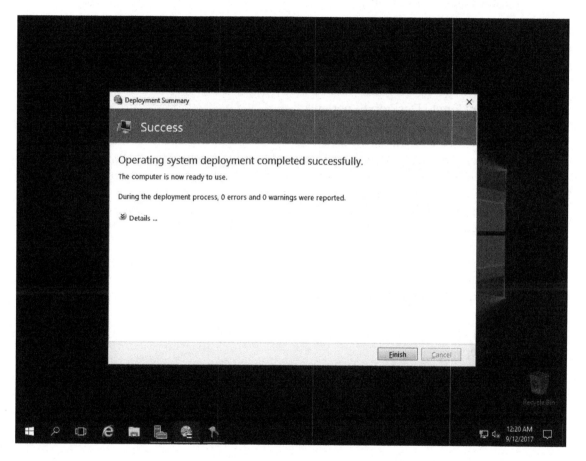

Figure 2.23. The MDT confirms Windows Server 2012 successful deployment

 You can download the Windows ADK from `https://developer.` `microsoft.com/en-us/windows/hardware/windows-assessment-` `deployment-kit`, and the MDT from `https://www.microsoft.com/en-us/` `download/details.aspx?id=54259`.

Upgrade and migration overview (1.3.8)

Upgrade replaces your existing OS with a new one. This means that you retain your files and settings. This is often called an *in-place upgrade* because it happens in place on a machine with an OS already installed. It is recommended to make a backup of Windows state, files, and folders before running an upgrade. You can upgrade to Windows Server 2016 if your existing server runs Windows Server 2012 or Windows Server 2012 R2, but you cannot upgrade from the following:

- Windows Server 2008
- A 32-bit OS to a 64-bit OS
- One language to another
- A **Technical Preview** (**TP**) to a retail version
- Server Core to Desktop Experience
- A retail version of an evaluation version

A migration takes place when you bring in a new machine (physical or virtual) and you want to move the roles, features, apps, and settings into it. To do so, first you would want to install the OS on a new server, and then proceed with the migration. Prior to running a migration, make sure to check whether Windows Server 2016 supports your existing apps. The migration requires the **Windows Server Migration Tool** (**WSMT**) feature to be installed on a new server (see *Figure 2.30*).

Performing an upgrade (1.3.8.1)

To perform an upgrade from Windows Server 2012 R2 to Windows Server 2016, complete the following steps:

1. Insert the Windows Server 2016 DVD disk, or plug in the USB flash drive, and run the setup file, as in *Figure 2.24*:

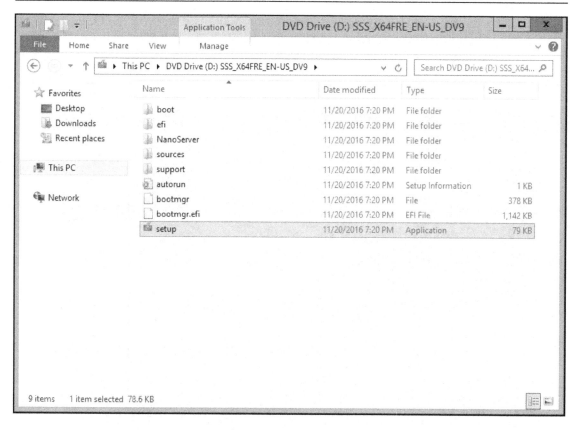

Figure 2.24. Running Windows Server's 2016 setup

2. Shortly, the **Get important updates** window will display. With the **Download and install updates (recommended)** option selected, click **Next** to continue, as shown in *Figure 2.25*:

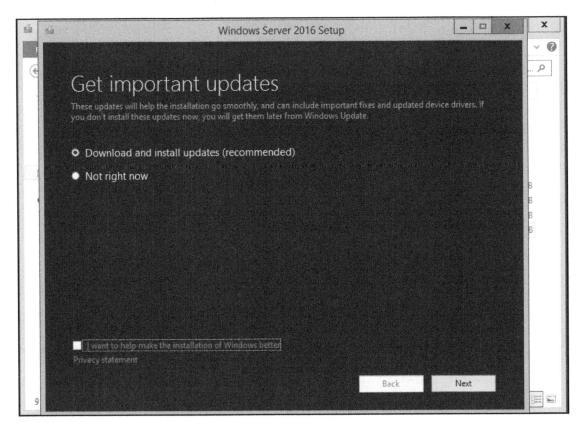

Figure 2.25. Getting important updates to help ease the upgrade

3. Type in the product key and click **Next**.
4. Select the edition that you want to install and click **Next**.
5. Click the **Accept** button to accept the license terms.
6. *Choose what to keep*, and then click **Next** to continue.
7. *Confirm* that you have compatible software installed on an existing server (that is Windows Server 2012 R2).

8. After the **Windows Server 2016 Setup** ensures that there is enough disk space on your server, you are **Ready to install**. Click the **Install** button to continue with the upgrade, as in *Figure 2.26*:

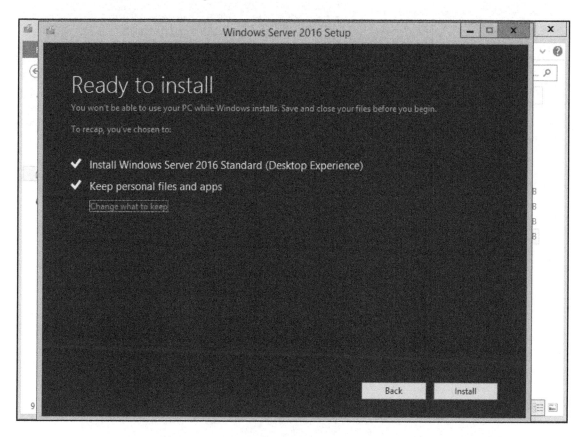

Figure 2.26. Ready to upgrade

9. Either sit back and relax, or you may want to do some other work until the upgrade completes:

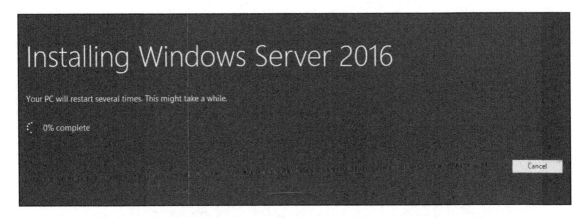

Figure 2.27. Upgrading from Windows Server 2012 R2 to Windows Server 2016

10. After the first restart, the screen, as shown in *Figure 2.28*, will show up:

Figure 2.28. The upgrade is comprised of several steps

11. After a few restarts, the upgrade from Windows Server 2012 R2 to Windows Server 2016 is completed successfully, as shown in *Figure 2.29*:

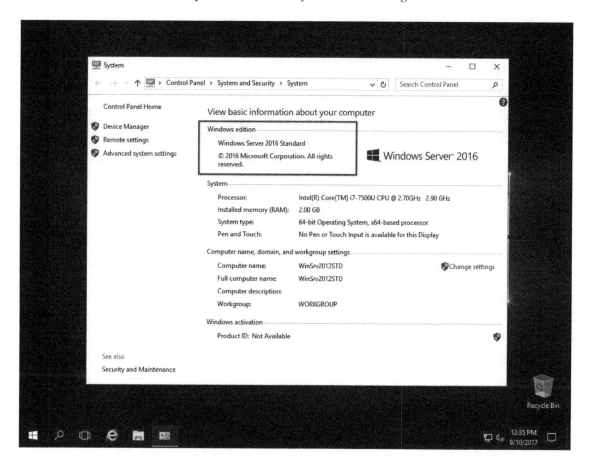

Figure 2.29. The System window confirms the upgrade

Performing a migration (1.3.8.2)

To perform the migration of roles from an *old server* (Windows Server 2012 R2) into a *new server* (Windows Server 2016), complete the following steps:

1. In a new server, install the WSMT feature through the **Server Manager,** as in *Figure 2.30*:

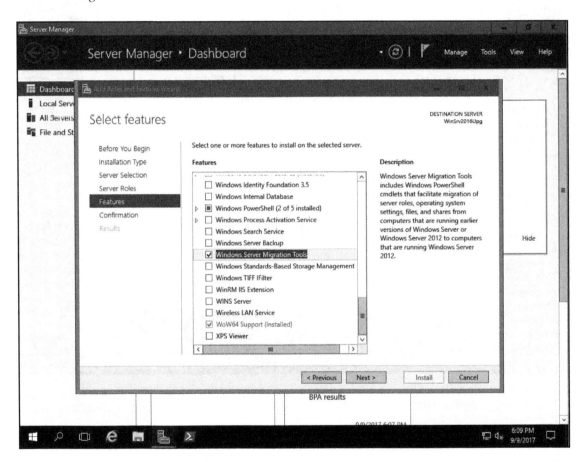

Figure 2.30. Adding WSMT feature in Windows Server 2016

2. After the installation is complete close the **Add Roles and Feature Wizard**, and the **Server Migration Tools** folder is created at
    `C:\Windows\System32\ServerMigrationTools`.

3. Open Windows PowerShell with elevated admin rights, and locate the Server Migration Tools entering the following command:

```
cd ServerMigrationTools
```

4. From the same Windows PowerShell session, create the `MigrationTools` folder entering the following command (see *Figure 2.31*):

```
.\SmigDeploy.exe /package /architecture amd64 /OS WS12R2 /path
C:\MigrationTools
```

Figure 2.31. Creating MigrationTools folder with Windows PowerShell in Windows Server 2016

5. Share the newly created `MigrationTools` folder on a new server (that is Windows Server 2016 server).
6. Try accessing the shared `MigrationTools` folder, and copy that into an old server (that is Windows Server 2012 R2).
7. After copying is complete, open up the `MigrationTools\SMT_ws12R2_amd64` folder on an old server and run the `SmigDeploy` app to complete the registration. Exit Windows PowerShell.

8. From an old server try to open the Windows Server Migration Tools (it is an additional PowerShell console) with elevated admin rights. The Windows Server Migration Tools (PowerShell console) was added by running the `SmigDeploy` app. List the roles installed on an old server by entering the following command:

    ```
    Get-SmigServerFeature
    ```

9. Prior to migrating, the DHCP role from an old server into a new one requires the DHCP service to be stopped. After stopping the DHCP service on an old server, export it by entering the following command:

    ```
    Export-SmigServerSetting -FeatureID DHCP -Path C:\DHCP\Store
    -Verbose
    ```

10. Provide the administrator's password to complete the export, as in *Figure 2.32*:

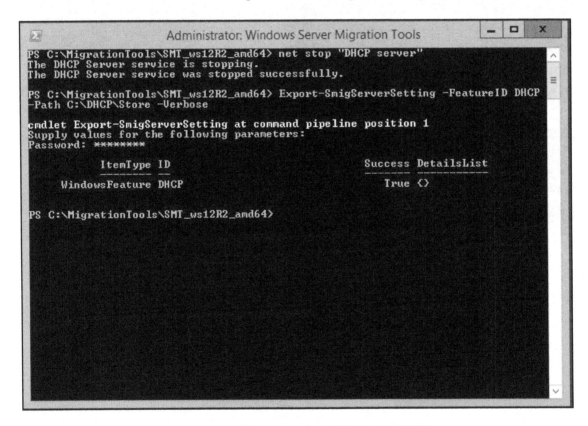

Figure 2.32. The Export of DHCP in an old server (that is Windows Server 2012 R2)

11. On a new server, add the DHCP role using the Server Manager.

12. On an old server share the `DHCP\Store` folder.

13. From the new server try accessing the shared `DHCP\Store` folder and copy that into the `MigrationTools` folder. Then open the Windows Server Migration Tools (PowerShell console), and enter the following command to import DHCP:

```
Import-SmigServerSetting -FeatureID DHCP -Path
C:\MigrationTools\DHCP\Store -Force
```

14. Provide the administrator's password to complete the import, as in *Figure 2.33*:

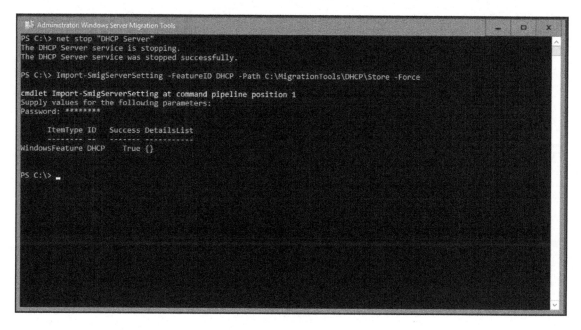

Figure 2.33. The Import of DHCP role into a new server (that is Windows Server 2016)

15. The DHCP role, as shown in *Figure 2.34*, is migrated successfully to a new server through Windows Server Migration Tools.

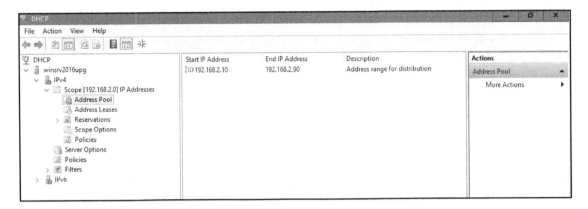

Figure 2.34. The successful migration of the DHCP role in a new server (that is Windows Server 2016)

References from Windows IT Pro Center

1. Install Server with Desktop Experience (https://docs.microsoft.com/en-us/ windows-server/get-started/getting-started-with-server-with-desktop-experience)

2. Install Server Core (https://docs.microsoft.com/en-us/windows-server/get-started/getting-started-with-server-core)

3. Install Nano Server (https://docs.microsoft.com/en-us/windows-server/get-started/getting-started-with-nano-server)

Summary

We summarize the chapter with following points:

- The disk partition is a logical division of the disk so that the operating system can manage data.
- MBR is an old partition scheme known today as a legacy boot option.
- GPT is a new partition scheme that overcomes the limitations of the MBR partition scheme.
- Desktop Experience is an installation option that contains everything from Windows Server 2016.
- Server Core is an installation option recommended by Microsoft due to its minimal hardware resource consumption and higher security.
- Nano Server, a replacement for Server Core, takes far fewer hardware resources than the two other installation options, has fewer updates, and supports only 64-bit applications.
- A clean installation overwrites the existing operating system on a hard disk.
- The WDS server enables installation over a network.
- An unattended installation has little or no interactivity with the operating system installation.
- Tools like the Windows ADK and MDT provide a unique platform to automate desktop and server deployments.
- An upgrade replaces your existing OS with a new one.
- Migration takes place when you bring in a new machine (physical or virtual) and you want to move the roles, features, apps, and settings into it.

Questions

1. _____ is a new partition scheme that overcomes the limitations of the MBR partition scheme.
2. A clean installation enables automated installation over a network. (True | False)
3. _____, a replacement for Server Core, takes up far fewer hardware resources than the two other installation options, has fewer updates, and supports only 64-bit applications.
4. Which of the following tools are provided by Microsoft to automate the Windows Server 2016 installation? (Choose two)
    1. Windows ADK
    ? MDT
    3. SharePoint Server 2016
    4. SQL Server 2016
5. An unattended installation requires interactivity during the installation of an operating system. (True | False)
6. _____ takes place when you bring in a new machine (physical or virtual) and you want to move the roles, features, apps, and settings into it.
7. Which of the following are installation options in Windows Server 2016? (Choose three)
    1. Desktop Experience
    2. Server Core
    3. Nano Server
    4. KDE and GNOME
8. Discuss the boot options: installation media (DVD) vs. USB flash drive vs. network boot.
9. Discuss the installation types: clean installation vs. network installation vs. unattended (automated) installation vs. upgrade vs. migration.

3
Post-Installation Tasks in Windows Server

This chapter explains some steps to take in Windows Server post-installation, including managing devices and device drivers, checking the registry and the status of services, and taking care of the initial server configuration. As you may notice, this chapter is divided into three parts. The first part explains the importance of device drivers after every installation of an operating system. Tasks such as installation, removal, disabling, update/upgrade, rollback, and other related things concerning device drivers are part of a system administrator's day-to-day job. The second part of the OS registry and services talks about the hierarchical database and the background programs that *keep alive* the operating system. Topics such as understanding the registry and services and how to manage the registry and services in a server environment are covered in this part. The third part provides instructions on how to perform the initial server configuration. Each topic is accompanied by step-by-step instructions driven by targeted, easy-to-understand graphics.

In this chapter, we will cover:

- Understanding devices and device drivers
- Working with devices and device drivers
- Explaining **Plug and Play (PnP)**, IRQ, DMA, interrupts, and driver signing
- Understanding the registry and services
- Working with the registry and services
- Explaining registry entries, service accounts, and dependencies
- Performing an initial server configuration

Understanding devices and device drivers (1.1)

Knowing that computer hardware is nothing more than a collection of devices and that the operating system is just a collection of programmed instructions, it is very intriguing to see the interaction between these two computer components. This raises the question, How does the operating system recognize the devices that make up the physical part of a computer?

Computer devices and device drivers

In general, if we agree that the computer system is comprised of a computer case, monitor, keyboard, and mouse, as shown in *Figure 3.1*, then computer devices are organized into internal, external, peripheral, and network devices:

- An *internal device* is any device that is located in the computer's case. Examples of a computer's internal devices are the power supply, motherboard and accompanying components, hard drives, extension cards, and other internal hardware components that constitute the core computer architecture (that is everything inside a computer case).

- An *external device* is any device that is attached or connected to a computer's case, and as such constitutes the whole computer system. Examples of a computer's external devices are the keyboard, monitor, mouse, speakers, earphones, webcam, microphone, and other external hardware components.

- A *peripheral device* is considered to be any device that is geographically located near to the computer, and as such is not an essential part of the computer system as a whole. Examples of peripheral devices are printers, scanners, projectors, plotters, and other peripheral devices.

- A *network device* is actually a peripheral device connected to a computer over a network cable. Examples of network devices are network printers, network scanners, network backup libraries, **Network Attached Storage (NAS)**, **Storage Area Network (SAN)**, and other network devices.

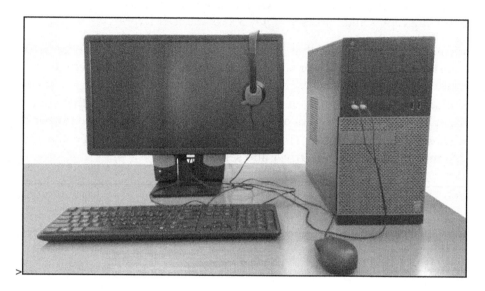

Figure 3.1. The computer

Another categorization of computer devices are *input* and *output* devices. These devices either create input or output for the computer core architecture. Lately, with the advancement of technology, there are devices that act as an input and output device at the same time. Touch-enabled devices are an example of both input/output devices.

 Note that, in today's literature, often external devices are referred to as peripheral devices too because these devices are connected to a computer case to add functionality. This perspective brings us to the conclusion that almost any device that resides outside of the core computer architecture is considered to be a peripheral device.

A *device driver* is a program that acts as a translator between computer hardware and an operating system. So, an OS operates the computer hardware by way of device drivers. Usually, the device drivers come with a DVD disk accompanying the device or can be downloaded from the manufacturer's website. However, there will often be no device driver accompanying the device, since nowadays, devices are PnP. PnP is explained in the *Explaining PnP, IRQ, interrupts, and driver signing* section of this chapter.

Working with devices and device drivers

Usually, devices in Windows settings are used to manage devices, while Device Manager is used to managing device drivers. In Device Manager, note that, other than the proper representation of device drivers (that is, when a proper device driver is installed), there are also the following representations (see *Figure 3.2*) of device drivers:

- **Generic:** This indicates that a generic (that is an alternative) device driver is installed. A generic driver is not always the best or most efficient device driver to use with any given device.
- **Black exclamation point on a yellow triangle:** This indicates that either the device driver is missing, or an installed device driver is not the proper one.
- **Downward black arrow:** This indicates a disabled driver. To enable it, you simply click on a device driver and select **Enable**.

Figure 3.2. Device drivers representation in Device Manager

Accessing devices and Device Manager

To access **Devices**, complete the following steps:

1. Click the **Start** button.
2. On the **Start** menu, click the **Settings** icon.
3. In **Windows Settings**, click **Devices**.

To access **Device Manager**, complete the following steps:

1. Right-click the **Start** button.
2. In the **Power User** menu, select **Device Manager**.
3. Shortly, the **Device Manager** opens.

Other than right-clicking the **Start** button to open the Windows menu, you can use the combination, *Windows key* + *X*. At the same time, to open **Device Manager**, enter `devmgmt.msc` in a **Run** window.

Adding devices and installing device drivers (1.1.1)

To *add a device*, complete the following steps:

1. In the **Devices** navigation menu, click **Printers & scanners** to add a printer or a scanner.
2. In the **Devices** navigation menu, click **Connected devices** to add a device.

To *install a device driver* on Windows Server 2016, complete the following steps:

When the device driver is on a DVD disk or you have downloaded it from the manufacturer's website, perform the following:

1. Insert the *DVD disk* in a DVD drive or locate the downloaded *device driver file* on your server.
2. Through **Windows Explorer**, run the `setup` or `install` file.
3. Follow the instructions in the **Setup or Install Wizard**.

Updating device drivers (1.1.4)

Using **Device Manager** to update the device driver perform the following:

1. **Expand** the device's category.
2. Right-click the device and select **Update driver**.
3. Select **Browse my computer for driver software** as shown in *Figure 3.3*.
4. Follow the instructions in the **Setup or Install Wizard**.

How do you want to search for driver software?

→ Search automatically for updated driver software
Windows will search your computer and the Internet for the latest driver software for your device, unless you've disabled this feature in your device installation settings.

→ Browse my computer for driver software
Locate and install driver software manually.

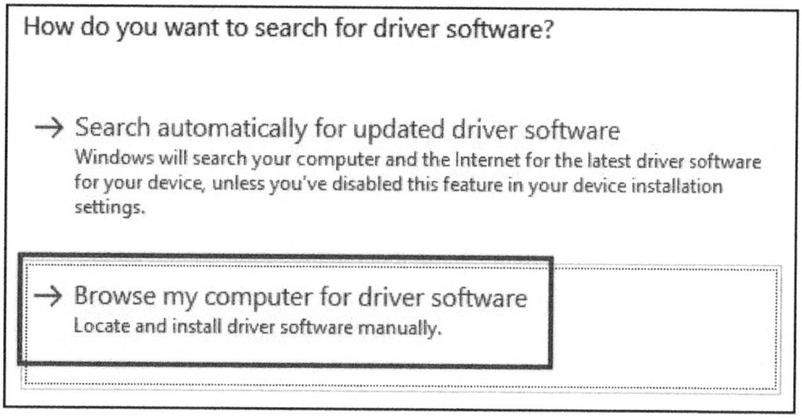

Figure 3.3. Installing a device driver

If you cannot find the device drivers on the internet, then let the **Update Driver Software Wizard** do the work for you by clicking on **Search automatically for updated driver software**.

 Whether you install or update the driver through **Device Manager** or not, you will always use the **Update driver** option.

Removing devices and uninstalling device drivers (1.1.2)

To *remove a device*, complete the following steps:

1. In the **Devices** navigation menu, click **Connected devices** and select the device that you want to remove.
2. Click the **Remove device** button as shown in *Figure 3.4*:

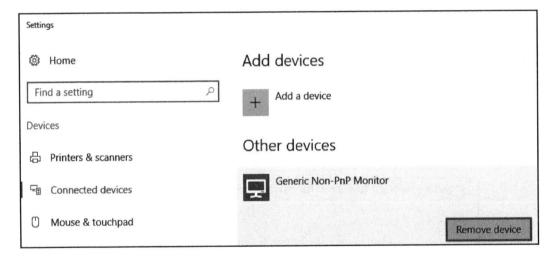

Figure 3.4. Removing a device

To *uninstall a device driver*, complete the following steps:

1. Expand the device's category.
2. Right-click the device and select **Uninstall device**.
3. Click **Uninstall**.

Managing devices and disabling device drivers (1.1.3)

To *manage a device*, complete the following steps:

1. In the **Devices navigation** menu, click **Printers & scanners** and select the device that you want to manage.
2. Click the **Manage** button.

To *disable a device driver*, complete the following steps:

1. Expand the device's category.
2. Right-click the device and select **Disable device**.
3. Click **Yes** as shown in *Figure 3.5*:

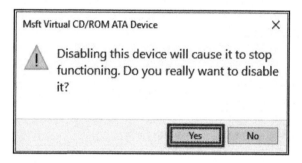

Figure 3.5. Disabling the device driver

Rolling back device drivers (1.1.5)

To *roll back a device driver*, complete the following steps:

1. Expand the device's category.
2. Right-click the device and select **Properties**.

3. Select the **Driver** tab and then click the **Roll Back Driver** button as shown in *Figure 3.6:*

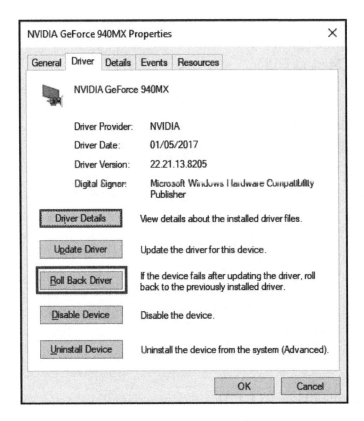

Figure 3.6. Rolling back a device driver

 You will want to roll back a driver if you have installed multiple device drivers or have updated the existing device driver with a newer one and the device is not performing as expected.

Troubleshooting a device driver (1.1.6)

In case there are issues with a device driver, there are several techniques (see *Figure 3.7*) to overcome device driver problems:

- **Update driver:** This enables to update the driver automatically or browse your server for driver software.

- **Roll-back driver:** This enables to roll-back driver if your current driver is causing problems.
- **Disable driver:** This enables to disable driver if the current driver is causing major issues such as server instability.
- **Uninstall driver:** This enables to uninstall current driver if you have found the appropriate driver from the device manufacturer.

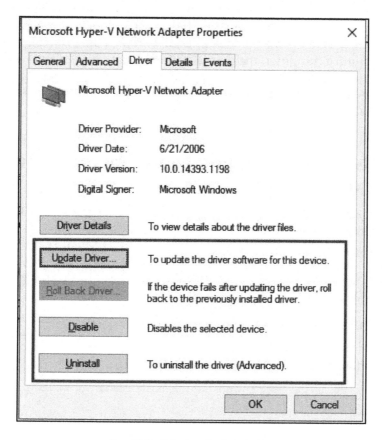

Figure 3.7. Troubleshooting options for device driver

Explaining PnP, IRQ, DMA, and driver signing

In computer hardware, devices use system resources to communicate with each other.

Plug and Play (1.1.7)

From time to time, you hear people say that *"Windows is all about PnP,"*and it really is! As a joint project between Intel and Microsoft, PnP have tremendously simplified the work with devices and device drivers. As the name implies, it works on the principle that when a device is plugged into a computer, the device is immediately recognized by the operating system. In that case, after the Windows server identifies the device then it uses its *Driver Store* to install the device driver. In Windows Server 2016, the *DriverStore* is located at `C:\Windows\System32\DriverStore.`

Interrupt Request (IRQ) and Direct Memory Access (DMA) (1.1.8)

An **Interrupt Request** (IRQ) in modern computers is a number from 0 to 31. It is a signal sent by a device through communication channels to get the attention of a processor whenever that device requires processing. In contrast, **Direct Memory Access (DMA)**, a number from 0 to 8, is a system resource used by a device to bypass the processor whenever that device needs access to RAM. To view IRQ and DMA resource settings in Windows Server 2016, complete the following steps:

1. Open the **Device Manager**.
2. Expand the device's category.
3. Right-click the device and select **Properties**.

4. Click the **Resources** tab and check out the **Resource settings** section as shown in *Figure 3.8:*

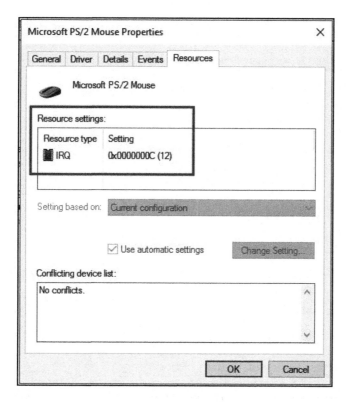

Figure 3.8. Driver's Resource Settings

Driver signing (1.1.9)

Driver signing is a driver's digital signature to identify the publisher of the driver package. Technically, a driver's digital signature proves that Microsoft has tested and approved the driver package ensuring that its installation will not cause any reliability or security issues. To view a driver's digital singing information in Windows Server 2016, complete the following steps:

1. Open the **Device Manager**.
2. Expand the device's category.
3. Right-click the device and select **Properties**.

4. Click the **Driver** tab and check out the **Digital Signer** information as shown in *Figure 3.9*:

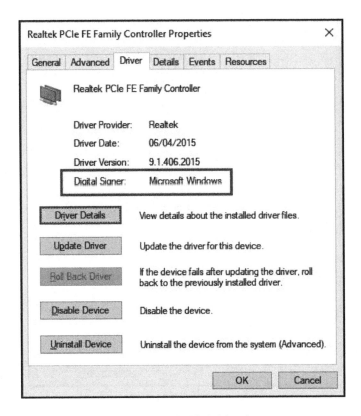

Figure 3.9. Driver's Digital Signing information

Understanding the registry and services (1.2)

Often, the Windows Registry refers to the heart of a Windows OS, and the services are the background programs that *keep alive* the Windows OS applications and utilities. These two software components make up the Windows OS core architecture.

Windows Registry

Any changes made to your server are stored in the registry. That said, the *Windows Registry* is a hierarchical database that stores the hardware/software configuration and system security information. After you access the registry, you will notice that its console tree (left-hand side) consists of five registry keys known as hives (that is HKEYs). Note that the syntax of the registry keys and sub-keys follows the standard of the Windows file path separated by a backslash. In Windows Server 2016 there are five HKEYs:

1. HKEY_CLASSES_ROOT: It stores information on installed applications and their extensions.
2. HKEY_CURRENT_USER: It stores information on the user that is currently logged-in.
3. HKEY_LOCAL_MACHINE: It stores information specific to the local computer.
4. HKEY_USERS: This contains information on logged user profiles.
5. HKEY_CURRENT_CONFIG: This contains information gathered during the boot process.

Windows services (1.2.1)

Whether you are running an application or a network service, working behind the scenes are **Services** that support their execution. These background programs can be started, stopped, restarted, and paused through **Services Control Manager**, as they lack their own user interface.

Services startup types (1.2.3)

When accessing services through **Services Control Manager**, you will notice that for each service there is a description which helps us understand its purpose. Each service has the following start-up types:

- **Automatic:** This service starts automatically when the OS starts.
- **Automatic (Delayed start):** This service starts approximately 2 minutes after all marked automatic services have started.
- **Manual:** This service must be started either by a user or dependent services.
- **Disable:** This service cannot be started by the OS, user, or dependent services.

Working with the registry and services (1.2.2)

While Windows Registry is accessed and managed by the Registry Editor, Windows services are accessed and managed via **Control Manager**.

Accessing and managing Windows Registry keys and values

To *access the Windows Registry*, complete the following steps:

1. Click the **Search Windows** icon in the taskbar.
2. Enter regedit and press *Enter*.
3. Shortly, the **Registry Editor** opens.

Modifying a registry value

To *modify the registry value*, complete the following steps:

1. On the left-hand side of the **Registry Editor**, locate the *registry key* and its *sub-key(s)*.
2. On the right-hand side of the **Registry Editor**, right-click the **registry value** that you want to change and select **Modify,** as shown in *Figure 3.10:*

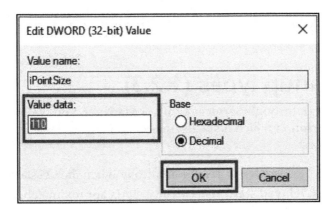

Figure 3.10. Modifying the registry value

Renaming a registry value

To *rename the registry value,* complete the following steps:

1. On the left-hand side of the **Registry Editor,** locate the registry key and its sub-key(s).
2. On the right-hand side of the **Registry Editor,** right-click the registry value that you want to rename and select **Rename,** as shown in *Figure 3.11:*

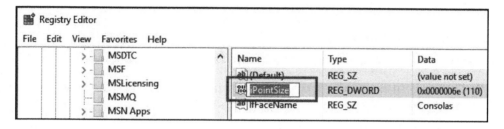

Figure 3.11. Renaming the registry value

Deleting a registry value

To *delete a registry value,* complete the following steps:

1. On the left-hand side of the **Registry Editor,** locate the registry key and its sub-key(s).
2. On the right-hand side of the **Registry Editor,** right-click the registry value that you want to delete and select **Delete,** as shown in *Figure 3.12:*

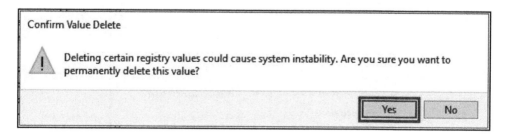

Figure 3.12. Deleting the registry value

 We work with registry keys in the same way we do with registry values. Delete, rename, and export is some of the operations that you can accomplish with registry keys.

Accessing and managing Windows services

To access the **Windows services**, complete the following steps:

1. Click the **Start** button.
2. In the **Start** menu, select the **Windows Administrative Tools**.
3. Scroll down and select **Services**.
4. Shortly, the **Windows Services Control Manager** opens up.

Service recovery options (1.2.4)

In case a service fails, you can set up **service recovery options** as follows:

1. On the right-hand side of the **Services** window, right-click the service that you want to set up recovery options for.
2. In the context menu, select **Properties**.
3. From the opened window, click the **Recovery** tab.
4. Select the computer's response if the service fails by specifying **First Failure**, **Second Failure**, and **Subsequent failures** actions, as in *Figure 3.13*:

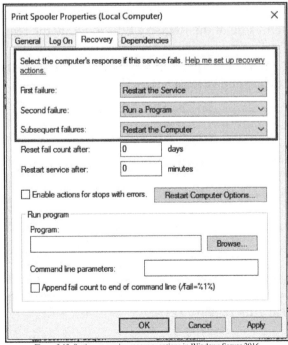

Figure 3.13. Setting up service recovery options in Windows Server 2016

5. Click **OK**.

Service delayed startup (1.2.5)

Usually, services start when the server is booted. If you want to delay the start of a service, complete the following steps:

1. On the right-hand side of the **Services** window, right-click the service that you want to delay.
2. In the context menu, select **Properties**.
3. From the **General** tab, click the **Startup type** drop-down list.
4. Select **Automatic (Delayed start)** as shown in *Figure 3.14*:

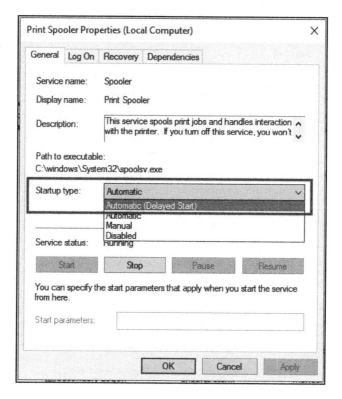

Figure 3.14. Setting up service delayed startup in Windows Server 2016

5. Click **OK**.

Run As settings for a service (1.2.6)

To set up the **Log on** settings for a service, complete the following steps:

1. On the right-hand side of the **Services** window, right-click the service that you want to delay.
2. In the context menu, select **Properties**.
3. In the opened window, click the **Log on** tab.
4. In the **Log on as:** section, click the**This account** option.
5. Enter a user account including domain with backslash, **Password**, and **Confirm password** as in *Figure 3.15*:

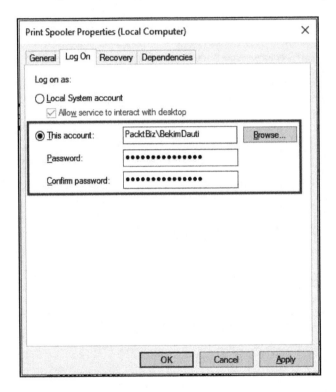

Figure 3.15. Setting up Log on settings for a service in Windows Server 2016

6. Click **OK**.

Starting the service (1.2.7)

To start the service, complete the following steps:

1. On the right-hand side of the **Services** window, right-click the service that you want to start.
2. In the context menu, select **Start** as shown in *Figure 3.16*:

Figure 3.16. Starting the service

Stopping the service (1.2.7)

To stop the service, complete the following steps:

1. On the right-hand side of the **Services** window, right-click the service that you want to stop.
2. In the context menu, select **Stop** as shown in *Figure 3.17*:

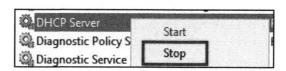

Figure 3.17. Stopping the service

Restarting the service (1.2.7)

To restart the service, complete the following steps:

1. On the right-hand side of the **Services** window, right-click the service that you want to restart.

2. In the context menu, select **Restart** as shown in *Figure 3.18*:

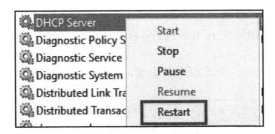

Figure 3.18. Restarting the service

Explaining registry entries, service accounts, and dependencies (1.2.8)

In most cases, you will end up adding a new registry key or a registry value when you are fixing an issue, or adding a new feature to your Windows Server. No matter what, you should always be careful when working with the registry. In regard to services, the service account is the Windows Server's native account or an account created by you to manage the running services. From a security standpoint, the service account enables the services to access both local and network resources. From the perspective of the accounts that the services run, the following service accounts are available in Windows Server 2016:

- **Local System:** This is a built-in account with the most privileges in a Windows OS. It is also known as a superuser, and this account is more powerful than your admin account.
- **NT Authority\LocalService:** This is a built-in account with the same privileges as members of the Users group.
- **NT Authority\NetworkService:** This is a built-in account that has more privileges than members of the Users group.

As far as service dependency is concerned, what often happens is that applications use more than one service. So, if you try to stop a service, you need to stop a few others too. Conversely, if you try to start a service, a few others will need starting too. Thus, dependencies are created between the services.

Adding a new registry key

To add a new registry key, complete the following steps:

1. On the left-hand side of the **Registry Editor**, right-click the registry key or its sub-key(s).

2. In the context menu, select **New | Key** as shown in *Figure 3.19*:

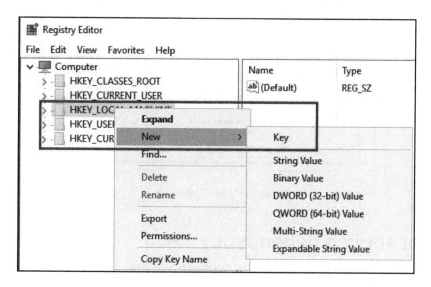

Figure 3.19. Adding the registry entry

 To add a new registry value, right-click the empty space on the right-side of the **Registry Editor** after you have located the registry key or its sub-key(s). In the context menu, select **New |** and the type of value you want to add.

Adding service accounts

To add a service account, complete the following steps:

1. On the right-hand side of the **Services** window, right-click the service that you want to add a service account too.

2. In the context menu, select **Properties**.

3. In the **Properties** window, click the **Log On** tab, as shown in *Figure 3.20*.

4. In the **Log on as:** section, select **This account** option and click the **Browse** button.

5. Specify the service account in your organization's **Active Directory**.
6. Enter the service account's **Password** and **Confirm the password**.
7. Click **OK** to close the **Properties** window.

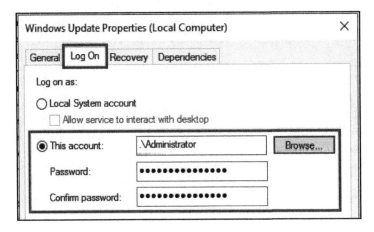

Figure 3.20. Adding the service account

Adding a service dependency

To add a service dependency, complete the following steps:

1. On the left-hand side of the **Registry Editor**, locate the **service** (HKEY_LOCAL_MACHINE\SYSTEM\CurrentControlSet\Services\) that you want to add a dependency too.
2. On the right-hand side of it, modify the value if there is a DependOnService value.
3. If not, then right-click in empty space, and select **Multi-string value** to create a DependOnService value.
4. Rename the DependOnService value with the exact name of the service that you want to create a dependency for.
5. Restart the server.
6. With **Services** open, locate the service that you have created a dependency for and right-click it to select **Properties**.
7. In the **Properties** window, click the **Dependencies** tab to see the added dependency.

Windows Server initial configuration

After setting up the device drivers and ensuring that the OS services are up and running, *initial server configuration* is a must. It is an activity that involves changing the server name, joining a domain (depends on the role of the server), enabling remote desktop, setting up the static IP address, changing the time zone, activating Windows Server 2016, turning off **Internet Explorer** (**IE**) enhanced security, and checking for updates. This ensures that the server is ready to take a new role in an organization's IT infrastructure.

Performing a server's initial configuration

The server's initial configuration is a very important task as it determines the functional status of the server just before taking on the task of adding roles. Thus, from my experience, first you will want to set up the IP address, change the time zone, activate your Windows Server 2016, and then proceed with checking for updates, changing the default server name, joining the domain, enabling remote desktop, and finally turning off IE enhanced security. With that in mind, let us perform the server's initial configuration both for Desktop Experience and Server Core installation options.

Desktop Experience

In Desktop Experience, the initial server configuration can be accomplished using **Server Manager,** as shown in *Figure 3.21*. After first logging into Windows Server 2016, the **Server Manager** starts automatically. It will always start automatically unless you change it.

To run the server's initial configuration, click **Configure this local server**:

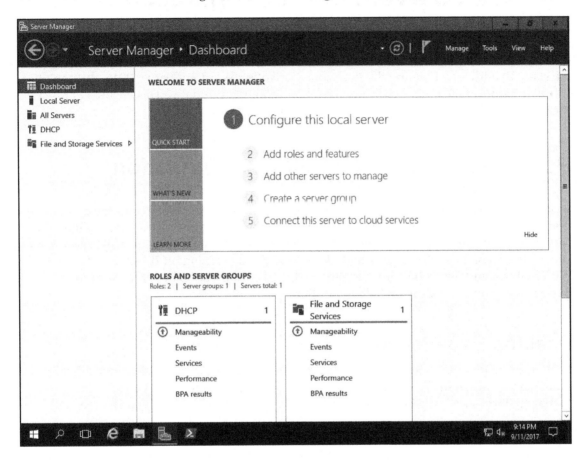

Figure 3.21. Server Manager in Windows Server 2016

Changing the server name

To change the server name as in *Figure 3.22*, complete the following steps:

1. In the **Properties** section, click the highlighted default **Computer Name**.
2. In the **System Properties** window, click the **Change** button.
3. In the **Computer Name/Domain Changes** window, delete the existing computer name and provide the name for your server. Then click **OK**:

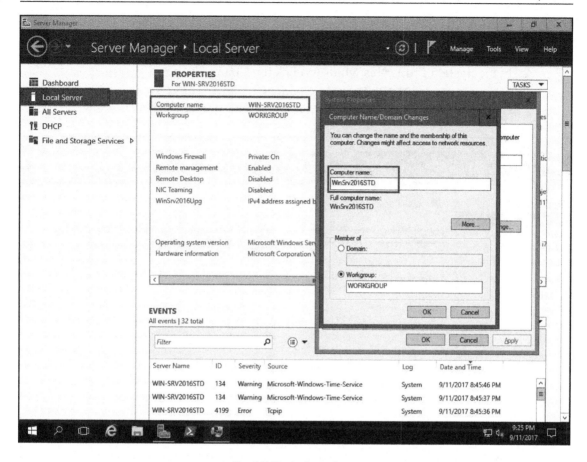

Figure 3.22. Changing the server's name

4. Click **OK** to confirm that you will **restart your server to apply these changes**.
5. In the **System Properties** window, click the **Close** button.
6. In the Microsoft Windows dialog box, click **Restart Now**.

Joining the domain

Before joining the server to a domain, evaluate the role of your server. If your server is going to be a DC then there is no need for it to join a domain, as adding the AD DS role will automatically make your server a domain controller. Otherwise, if your server is going to have a role other than AD DS, then as a domain member it must join the domain as in *Figure 3.23*.

To do so, complete the following steps:

1. In the **Properties** section, click the highlighted **Workgroup**.
2. In the **System Properties** window, click the **Change** button.
3. In the **Computer Name/Domain Changes** window, select the **Domain** option and click the text box to provide your organization's domain. Then click **OK**:

Figure 3.23. Joining a server to a domain

4. In the Windows Security window, enter the name and password of an account with a permission to join the domain. Then click **OK**.
5. The **Computer Name/Domain Changes** dialog box welcomes your server to your organization's domain. Click **OK** to close it.
6. Click **OK** to confirm that you will restart your server to apply these changes.

7. In the **System Properties** window, click the **Close** button.
8. In the Microsoft Windows dialog box, click **Restart Now**.

Enabling Remote Desktop

To enable Remote Desktop, as in *Figure 3.24*, complete the following steps:

1. In the **Properties** section, click the highlighted **Remote Desktop** setting.
2. In the **System Properties** window, select the **Allow remote connections to this computer** option.
3. The **Remote Desktop Connection** dialog box informs you that the **Remote Desktop Firewall exception will be enabled**. Click **OK** to close it:

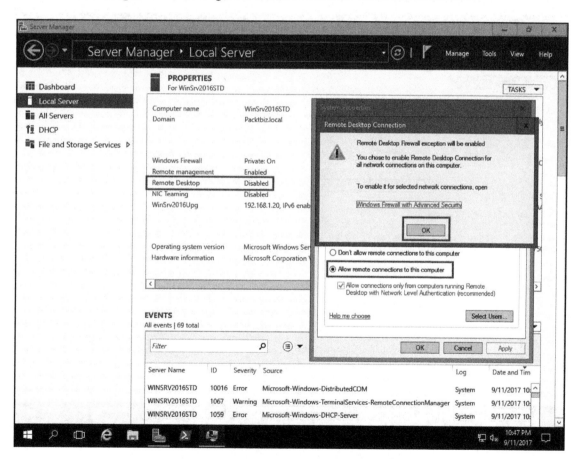

Figure 3.24. Enabling Remote Desktop

4. To add Remote Desktop users, click the **Select Users...** button.

5. In the **Remote Desktop Users** window, click the **Add** button to add users. Select users or groups from your AD DS. When you have finished adding RD users, click **OK** to close the **Remote Desktop Users** window.

6. Again, click **OK** to close the **System Properties** window.

Setting up the IP address

To set up the IP address, as in *Figure 3.25*, complete the following steps:

1. In the **Properties** section, click the highlighted **Ethernet** setting:

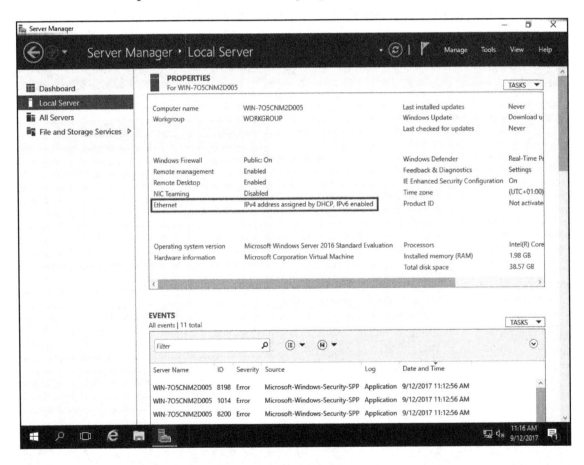

Figure 3.25. Setting up the IP address

2. In the **Network Connections** window, right-click your server's Ethernet and select **Properties**.

3. In the **Ethernet Properties** window, select **Internet Protocol Version 4 (TCP/IPv4)** and click the **Properties** button.

4. In the **Internet Protocol Version 4 (TCP/IPv4) Properties** window, select the option **Use the following IP address:** and enter the IP address, Subnet mask, and Default gateway. Additionally, select **Use the following DNS server addresses:** option and enter the **Preferred DNS server** and **Alternate DNS server**. Click **OK** to close.

5. Click the **Close** button to close the **Ethernet Properties** window.

6. In the upper-right corner, click **Close** (the red X) to close the **Network Connections** window.

Checking for updates

To check for updates, as in *Figure 3.26*, complete the following steps:

1. In the **Properties** section, click the highlighted **Last checked for updates** setting.

2. In the **Settings** window on the right-hand side of the Windows **Update** section, the Available updates are listed (if any). If any updates are ready for installation, then click the **Install now** button:

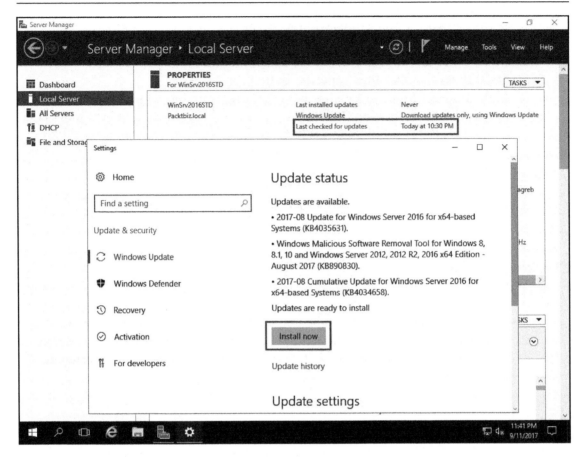

Figure 3.26. Checking for updates

3. Installing updates might take some time! When the installation is done, often you will be asked to **Restart** the server for the updates to take place.

Turning off IE enhanced security

To turn off the IE enhanced security settings, as in *Figure 3.27*, complete the following steps:

1. In the **Properties** section, click the highlighted **IE Enhanced Security Configuration** setting.
2. In the **IE Enhanced Security Configuration** window within the **Administrators** section, select the **Off** option.

3. Click **OK** to close the **Internet Explorer Enhanced Security Configuration** window.

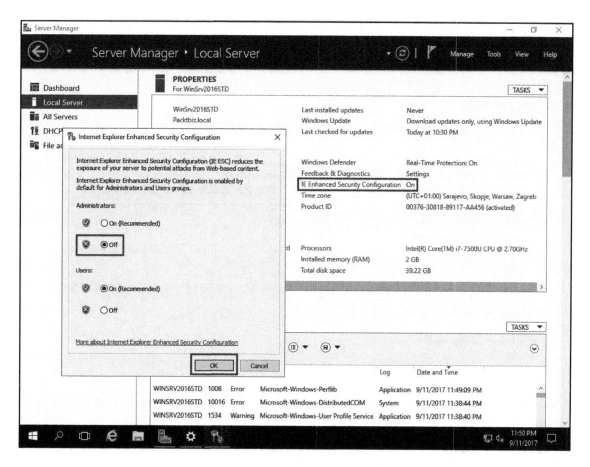

Figure 3.27. Turning off IE enhanced security

Changing the time zone

To change the time zone, as in *Figure 3.28*, complete the following steps:

1. In the **Properties** section, click the highlighted **Time Zone** setting.
2. In the **Date and Time** window, click the **Change time zone...** button.
3. In the **Time Zone Settings** window, click the drop-down list to select your **time zone**.

4. Click **OK** to close the **Time Zone Settings** window.

5. Again, click **OK** to close the **Date and Time** window:

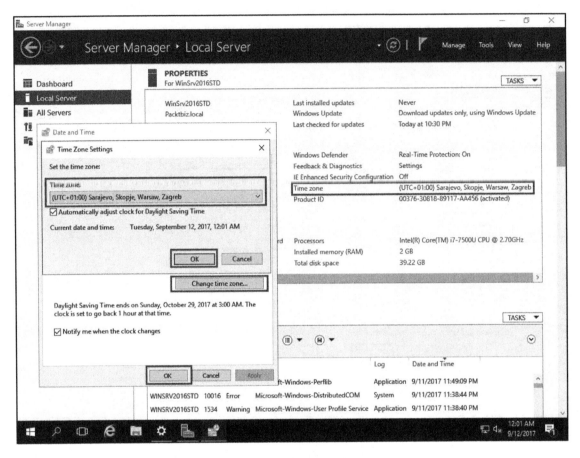

Figure 3.28. Changing time zone

Activating Windows Server 2016

To activate your Windows Server 2016 (Desktop Experience), as in *Figure 3.29*, complete the following steps:

1. In the Properties section, click the highlighted **Not activated** setting of **Product ID**:

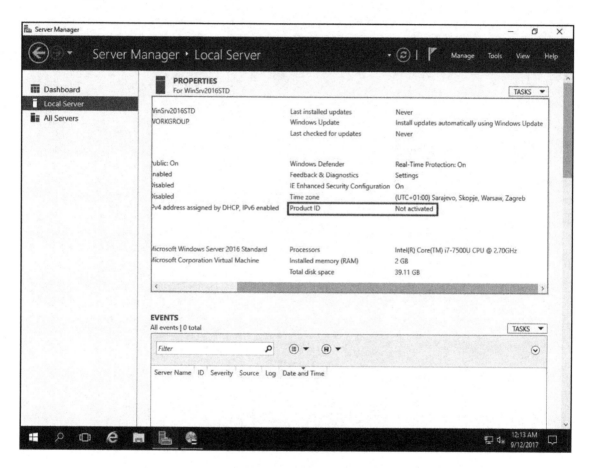

Figure 3.29. Activating Windows Server 2016

2. In the **Enter a product key** window, enter your Windows Server 2016 product key and press *Enter*.

3. Microsoft's Activation Server checks the product key you entered. If it is valid, click **Next** in the **Activate Windows** window.

4. When activation finishes, click **Close** to close the **Thank you for activating** the window.

Server Core

In Server Core, the initial server configuration can be accomplished through the **Server Configuration** tool, as shown in *Figure 3.30*. In contrast to **Server Manager**, the **Server Configuration** tool is accessed by entering `SConfig.cmd` at Command Prompt:

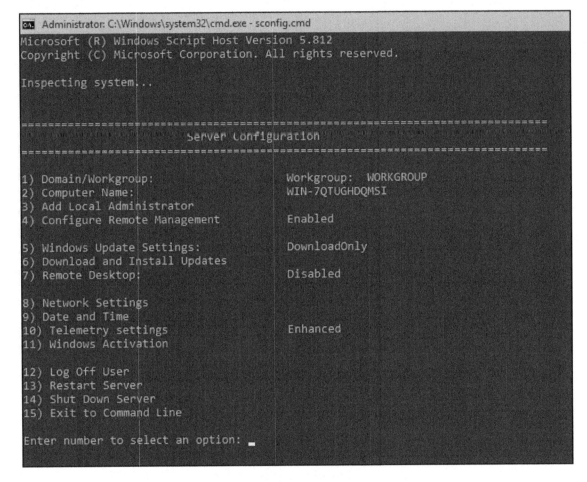

Figure 3.30. Server Configuration in Windows Server 2016

Changing the server name

To change the server name, as in *Figure 3.31*, complete the following steps:

1. Enter 2 as a selected option and press *Enter*.
2. Enter the new server name and press *Enter*.

3. In the **Restart** dialog box, click **Yes** to restart the server:

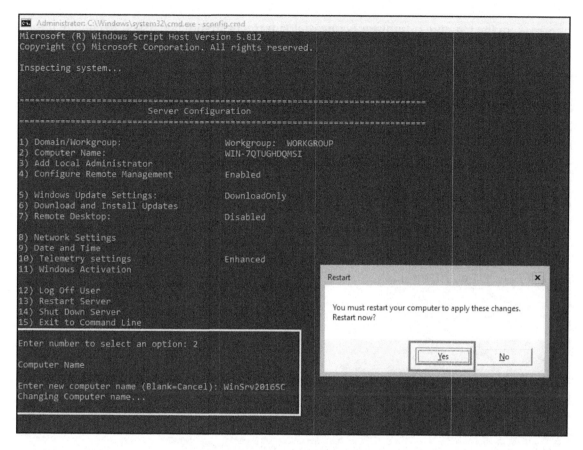

Figure 3.31. Changing the server's name

4. Your server is restarting so it can apply the server name change.

Joining the domain

Before joining the domain, take into consideration the notes explained earlier in the *Desktop Experience - Joining the domain* section. To join the domain, as in *Figure 3.32*, complete the following steps:

1. Enter 1 as a selected option and press *Enter*.
2. To join your server to your organization's domain, enter D and press *Enter*.
3. Enter your organization's domain and press *Enter*.

4. Enter the authorized domain user and press *Enter*.

5. Enter the password and press *Enter*.

6. In the **Change Computer Name** dialog box, click **No** when asked to change the name of your server:

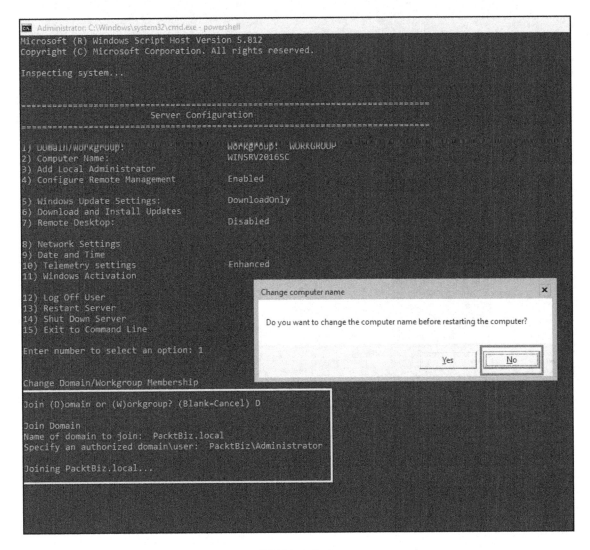

3.32. Joining the domain

Enabling Remote Desktop

To enable Remote Desktop, as in *Figure 3.33*, complete the following steps:

1. Enter 7 as a selected option and press *Enter*.
2. To enable Remote Desktop, enter E and press *Enter*.
3. Enter 1 and press *Enter* for more secure access.
4. In the **Remote Desktop** dialog box, click **OK** to confirm Remote Desktop enabling:

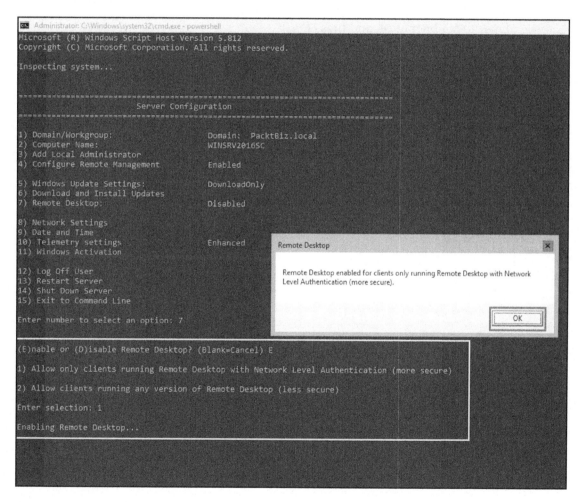

Figure 3.33. Enabling Remote Desktop

Setting up the IP address

To set up the IP address, as in *Figure 3.34*, complete the following steps:

1. Enter 8 as a selected option and press *Enter*.
2. Enter the number of the network adapter that you want to set up the IP address for and press *Enter*.
3. Enter 1 in the sub-menu to Set Network Adapter Address and press *Enter*.
4. Enter s for Static IP address and press *Enter*.
5. Enter the Static IP address and press *Enter*.
6. Enter the Subnet mask and press *Enter*.
7. Enter the Default gateway and press *Enter*.
8. Enter 2 in the sub-menu to Set DNS Servers and press *Enter*.
9. Enter the new preferred DNS server and press *Enter*.
10. In the **Network Settings** dialog box, click **OK** to close it.
11. Enter the alternate DNS server and press *Enter*.
12. Enter 4 in the sub-menu to exit and **Return to Main Menu**.

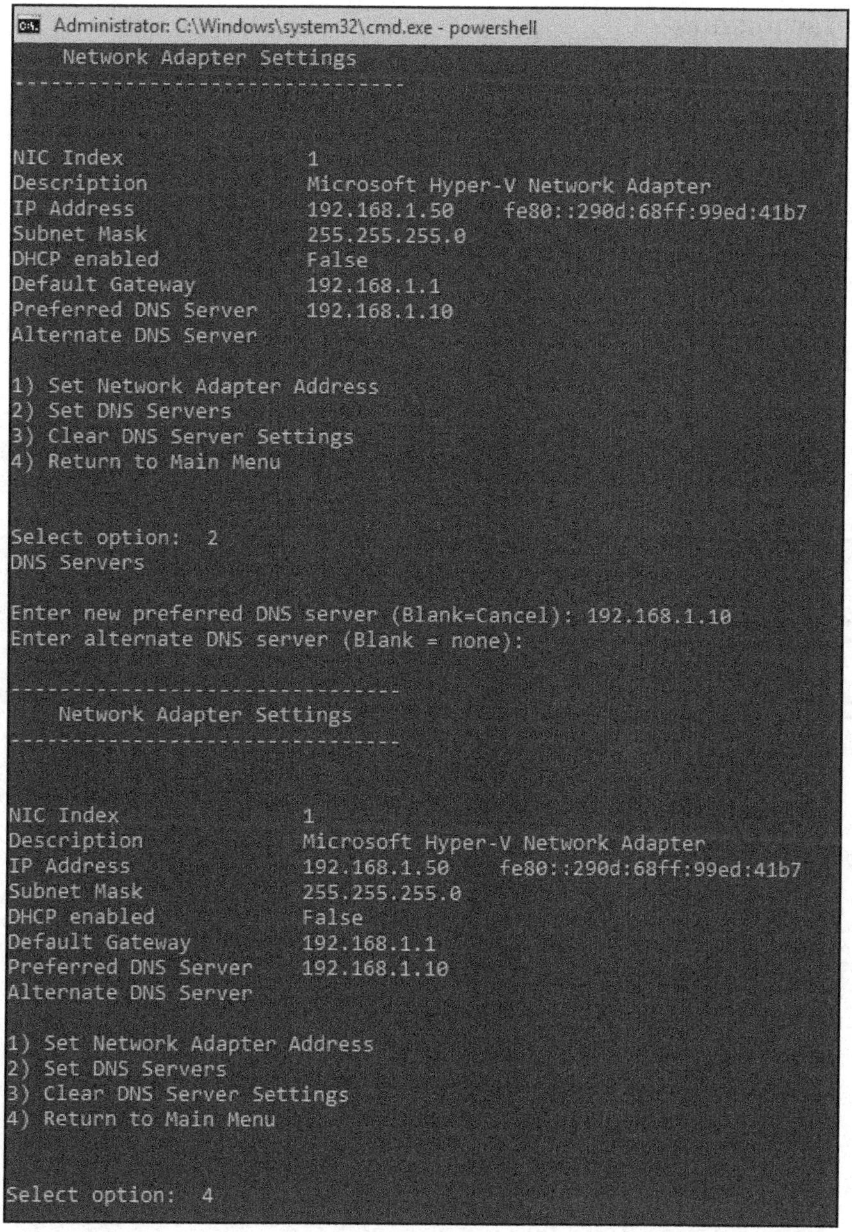

```
■ Administrator: C:\Windows\system32\cmd.exe - powershell
    Network Adapter Settings
------------------------------------


NIC Index               1
Description             Microsoft Hyper-V Network Adapter
IP Address              192.168.1.50      fe80::290d:68ff:99ed:41b7
Subnet Mask             255.255.255.0
DHCP enabled            False
Default Gateway         192.168.1.1
Preferred DNS Server    192.168.1.10
Alternate DNS Server

1) Set Network Adapter Address
2) Set DNS Servers
3) Clear DNS Server Settings
4) Return to Main Menu


Select option:  2
DNS Servers

Enter new preferred DNS server (Blank=Cancel): 192.168.1.10
Enter alternate DNS server (Blank = none):

------------------------------------
    Network Adapter Settings
------------------------------------


NIC Index               1
Description             Microsoft Hyper-V Network Adapter
IP Address              192.168.1.50      fe80::290d:68ff:99ed:41b7
Subnet Mask             255.255.255.0
DHCP enabled            False
Default Gateway         192.168.1.1
Preferred DNS Server    192.168.1.10
Alternate DNS Server

1) Set Network Adapter Address
2) Set DNS Servers
3) Clear DNS Server Settings
4) Return to Main Menu


Select option:  4
```

Figure 3.34. Setting up the IP address

Checking for updates

To check for updates, as in *Figure 3.35*, complete the following steps:

1. Enter 6 as a selected option and press *Enter*.
2. In a new window, enter A for All or R for Recommended updates and press *Enter*.
3. Shortly, Windows Update starts searching for updates.
4. If applicable updates are found then enter A for All, N for No updates, or S for Single update, and press *Enter*.
5. When the updates are downloaded, the installation takes place. Click **Yes** to **Restart** your server:

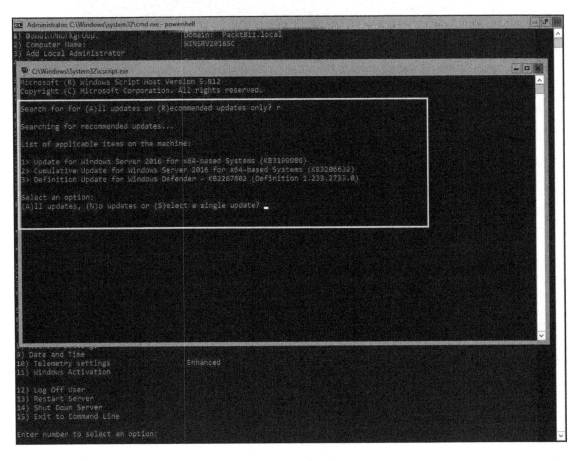

Figure 3.35. Checking for updates

Changing the time zone

To change the time zone, as in *Figure 3.36*, complete the following steps:

1. Enter 9 as a selected option and press *Enter*.
2. In the **Date and Time** window, click the **Change time zone...** button.
3. In the **Time Zone Settings** window, click the drop-down list to select your **time zone**.
4. Click **OK** to close the **Time Zone Settings** window.
5. Again, click **OK** to close the **Date and Time window**:

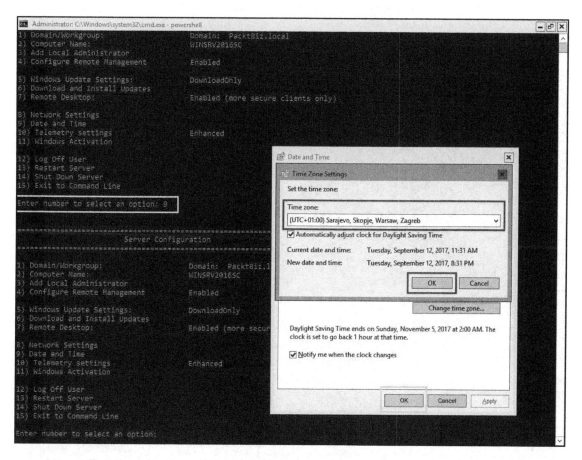

Figure 3.36. Changing Time Zone

Activating Windows Server 2016

To activate Windows Server 2016 Server Core, as in *Figure 3.37*, complete the following steps:

1. Enter 11 as a selected option and press *Enter*.
2. Enter 3 in the sub-menu to install the product key and press *Enter*.
3. In the **Enter Product Key** window, enter the Windows Server's 2016 product key and click **OK**.
4. Enter 2 from the sub-menu to **Activate Windows** and press *Enter*.
5. Shortly, your Windows Server 2016 will activate. Enter Exit to close the Activation window.
6. Enter 4 from the sub-menu to exit and **Return to Main Menu**:

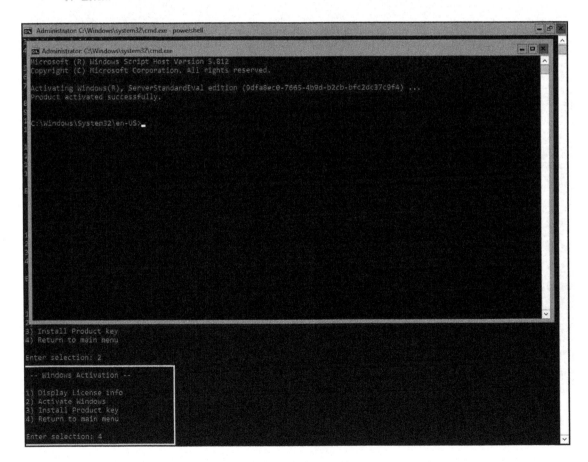

Figure 3.37. Activating Windows Server 2016

References from Windows IT Pro Center

1. Server Manager in Windows Server 2016 (`https://docs.microsoft.com/en-us/windows-server/administration/server-manager/server-manager`)
2. Keyboard Shortcuts for Server Manager in Windows Server 2016 (`https://docs.microsoft.com/en-us/windows-server/administration/server-manager/keyboard-shortcuts-for-server-manager`)
3. Configure a Server Core installation of Windows Server 2016 (`https://docs.microsoft.com/en-us/windows-server/get-started/sconfig-on-ws2016`)

Summary

We summarize the chapter with following points:

- A computer system is comprised of the computer case, monitor, keyboard, and mouse.
- An internal device is any device that is located in the computer's case.
- An external device is any device that is attached or connected to a computer's case, and as such constitutes the whole computer system.
- A peripheral device is considered to be any device that is geographically located near to a computer, and as such is not an essential part of the computer system as a whole.
- A network device is actually a peripheral device connected to a computer by a network cable.
- A device driver is a program which acts as the translator between the computer hardware and an operating system.
- A generic driver indicates that a generic (that is, alternative) device driver is installed instead of a proper one.
- A black exclamation point on a yellow triangle next to a device indicates that either the device driver is missing, or an installed device driver is not the proper one.
- A downwards black arrow on a device indicates a disabled driver.
- In computer hardware, devices use system resources to communicate with each other.

- Plug and play work on the principle that when a device is plugged into a computer, the device is immediately recognized by the operating system.
- An IRQ, in modern computers a number from 0 to 31, is a signal sent by a device through communications channels to get the attention of a processor whenever that device requires processing.
- DMA, a number from 0 to 8, is a system resource used by a device to bypass the processor whenever that device needs access to RAM.
- Driver signing is a driver's digital signature to identify the publisher of the driver package.
- The Windows Registry is a hierarchical database that stores the hardware and software configurations, and system security information.
- HKEY_CLASSES_ROOT stores information on the installed applications and their extensions.
- HKEY_CURRENT_USER stores information on the user that is currently logged-in.
- HKEY_LOCAL_MACHINE stores information specific to the local computer.
- HKEY_USERS contains information on the logged user profiles.
- HKEY_CURRENT_CONFIG contains information gathered during the boot process.
- The services are the background programs that *keep alive* the Windows OS, applications and utilities.
- Automatic services start automatically when the OS starts.
- Automatic (Delayed start) services start approximately 2 minutes after all marked Automatic services have started.
- Manual services must be started either by a user or dependent services.
- Disable services cannot be started by the OS, user, or dependent services.
- Local System is the built-in account with the most privileges in a Windows OS. Known as a superuser, this account is more powerful than your admin account.
- NT Authority\LocalService is the built-in account with the same privileges as members of the Users group.
- NT Authority\NetworkService is a built-in account that has more privileges than members of the Users group.
- The service account is the Windows Server's native account or an account created by you to manage the running services.
- After setting up the device drivers and ensuring that the OS services are up and running, initial server configuration is a must.

Questions

1. A device driver is a program which acts as the translator between computer hardware and an operating system. (True | False)

2. _____ works on the principle that when a device is plugged into a computer, the device is immediately recognized by the operating system.

3. Which of the following are known as a computer's system resources? (Choose two)
    1. IRQ
    2. DMA
    3. SAN
    4. NAS

4. A driver's digital signature identifies its publisher. (True | False)

5. _____ is a hierarchical database that stores the hardware and software configurations, and system security information.

6. Which of the following Windows Server tools are used to operate devices and device drivers? (Choose two)
    1. Devices
    2. Device Manager
    3. Registry Editor
    4. Control Manager

7. Which of the following Windows Server tools are used to operate the registry and services? (Choose two)
    1. Services Control Manager
    2. Registry Editor
    3. Device Manager
    4. Devices

8. The _____ is the Windows Server's native account, or an account created by you to manage the running services.

9. Discuss the Windows Registry keys.

10. Discuss the Windows Services start-up types.

4
Directory Services in Windows Server

Now that you have learned how to install Windows Server 2016 and run the initial server configuration, it is time to set up the very first services in your organization's IT infrastructure. With that in mind, this chapter explains directory services. Specifically, this chapter will cover Microsoft's **Active Directory** (**AD**) infrastructure and **Domain Name System** (**DNS**) in Windows Server 2016 so that you will become familiar with topics such as domains, forests, trees, domain controllers, functional levels, trust relationships, organizational units, groups, forward lookup zones, reverse lookup zone, DNS records, and many others. Other than that, you will get to know the **Active Directory Domain Services** (**AD DS**), and DNS roles so that you can set up a domain controller and a DNS server in your organization's IT infrastructure. Additionally, you will become familiarized with **Organizational Units** (**OUs**), default containers, user accounts, and groups so that you can organize the user and computer accounts in your domain.

In this chapter, we will cover:

- Understanding the AD infrastructure
- Adding the AD DS role
- Understanding DNS
- Adding the DNS role
- Understanding OUs and default containers
- Operating with OUs
- Understanding accounts and groups
- Operating with groups

Understanding the Active Directory infrastructure (3.3)

AD a Microsoft technology is a distributed database that stores objects in a hierarchical, structured, and secure format. AD's objects typically represent users, computers, peripheral devices, and network services. Each object is uniquely identified by its **name** and **attributes**. The domain, the forest, and the tree represent logical divisions of an AD infrastructure. AD uses the following protocols and services:

- **Lightweight Directory Access Protocol** (**LDAP**): It is used to access the directory services data
- **Kerberos:** Kerberos securely authenticates and proves identity between users and servers on the network
- **Domain Name System** (**DNS**): DNS is used to translate domain names into IP addresses

AD is managed through the following snap-ins in **Microsoft Management** (**MMC**) (`mmc.exe`):

- **Active Directory Administrative Center** (`dsac.exe`): Shown in *Figure 4.1*, it is the one stop-place that is used to manage Windows Server's directory services
- **Active Directory Users and Computers** (`dsa.msc`): This console is used to manage users, computers, and relevant information
- **Active Directory Domains and Trusts** (`domain.msc`): This console is used to manage domains, trusts, and relevant information
- **Active Directory Sites and Services** (`dssite.msc`): This console is used to manage the replication and services between sites

- **Active Directory Module for Windows PowerShell**: This console is used to manage the Windows Server's directory services through `cmdlets`

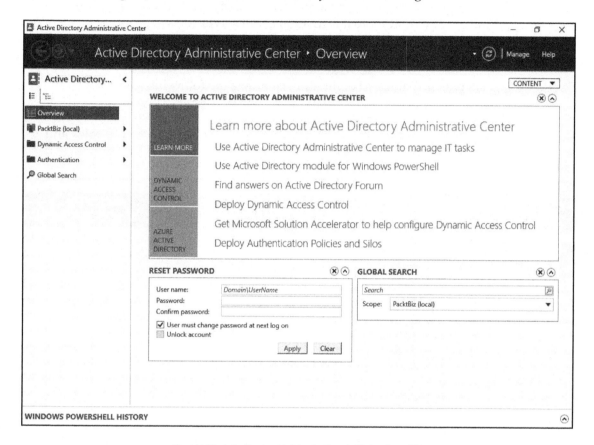

Figure 4.1. The Active Directory Administrative Center in Windows Server 2016

 You can access Microsoft's Script Center at `https://technet.microsoft.com/en-us/scriptcenter/bb410849.aspx`, and PowerShell Gallery at `https://www.powershellgallery.com/`. Both are well-known repositories of free and public domain PowerShell scripts. Additionally, substantial collections of AD- and DNS-related entries are included.

Adding the Active Directory Domain Services role

To set up domain services in your organization's IT infrastructure, add the AD DS role to your server. While you can find more information about server roles in `Chapter 5`, *Adding Roles to Windows Server*, AD DS is a role in Windows Server 2016 that lets system administrators manage and store a network's information resources.

To add the AD DS role in Windows Server 2016, complete the following steps:

1. Open up the **Server Manager.**
2. Within the **WELCOME TO SERVER MANAGER** section, click **Add roles and features** as shown in *Figure 4.2*:

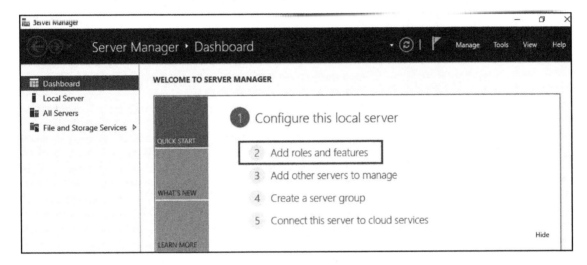

Figure 4.2. Adding roles and features to your server with Server Manager

3. With the **Add roles and features** Wizard open, click **Next**.
4. Select the **Role-based or feature-based installation** option and click **Next**.
5. With the **Select a server from the server pool** option checked, click **Next**.

6. Select the **Active Directory Domain Services** role as in *Figure 4.3*, then click **Next**:

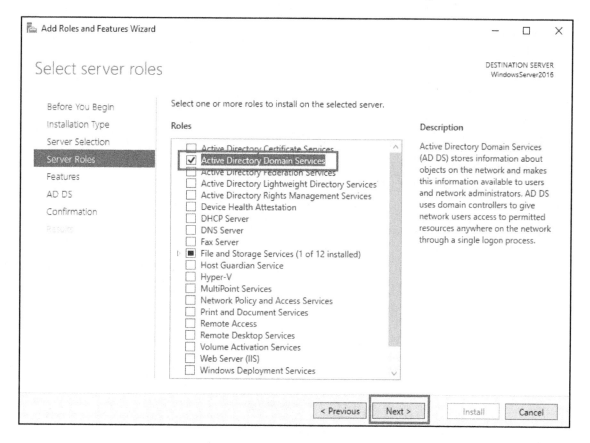

Figure 4.3. Add Roles and Features Wizard in Windows Server 2016

7. Click the **Add Features** button when the *Add features that are required for AD DS* window is displayed. Click **Next**.
8. Accept the default settings in the **Select features** step, and click **Next**.
9. Take your time to read the *AD DS* definition and the things to note regarding AD DS installation. Then, click **Next**.
10. Confirm installation selections for the AD DS role, and click the **Install** button.
11. Either hit **Close**, or wait until the installation progress reaches its end.
12. Click **Close** to close the **Add roles and features** Wizard.
13. In *Notifications*, click **Promote this server to a domain controller**.

14. In the AD DS **Configuration** Wizard, select the **Add a new forest** option as in *Figure 4.4*, then enter **Root domain name**. Click **Next**:

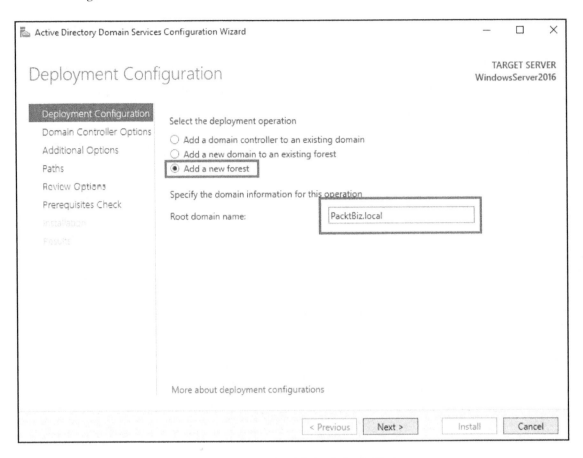

Figure 4.4. Acive Directory Domain Services Configuration Wizard

15. Accept the defaults for the Forest and Domain functional levels, and enter the **Directory Services Restore Mode (DSRM)** password. Click **Next**.

16. If you have an existing DNS on your network, then manually create a delegation for that DNS server to enable reliable name resolution from outside of your domain. Otherwise, no action is required. Click **Next**.

17. Either accept the default NetBIOS entry, or change it accordingly. Click **Next**.

18. Either accept the default paths, or change them accordingly. Click **Next**.

19. Review your options, and click **Next**.

20. Since the prerequisites are met, click **Install**.
21. The server will restart to complete promoting itself as a domain controller.

Domain controller (3.3.1)

A **domain controller (DC)** (see *Figure 4.5*) is a server that is responsible for securely authenticating requests for accessing resources in your organization's domain. In Windows NT, there was one domain controller per domain configured as **Primary Domain Controller** (PDC), and all other domain controllers acted as **Backup Domain Controllers** (BDC). With Windows Server 2016, there are no primary and backup concepts, instead numbers are used next to DCs to identify priorities (for example, DC1 and DC2):

Figure 4.5. Accessing Domain Controllers through Active Directory Administrative Center

 A server that is not acting as a domain controller in an organization's network, is known to be a member server.

Domain

A domain is a logical grouping of users, computers, peripherals, network services, and security settings. From the perspective of network service access, domains are usually centralized network environments where authentication is governed by a domain controller. In Windows Server-based networks, the domain is powered by the AD DS role.

Figure 4.6 presents the step in the Active Directory Domain Services Configuration Wizard to specify the domain:

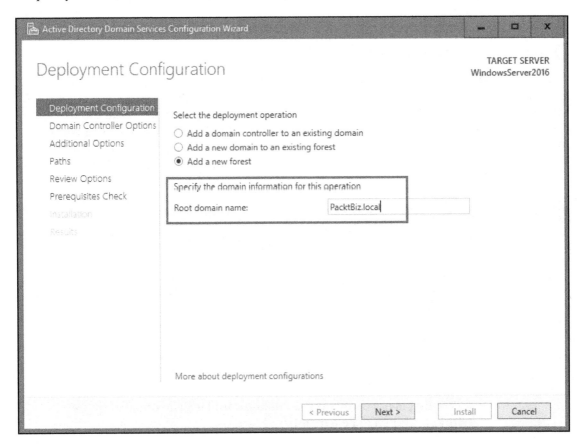

Figure 4.6. Setting up a root domain in Windows Server 2016

You must understand that there is a profound difference in the meaning of *domain* in the context of a directory domain or a domain server, and in the context of *domain name*. The former means a database of users, servers, devices, and resources within a specific collection of such things. The latter means the logical naming system that governs the internet, including web servers and websites.

Tree

A Tree in an AD structure is comprised of one or more domains. Domains in a tree are linked through a transitive trust. In a transitive trust, if A trusts B, and B trusts C, then A trusts C. That said, in a tree domain when a new domain joins an existing tree, then the new domain automatically trusts all existing domains in the tree. Similar to adding a domain, the tree domain is configured during the *Promote this server to a domain controller* process as in *Figure 4.7*:

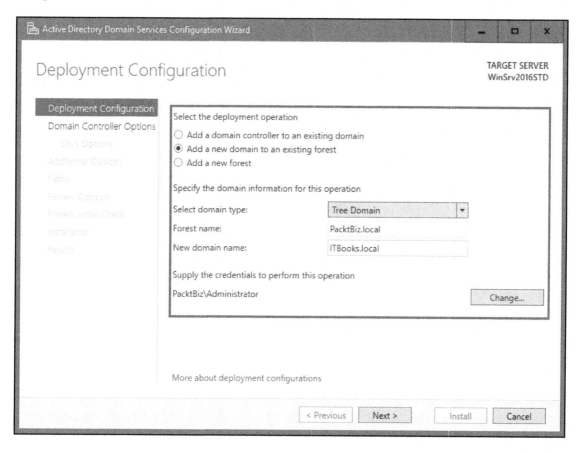

Figure 4.7. Setting up a tree domain in Windows Server 2016

Forest (3.3.2)

As you know, in real life, a forest consists of trees. Likewise, in AD, a forest consists of a collection of trees. Now that you are familiar with the concepts of domain, tree, and forest, it can be concluded that the domain is within the tree domain, that the tree domain is in the forest, and that the forest is a domain too. Isn't this a closed circle? To set up the forest in Windows Server 2016, as with domains and tree domains, use the **Active Directory Domain Services Configuration Wizard** shown in *Figure 4.8:*

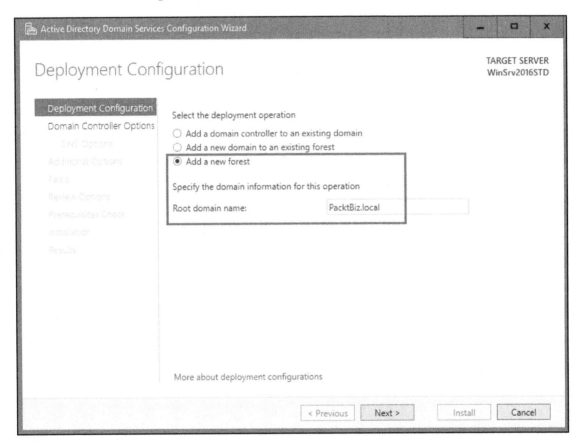

Figure 4.8. Setting up the forest in Windows Server 2016

Child domain (3.3.5)

To understand the child domain, let's illustrate it with a real tree. A tree consists of roots, a trunk, branches, and leaves. Then, in our illustration, if we rotate the tree with the roots above and the leaves below, we conclude that the parent domain is the root, and the child domain is its branches. This, as a whole, constitutes a tree domain. Furthermore, many tree domains of this kind constitute the forest. From the above examples, `PacktBiz.local` represents a forest, `ITBooks.local` represents a tree domain within the forest, and `SysAdmin.ITBooks.local` represents a child domain within the tree domain. To set up the child domain in Windows Server 2016, use almost the identical steps for setting up the tree domain earlier using the **Active Directory Domain Services Configuration Wizard**, as shown in *Figure 4.9*:

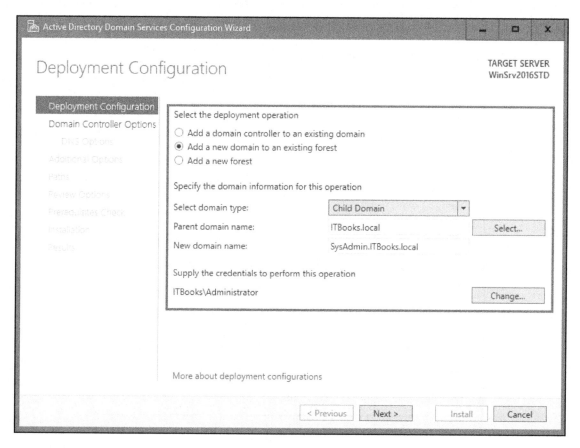

Figure 4.9. Setting up a child domain in Windows Server 2016

Operations master roles (3.3.3)

AD DS is complex! However, as soon as you start deploying it, everything becomes clearer. Let's look at the operations master role this way. Earlier in the *Domain* section, we created the root domain `PacktBiz.local` that actually represents the domain controller in our forest. In that domain controller, AD DS automatically assigns five master operations roles. The first two, **master schema** and **domain naming master**, are ForestWide operations master roles. While the remaining three, **relative identifier (RID)**, **primary domain controller (PDC) emulator**, and **infrastructure master** are DomainWide operations master roles. From there (see *Figure 4.10*), there is only one master schema and one domain name in the whole forest, that is, `PacktBiz.local`, and each domain, that is, `ITBooks.local` in a forest has its own RID master, PDC emulator, and infrastructure master.

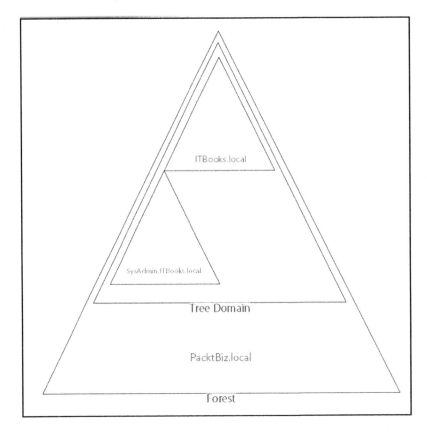

Figure 4.10. AD DS structure

Domain versus workgroup (3.3.4)

In `Chapter 1`, *Introducing Windows Server*, in the *Understanding network architectures* section, peer-to-peer networking (P2P) and client/server networking were explained. From there, a client/server network is the best example of a domain where a dedicated server is used to provide services. Similarly, P2P networking represents the best example of a workgroup where computers share resources without using a dedicated server.

Trust relationship (3.3.6)

In AD DS, there is a trust relationship between a workstation and domain, and a trust relationship between domains. That said, after a computer joins a domain, the **Security Account Manager (SAM)** in the local computer trusts AD DS's authentication mechanism. Thus, the user is authenticated by a domain in a network, and not by the local SAM. Similarly, the authentication mechanism for each tree domain trusts the authentication mechanism for other trusted tree domains within a forest. Thus, if a user is authenticated by `ITBooks.local`, its authentication is accepted by `BusinessBooks.local` and `ScienceBooks.local` because these tree domains are part of the forest's root domain `PacktBiz.local`.

Functional level (3.3.7)

The functional level determines the available AD DS capabilities. Also, depending on what functional level you have set for your forest or domain, it determines which versions of Windows Server you can run in your forest or domain.

To set up the functional level in Windows Server 2016, use the **Active Directory Domain Services Configuration Wizard** as shown in *Figure 4.11*:

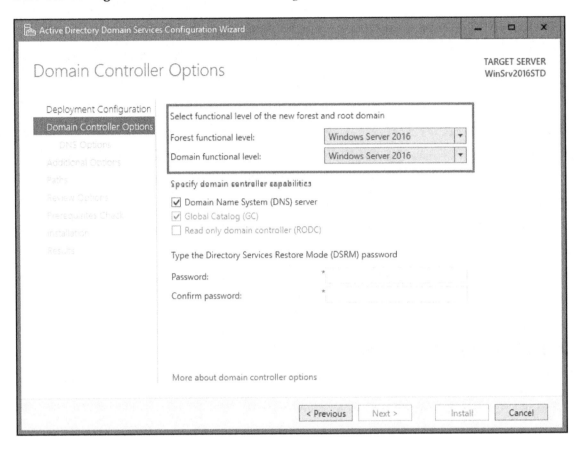

Figure 4.11. Setting up the functional level in Windows Server 2016

Namespace (3.3.8)

In our `PacktBiz.local` forest, we have created `ITBooks.local`, `BusinessBooks.local`, and `ScienceBooks.local` tree domains. Inside the `ITBooks.local` tree domain, we have created a child domain, `SysAdmin.ITBooks.local`. As you can see, all these tree domains share a common namespace within a forest. This is known as a *contiguous namespace* (see *Figure 4.12*):

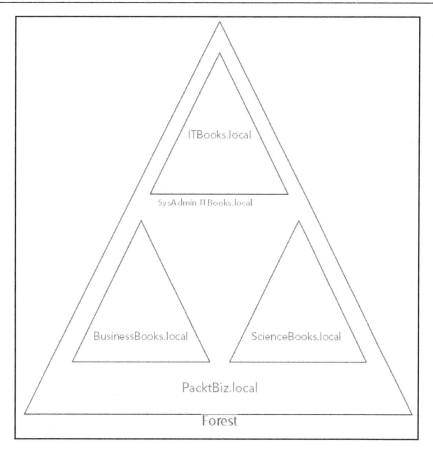

Figure 4.12. The namespace concept in AD DS

Site (3.3.9)

As with computer networks (see `Chapter 1`, *Introducing Windows Server, Understanding network architectures* section), in AD DS there are physical and logical topologies too. Thus, a domain represents the logical topology, and the site represents the physical topology of an AD DS infrastructure. From this, the site actually represents the physical location of the computer network.

Replication (3.3.10)

In AD DS infrastructure, replication is a process that synchronizes the common directory partition among all domain controllers in the forest. Additionally, replication topology is a set of communication paths through which the domain controllers' replication data travels.

Schema

If we recall the definition of AD, you will notice that it stores the objects. Since these objects are identified by their names and attributes, then that means that it is actually the schema which is a component stored in the directory. It is the replication that synchronizes the schema among all domain controllers in the forest.

Understanding Domain Name System (DNS)

DNS dates back to the '60s, also known as the ARPANET era. At that time, scientists engaged in the ARPANET project were trying to find a way of memorizing names instead of IP addresses. At the beginning of the '80s, in the form of **Requests for Comments** (**RFC**) documents, the first specification documents were published about the DNS. Essentially, DNS has a tree structure (hierarchical) where each branch represents the root zone and each leaf has zero or more resource records. Each zone represents a root domain or multiple domains, and sub-domains. A domain name consists of one or more parts, called labels, and are separated by points (for example, `packtpub.com`). DNS is maintained by a database that uses distributed clients/server architecture where network nodes represent the servers' names. This is how DNS works:

1. If you enter `www.packtpub.com` in your browser's address bar and press *Enter*, your browser will make a request on the internet to access the website `www.packtpub.com`.
2. The very first server that your browser runs into is the **Recursive Resolver** which may be provided by your **Internet Service Provider** (**ISP**).
3. The recursive resolver will then contact the root servers that are scattered all over the globe and contain the information about top-level domains, in our `example .com`.
4. The top-level domains will provide the DNS information to the recursive resolver.

5. Afterwards, the recursive resolver will contact the domain name server `packtpub.com` and, through the domain name server's local DNS, locate the IP address.

6. Then, that IP address is provided to your browser by the recursive resolver to access the web server content via its newly·accustomed IP address.

Adding the DNS role

Similar to AD DS, the DNS in Windows Server 2016 is a role that is added through Server Manager as shown in *Figure 4.13*:

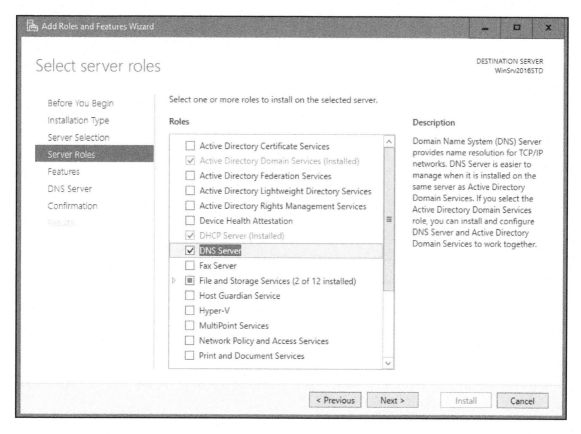

Figure 4.13. Adding DNS role in Windows Server 2016

Note that when adding the DNS role, either add it as a separate role (see *Figure 4.13*), or alongside AD DS (see *Figure 4.14*):

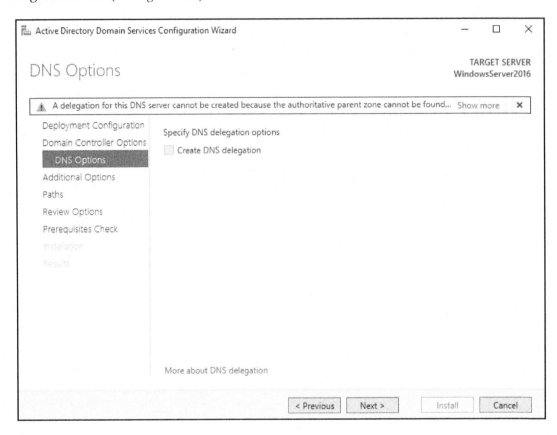

Figure 4.14. Adding DNS alongside AD DS in Windows Server 2016

Understanding hosts and lmhosts files

The `hosts` and `lmhosts` files are used for name resolution and are stored in the
`C:\Windows\system32\drivers\etc` directory as shown in *Figure 4.15*. The `host` files
contains the mapping of IP addresses to host names, and is used for DNS name resolution.
Unlike `hosts`, the **LAN manager hosts** (`lmhosts`) file contains the mapping of IP addresses
to computer names, and is used for NetBIOS name resolution. In both files, entries are
inserted manually, and each entry should be kept on an individual line. Table 1 presents the
examples of inserting `hosts` and `lmhosts` entries:

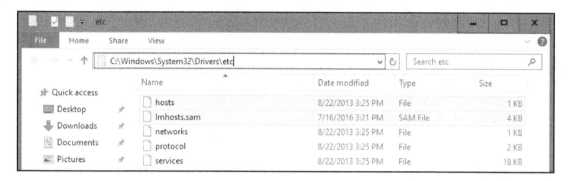

Figure 4.15. HOSTS and LMHOSTS files in Windows Server 2016

Table 1. Syntax for `hosts` and `lmhosts` entries

HOSTS entry:	IP address FQDN hostname #Comment
LMHOSTS entry:	IP address FQDN hostname Extension <tag>#Comment

Understanding hostname

Hostname is a logical element that is assigned to a device (see *Figure 4.16*). It is unique and used to identify the device in a computer network. Often, it is called a domain name too:

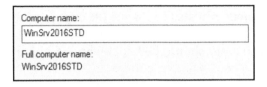

Figure 4.16. Assigning a hostname in Windows Server 2016

Understanding DNS Zones

It is a hierarchical structure that allows the existence of DNS zones. The AD DS namespace is jointly related to the DNS namespace. This is because the DNS namespace can be divided into zones that store information about domains. Thus, DNS offers three types of zones:

- **Primary zone**: This stores the primary copy of the DNS database and maintains all the DNS zone records
- **Secondary zone**: It acts as a backup of the primary zone and, whenever the first one is unavailable, it resolves DNS queries
- **Stub zone**: In principle, it is a secondary zone with no editable primary copy of the database and contains sufficient information to identify the authoritative DNS

Authoritative DNS, configured manually by a system administrator or dynamically by other DNSes, is a DNS server that holds the DNS records of the actual domain. Unlike an authoritative DNS, a **non-authoritative DNS** holds the cached information that has been constituted by previous DNS lookups.

Understanding WINS

To automate NetBIOS name resolution, you can use Microsoft's **Windows Internet Name Service (WINS)** server. A WINS server maps the IP addresses to NetBIOS names. The NetBIOS names are the names that are used when you connect to a shared folder or printer. WINS is a feature in Windows Server 2016, and can be added through Server Manager using the **Add roles and features Wizard** as shown in *Figure 4.17*:

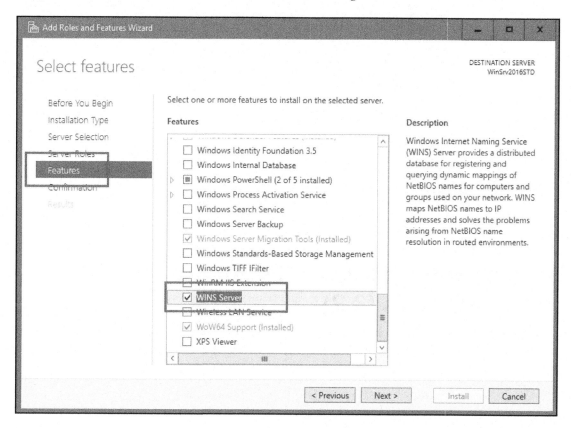

Figure 4.17. Setting up WINS feature in Windows Server 2016

Understanding Universal Naming Convention (UNC)

Universal Naming Convention (UNC), originally used in Unix, is a standard to identify a share in a computer network. Its format (see *Figure 4.18*) uses double backslashes to precede the name of the server, for example, `\\servername\folder`:

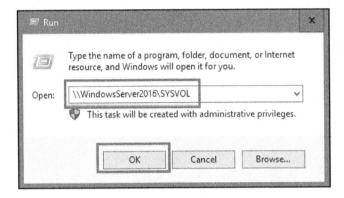

Figure 4.18. A UNC path in Windows Server 2016

Understanding organizational units (OUs) and containers (3.2)

To ease the administration of objects, the *AD Users and Computers* console DS provides OU and default containers. In the following sections, you will become familiarized with OUs and default containers.

Purpose of OUs (3.2.1)

To ease the administration of its objects, AD uses OU. Usually, users, groups, computers, and other organizational units are placed within OUs. Often, organizations create OUs to mirror their organizational business structures. Regardless of the number of tree domains in a forest, each domain can have its own OU hierarchy as shown in *Figure 4.19*:

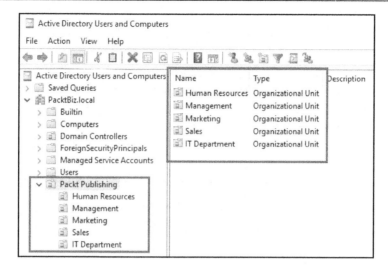

Figure 4.19. An example of OUs hierarchy in Windows Server 2016

Default containers (3.2.4)

After *Promoting the server to a domain controller*, several default containers are created (see *Figure 4.20*). These default containers are unique because you cannot rename, delete, create new ones, or associate **Group Policy Objects (GPO)** with these containers. The default containers in Windows Server 2016 are shown in *Figure 4.20*:

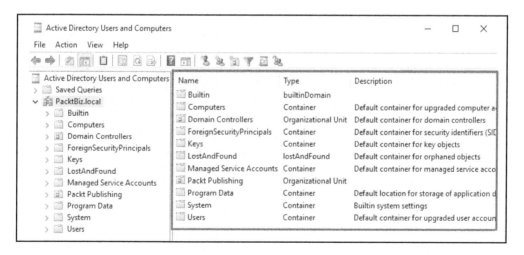

Figure 4.20. Default containers in Windows Server 2016

Default hidden and visible containers

Not all the default containers are needed for an system administrator day-to-day job! Because of that, there are certainly hidden containers. One reason why there are hidden containers by default is to avoid the **Active Directory Users and Computers** console looking messy. Additionally, when you begin to add your own OUs, the messiness might get worse. However, security is the biggest reason why there are hidden containers in AD. To make them visible as in *Figure 4.21*, enable the **Advanced Features** option from the **View** menu:

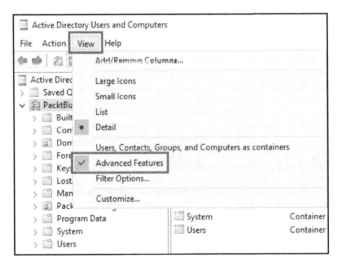

Figure 4.21. Default hidden containers in Windows Server 2016

Uses for different container objects (3.2.2)

The following are simple uses for some of the default containers in Windows Server 2016:

- **Computers**: It is a default container for upgraded computer accounts
- **Domain Controllers**: It is a default container for domain controllers
- **Foreign Security Principals**: It is a default container for security identifiers (SID)
- **Keys**: It is a default container for key objects
- **LostandFound**: It is a default container for orphaned objects
- **Managed Service Accounts**: It is a default container for managed service accounts
- **Users**: It is a default container for upgraded user accounts

Delegating control to an OU (3.2.3)

Knowing that OUs facilitate the organization of AD objects, whenever you want to grant permissions to a certain user, or group of users, in the AD then the choice is a delegation of control to an OU. However, it is required that prior to assigning permissions to a user, or group of users, they need to be placed into an OU (see *Figure 4.22*):

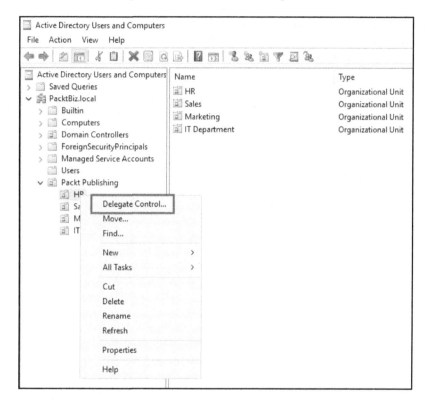

Figure 4.22. Delegating control to an OU in Windows Server 2016

Understanding accounts and groups (3.1)

To access network services, user and computer accounts are used. In a Windows Server-based network, both users and computer accounts reside in a centralized directory. In these centralized environments, groups are used to facilitate the process of assigning rights and permissions. In the following sections, you will become familiarized with accounts and groups.

Domain accounts (3.1.1)

Technically, the domain account exists in the AD and as such, it is authenticated by the same entity (that is, AD). The domain account can access both local and network services based on the access that is granted to the account, or to a group that an account belongs to. To create a domain account on Windows Server 2016, complete the following steps:

1. From **Windows Administrative Tools** open the **Active Directory Users and Computers** console.
2. Right-click the **Users** container and select **New | User**.
3. Enter the users required information, as shown in *Figure 4.23*, and click **Next**:

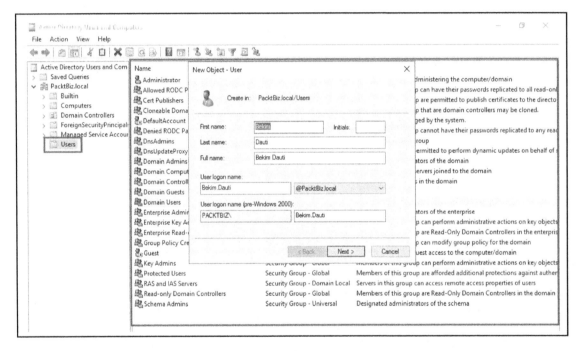

Figure 4.23. Creating a domain account in Windows Server 2016

4. Provide a temporary password, confirm, and click **Next**.
5. Click **Finish** to close the **New Object | User window**.

Local accounts (3.1.2)

Unlike domain accounts, the local account exists in a computer where that account has been created, and as such, it is authenticated by the Windows's SAM. The local account can access local services based on the access that is granted to the account. Additionally, the local account can access shared resources in a P2P network. To create a local account on Windows Server 2016 (*note that the server should not be a domain controller*), complete the following steps:

1. From **Windows Administrative Tools**, open the **Computer Management** console.
2. Expand **System Tools | Local Users and Groups,** right-click the **Users** container and select **New | User**.
3. Enter the user's required information, as shown in *Figure 4.24*, and click **Create**:

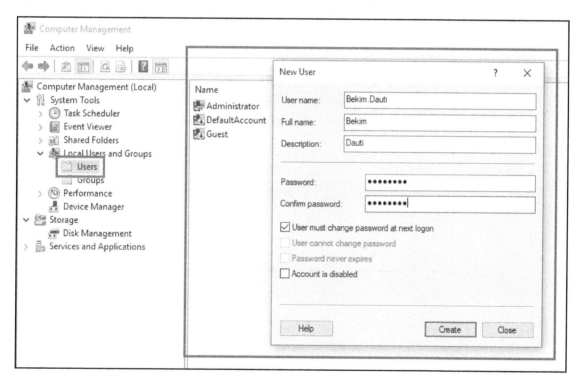

Figure 4.24. Creating a local account in Windows Server 2016

User profiles (3.1.3)

Usually, in Windows Server-based networks, the following user profiles are used:

- **Local user profile**: It is created when the user logs on to a computer for the first time and is stored on a local computer (see *Figure 4.25*)
- **Roaming user profile**: It is a local profile copied and stored to a network share
- **Mandatory user profile:** It is a kind of roaming profile where a user logs off and no changes in a profile are saved

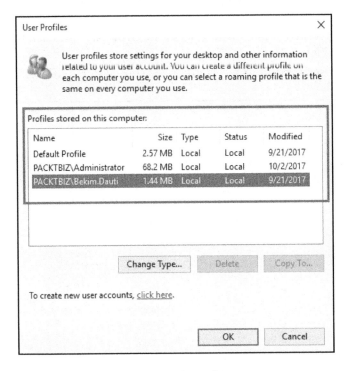

Figure 4.25. Local user profiles

Computer accounts

In AD, a computer account identifies a computer in a domain. Before a computer joins a domain, its name must be unique in a network. After a computer joins a domain, it continues to use its computer name for communication with other computers and servers in a network. Computer accounts are managed through the **Active Directory Users and Computers** console, as shown in *Figure 4.26*:

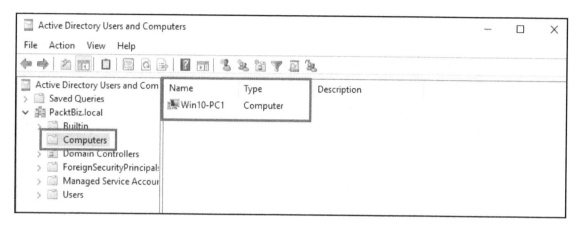

Figure 4.26. Computer accounts in Windows Server 2016

Group types (3.1.4)

In AD, a group is a collection of AD objects. Instead of assigning permissions and rights to each AD object individually, groups are used for a more structured administration. Note that a group is an object too, thus it can be placed inside an OU. Groups are managed through the **Active Directory Users and Computers** console as shown in *Figure 4.27*. In AD, there are two types of groups:

- **Security groups**: These are explicitly used to assign permissions to shared resources on a network.

- **Distribution groups**: These are particularly used to distribute email lists in an organization's network:

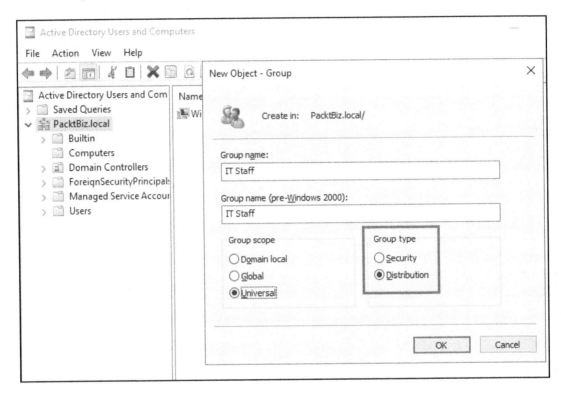

Figure 4.27. Group types in Windows Server 2016

Default groups

As discussed earlier, in the **Group types** section, groups are used to facilitate AD object administration. Thus, after *Promoting the server to a domain controller*, a significant number of default groups are created (see *Figure 4.28*):

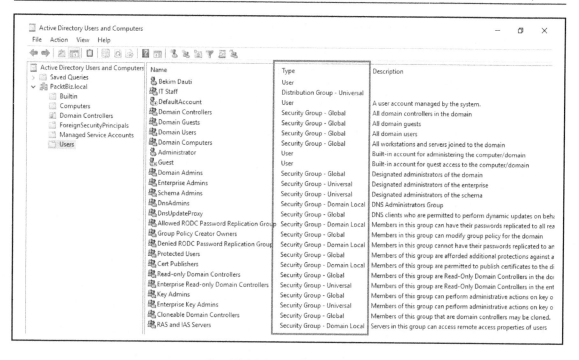

Figure 4.28. Default groups in Windows Server 2016

Group scopes (3.1.5)

Regardless of whether it is a security or universal group, try to understand the group scope as an extension option of the group in the domain, forest, or tree domain. In AD, there are three group scopes (see *Figure 4.29*):

- **Domain local group**: It includes accounts, domain local groups, global groups, and universal groups from the parent's domain local group domain
- **Global group**: It includes accounts and global groups from the parent's global group domain

- **Universal group**: It includes accounts, global groups, and universal groups from any domain in the forest where a universal group belongs:

Figure 4.29. Group scopes in Windows Server 2016

Group nesting (3.1.6)

The AD groups are objects too, thus they can be organized in a group nesting. This way, adding groups to other groups minimizes the number of individually assigned permissions to users or groups.

Understanding AGDLP and AGUDLP

Both **Accounts, Global, Domain Local, Permissions (AGDLP)** and **Accounts, Global, Universal, Domain Local, Permissions (AGUDLP)** are Microsoft's recommendation for effectively using group nesting when assigning permissions. Table 2 presents the flow of assigning permissions with AGDLP and AGUDLP.

Table 2. Assigning permissions with AGDLP and AGUDLP:

AGDLP	AGUDLP
Add the Accounts to Global group	Add the Accounts to Global group
Add the Global group scope to Domain Local group	Add the Global group to Universal group
To Domain Local group assign Permissions	Add Universal group to Domain Local group
	To Domain Local group assign Permissions

References from Windows IT Pro Center

1. What's new in Active Directory Domain Services for Windows Server 2016 (`https://docs.microsoft.com/en-us/windows-server/identity/whats-new-active-directory-domain-services`)

2. What's new in Active Directory Federation Services for Windows Server 2016 (`https://docs.microsoft.com/en-us/windows-server/identity/ad-fs/overview/whats-new-active-directory-federation-services-windows-server`)

3. Introduction to Active Directory Administrative Center Enhancements (`https://docs.microsoft.com/en-us/windows-server/identity/ad-ds/get-started/adac/introduction-to-active-directory-administrative-center-enhancements--level-100-`)

Summary

- Active Directory is a distributed database that stores objects in a hierarchical, structured, and secure format.
- Active Directory's objects typically represent users, computers, peripheral devices and network services.
- The domain, the forest, and the tree represent the logical division of an AD infrastructure.

- A DC, is a server that is responsible for securely authenticating requests to access resources in your organization's domain.
- A domain is a logical grouping of users, computers, peripherals, network services, and security settings.
- A tree in an AD structure is comprised of one or more domains.
- In an AD structure, the forest consists of a collection of trees.
- Master schema and domain naming master are ForestWide operations master roles.
- RID, PDC emulator, and infrastructure master are DomainWide operations master roles.
- The best example of a domain is a client/server network where a dedicated server on the network is used to provide services.
- P2P networking represents the best example of a workgroup where computers are connected and share resources without using a dedicated server.
- In an AD, there is a trust relationship between workstations and domains, and a trust relationship between domains.
- The functional level determines the available AD DS capabilities.
- Domain represents the logical topology, and the site represents the physical topology of AD DS infrastructure.
- In AD infrastructure, replication is a process that synchronizes the common directory partition among all domain controllers in the forest.
- Replication topology is a set of communication paths through which the domain controllers replication data travels.
- Schema are components that are stored in the directory. Replication, then synchonizes the schema among all domain controllers in the forest.
- A domain name consists of one or more parts, called labels, and are separated by points.
- When adding a DNS role, you should either add it as a separate role, or alongside an AD DS role.
- HOSTS files contain the mappings of IP addresses to host names, and is used for DNS name resolution.
- `Lmhosts` files contain the mappings of IP addresses to computer names, and are used for NetBIOS name resolutions.
- Hostname is a logical element that is assigned to a device.
- WINS server maps the IP addresses to NetBIOS names.
- NetBIOS names are the names that are used when connecting to a shared folder or printer.

- UNC, is a standard to identify a share in a computer network.
- To ease the administration of objects, AD DS provides OU.
- After promoting the server to a domain controller, several default conatainers are created.
- Security is one strong reason why there are hiden containers by defaults.
- Technically, the domain account exists in AD, and as such, it is authenticated by the same entity.
- A local account exists in a computer where that account has been created, and as such, it is authenticated by the Windows SAM.
- A local user profile is created when the user logs on to a computer for the first time, and it is stored on a local computer.
- A roaming user profile is a local profile copied and stored to a network share.
- A mandatory user profile is a kind of roaming profile where when a user logs off, no changes in a profile are saved.
- In an AD, a computer account identifies a computer in a domain.
- In an AD, the group is a collection of AD objects.
- Security groups are explicitly used to assign permissions to shared resources on a network.
- A distribution groups are particularly used to distribute e-mailing lists in an organization's network.
- A domain local group includes accounts, domain local groups, global groups, and universal groups from the parent's domain local group domain.
- A global group includes accounts, and global groups from the parent's global group domain.
- A universal group includes accounts, global groups, and universal groups from any domain in the forest where a universal group belongs.
- Group nesting minimizes the number of individually assigned permissions to users or groups.
- Both AGDLP and AGUDLP are Microsoft's recommendation for using group nesting effectively when assigning permissions.

Questions

1. An AD is a distributed database that stores objects in a hierarchical, structured, and secure format. (True | False)

2. _____ minimizes the number of individually assigned permissions to users or groups.

3. Which of the following user profiles are used mostly in Windows Server-based networks?
    1. Domain user profile
    2. Security user profile
    3. Roaming user profile
    4. Mandatory using profile

4. WINS server maps the IP addresses to BIOS names. (True | False)

5. _____ is a set of communication paths through which the domain controllers' replication data travels.

6. Which of the following are AD's group scopes?
    1. Organizational Units (OU)
    2. Security group
    3. Global group
    4. Universal group

7. UNC, is a standard to identify a share in a computer network. (True | False)

8. _____ is a server that is responsible for securely authenticating requests to access resources in your organization's domain.

9. Which of the following snapins for Microsoft Management Consoles (MMC) consoles are used to manage AD?
    1. Active Directory Administrative Center
    2. Active Directory Users and Computers
    3. UNC
    4. OU

10. The best example of a domain is a client/server network where a dedicated server on the network is used to provide services. (True | False)

11. _____ stores the primary copy of the DNS database and maintains all the DNS zone records.

12. Which of the following are forest-wide operations master roles?
    1. Master schema
    2. Domain naming master
    3. Lan Manager HOSTS
    4. Default containers

13. Discuss AD DS and DNS roles, and their implementation.

14. Discuss Microsoft's recommendations, AGDLP and AGUDLP, for assigning permissions.

5
Adding Roles to Windows Server

Now that you have added two very important roles, AD DS and DNS, in `Chapter 4`, *Directory Services in Windows Server*, it is time to get acquainted with the roles and features that Windows Server 2016 offers. At the same time, this chapter will provide a broader explanation of what a role is, as well as the importance of roles in determining the server's function when providing network services. Also, you will get to know all the roles and features that Windows Server 2016 supports. You will learn how to add roles to your server, as well as the requirements after you have added roles so you can set up your server whenever that is required. In that way, you will be able to understand what application servers, web services, remote access, and file and print services are. In addition to roles, features will also be explained along with the steps it takes to add them to a server.

In this chapter, we will cover:

- Understanding server roles and features
- Understanding application servers
- Understanding web services
- Understanding remote access
- Understanding file and print services

Understanding server roles and features (2)

When you add a role to Windows Server 2016, you have actually assigned the task that the server needs to do. So, the server role is a primary task that a server should perform. In the best scenario, the server has only one role. However, the server can have multiple roles too. Remember the *Understanding server hardware and software* section from Chapter 1, *Introducing Windows Server*, where the importance of selecting the server's hardware was mentioned including a list of the important hardware components that affect the overall performance of the server. Thus, the activity of selecting the server's hardware entirely depends on the role that your server will have. Just because of that, always try to understand the exact role that your server needs to perform so that you can then choose the right hardware for it.

In Windows Server 2016, when adding a role to your server you will encounter situations where, besides the role, you should also add role services. So the question arises, what are role services? Let us try to understand role services with the following example. Assume that you want to have an internet print server so that employees can print from outside the company's network. To do that, you add the **Print and Document Services** (**PDS**) role to your server and then you add **Internet Printing** as a role service. That way, you augment the functionality of the role.

Other than roles and role services, features are added to the server to support the given role. For example, there are situations where you are asked to install *.NET Framework 3.5 Features* so that you can complete the role you are adding, or you need to install an **IP Address Management** (**IPAM**) server to support the DHCP or DNS roles in your network infrastructure, or maybe you want to have a WINS server alongside DNS so you can solve problems arising from NetBIOS name resolution in routed environments, or other similar situations.

To add roles in Windows Server 2016, you will use **Server Manager**. Introduced with Windows Server 2008, **Server Manager** is an administrative tool used by system administrators to add, set up, and manage server roles. Its user interface is simple and easy to navigate. Usually (see *Figure 5.1*), the **Scope Pane** has the installed roles, and the **Details Pane** displays the details of a selected role. It acts as an entry point for adding roles, and as an administrative console for managing roles. Without a doubt, as its name implies, **Server Manager** is a *one-stop station* for adding roles, configuring services, managing resources, and administering tasks in Windows Server:

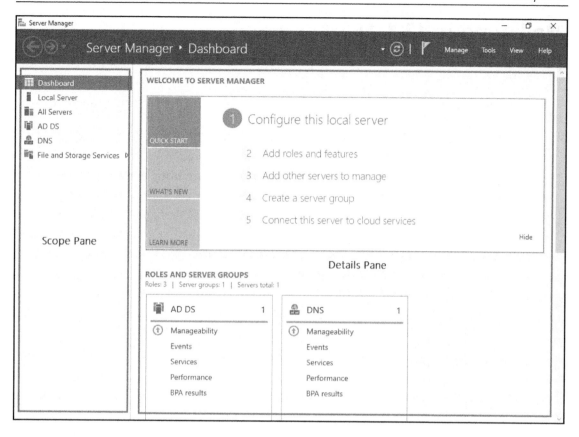

Figure 5.1. Server Manager's user interface in Windows Server 2016

Identifying application servers (2.1)

When searching for the meaning of the word *application* in the Merriam-Webster dictionary, one of the definitions is: *an act of putting something to use.* From that, the conclusion can be drawn that application servers are servers that offer usable services to the network. In the following sections, you will become familiar with some of the most applicable application servers around today.

Mail servers (2.1.1)

A mail server is a server that sends and receives emails. The main components of a mail server are:

- **Mail Transport Agent (MTA)**: This is responsible for transporting the mail between mail servers
- **Mail Delivery Agent (MDA)**: This is responsible for delivering the mail from the server into a user's inbox
- **Mail User Agent (MUA)**: This is responsible for providing a platform for composing and reading emails

Additionally, the mail server utilizes the following protocols:

- **Simple Mail Transfer Protocol (SMTP)**: SMTP uses port 25 and powers the MTA in transferring the mail between servers
- **Post Office Protocol (POP)**: POP uses port 110 and is responsible for downloading emails from the server to the user's local computer
- **Internet Message Access Protocol (IMAP)**: IMAP uses port 143 and is responsible for retrieving emails from the mail server and sending them to a user's mail application

To set up a mail server in Windows Server 2016, you must add the SMTP server feature to your server as shown in *Figure 5.2*:

1. Click **Add roles and features** in the **Server Manager** *Welcome to Server Manager* section.
2. In the **Before you begin** option, click **Next.**
3. Click **Next** in the **Installation type** option.
4. In the **Select destination server** option, click **Next.**
5. There is no **role to add**, so click **Next.**
6. Select **SMTP Server** from the **Features** list:

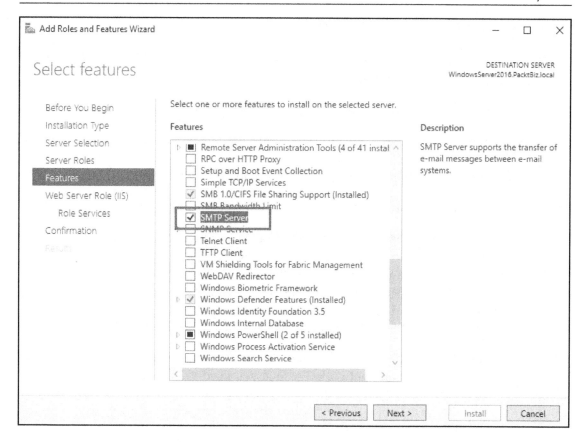

5.2. Adding the SMTP Server feature in Windows Server 2016

7. There is no **role service to add**, so click **Next.**

8. In the **Confirm installation Selections** option, click **Install.**

Exchange Server 2016 is Microsoft's application for setting up a mail server in an organization's network. To do it, you should install and configure Exchange Server 2016. You can download Exchange Server 2016 at the following URL: `https://www.microsoft.com/en-us/download/details.aspx?id=49161`.

Database servers (2.1.2)

In its simplest definition, the database server is the server that provides database services. The main components of the database server are:

- **Data**: Data is the raw material of the database and as such is the main component of a database server because without data there is no database
- **Database Application**: The application through which the user interacts with the database server
- **Users**: Users are the people who use the database

Additionally, the database server utilizes the following access protocols:

- **Open Database Connectivity (ODBC)**: ODBC is a protocol that enables applications to access data in a database server
- **Java Database Connectivity (JDBC)**: JDBC is Sun Microsystem's protocol that enables Java applications to access data in a database server
- **Object Linking and Embedding Database (OLEDB)**: OLEDB is Microsoft's protocol that enables applications to access data in a database server

SQL Server 2017 is Microsoft's application for setting up a database server in an organization's network. To do it, you need to install and configure SQL Server 2017. You can download SQL Server 2017 from the following URL: https://www.microsoft.com/en-us/sql-server/sql-server-downloads.

Collaboration servers (2.1.3)

In a nutshell, the collaboration server is the server that brings people together for a common project.

SharePoint Server 2016 is Microsoft's application for setting up a collaboration server in an organization's network. To do it, you need to install and configure SharePoint Server 2016. You can download SharePoint Server 2016 from the following URL: https://www.microsoft.com/en-us/download/details.aspx?id=51493.

Monitoring servers (2.1.4)

The general concept of a monitoring server can involve anything from monitoring a server's health to monitoring its performance.

System Center 2016 Operations Manager is Microsoft's application for setting up a monitoring server in an organization's network. To do that, you need to install and configure System Center 2016 Operation Manager. You can download System Center 2016 Operation Manager from the following URL: `https://www.microsoft.com/en-us/evalcenter/evaluate-system-center-2016`.

Threat management (2.1.5)

As the name suggests, the threat management server is a server that acts as a router, firewall, antivirus program, VPN server, proxy server, and other threat management roles.

System Center 2016 Endpoint Protection is Microsoft's application for setting up a threat management server in an organization's network. To do it, you need to install and configure System Center 2016 Endpoint Protection. You can download System Center 2016 Endpoint Protection from the following URL: `https://www.microsoft.com/en-us/evalcenter/evaluate-system-center-2016`.

Understanding web services (2.2)

A web service is the means of communication between two devices based on the request/response methodology using the **Hypertext Transfer Protocol (HTTP)**.

What is IIS? (2.2.1)

Internet Information Services (IIS) is Microsoft's web server. A web server that runs on IIS provides reliable, manageable, and scalable web applications. IIS supports communication protocols such as HTTP, HTTPS, FTP, FTPS, SMTP, and NNTP for communication between the browser and the web server. For dynamic content on the server side, Microsoft has developed scripting technology called **Active Server Pages (ASP)**. From a security perspective, Microsoft has constantly offered features and technologies to make IIS more secure.

In IIS version 10, Microsoft has significantly increased security with the support for scripts that take a long time to execute, including HTTP/2. Add to this Microsoft Edge, a new browser introduced with Windows 10. These and many other improvements have established IIS firmly in second place, right after Apache. To set up a web server in Windows Server 2016, you need to add IIS as a role to your server as shown in *Figure 5.3*:

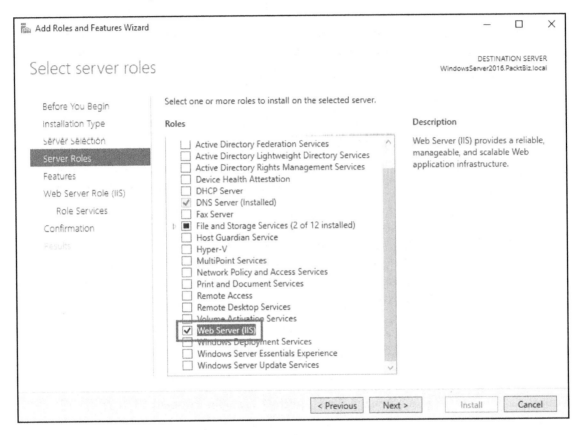

Figure 5.3 Adding the Web Server (IIS) role in Windows Server 2016

Additionally, **Internet Information Service (IIS) Manager** is a console that is used to manage the web server in Windows Server 2016 (see *Figure 5.4*):

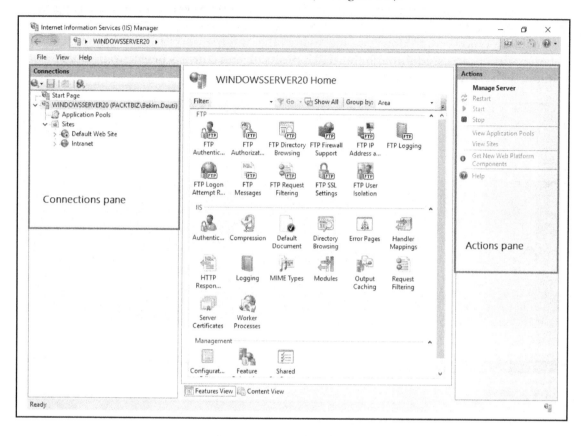

Figure 5.4. IIS Manager in Windows Server 2016

What is the WWW? (2.2.2)

Often, people confuse the internet with the **World Wide Web** (**WWW**). Perhaps using the WWW while connected to the internet means they get the feeling that the WWW is actually the internet! Who knows? However, like many other internet services, WWW too is an internet service, accessed through the HTTP protocol, and consists of electronic documents compiled with **Hypertext Markup Language** (**HTML**) as shown in *Figure 5.5*:

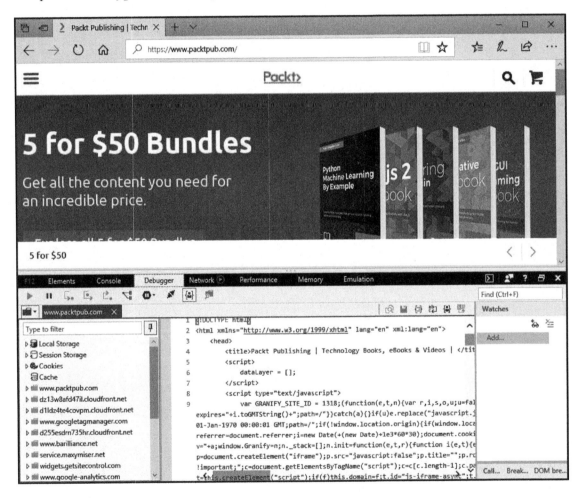

Figure 5.5. A website and its source code

What is FTP? (2.2.3)

File Transfer Protocol (FTP) does exactly what its name indicates. FTP transfers files from computer to computer, computer to the server, or vice-versa, on a LAN or WAN (or the internet). To set up an FTP server in Windows Server 2016, first you need to add **Web Server Role (IIS)** as a role, and then **FTP Server** as a role service (see *Figure 5.6*):

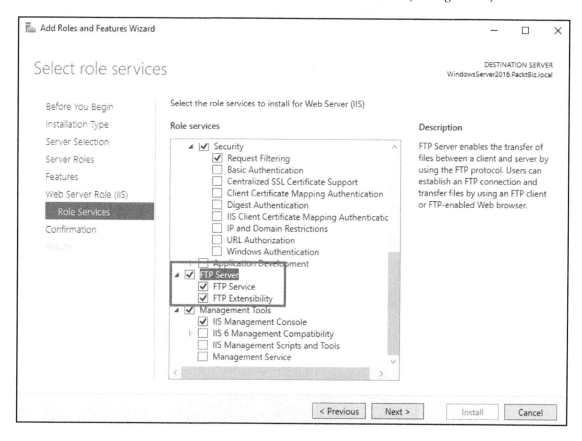

Figure 5.6 Adding FTP Server as a role service in Windows Server 2016

Separate worker processes (2.2.4)

From an IIS perspective, a web directory represents a website that has an application pool. As we are talking about a pool of applications, then it is understood that there is more than one application. From there, each application in the application pool is supported by the same worker process. This means that a **worker process** that serves an application pool is separated by another worker process that serves another application pool. Thus, if one web application does not work then that does not affect the applications that run in other application pools. To access an application's pool worker processes select **Application Pools**, then from the **Actions** pane on the right-hand side of the *IIS* window select **Advanced Settings** as shown in *Figure 5.7*:

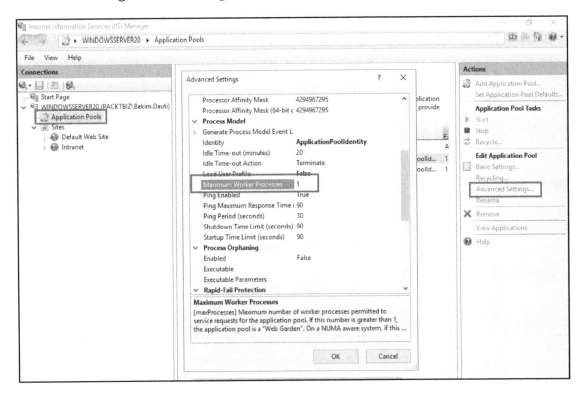

Figure 5.7. An application's pool worker process in IIS

Adding components (2.2.5)

In the process of adding the web server (IIS) role, you will encounter the **Role Services** step (see *Figure 5.6* in the *What is FTP?* section) from where you will add the required components for the IIS. Additionally, you can add the required components to your web server even after you have added IIS as a role. That means you must use the **Add roles and features wizard** again to add additional required components to your IIS Windows Server.

Sites (2.2.6)

A **site** is a collection of web pages whose purpose is to publish content on the intranet, or internet, through web services. When you add **Web Server (IIS)** as a role to your server, the default website is created as shown in *Figure 5.8*:

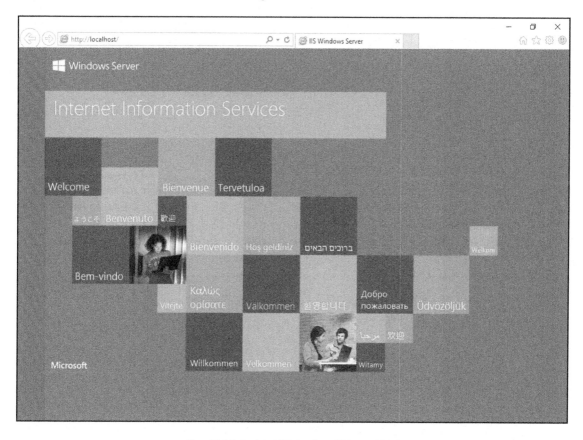

Figure 5.8. Default website in Windows Server 2016 powered by IIS

However, if you right-click **Sites** and select **Add Website...** as in *Figure 5.9* you can add additional websites to your IIS Windows Server:

Figure 5.9. Adding additional websites... through IIS Manager in Windows Server 2016

Ports (2.2.7)

In the broader context, there are hardware and software ports. In the narrower context, a **hardware port** is any physical interface in a computer, peripheral device, or network device that allows interconnection for communication purposes. By contrast, a **software port** (often known as an application port) is any logical endpoint where applications from your computer communicate with other applications on other computers, both on LAN and WAN (or the internet). A web server uses ports 80 and 443 for the HTTP protocol and HTTPS protocol respectively. Table 5.1 shows the application ports that are used most often.

Table 5.1. Common TCP/UDP port addresses for internet services:

Protocol	Port	Transportation Protocol
FTP	21	TCP
SSH	22	TCP
Telnet	23	TCP
SMTP	25	TCP
HTTP	80	TCP and UDP
POP3	110	TCP
NNTP	119	TCP
NTP	123	TCP
IMAP4	143	TCP
HTTPS	443	TCP

Secure Sockets Layer (2.2.8)

Secure Sockets Layer (SSL) is a communication technology that encrypts the communication channel between a website on a web server and a browser on a computer. The browser connects to a secured website with SSL through the HTTPS protocol that operates on port 443. In such a secure infrastructure, certificates play an important role in encrypting all transmitted data. Certificates are used mutually by the website and browser in negotiating a secure session between browser-to-server or server-to-server communication as shown in *Figure 5.10*:

Figure 5.10. Secured communication between browser and website

Certificates (2.2.9)

As discussed previously, a certificate is responsible for securing the communication channel between a website and browser. As such, the certificate, known also as the **digital certificate**, is an electronic document that ensures that entities can exchange data securely on the internet. Usually, certificates are issued by a secure entity known as a **Certificate Authority (CA)** as shown in *Figure 5.11*. This infrastructure uses **Public Key Infrastructure (PKI)**, which uses certificates to prove the ownership of the public key:

Figure 5.11. Certificate issued by Certificate Authority (CA)

 You can learn more about Public Key Infrastructure from `https://docs.oracle.com/cd/B10501_01/network.920/a96582/pki.htm`.

Understanding Remote Access (2.3)

The **Remote Access** role in Windows Server 2016 enables remote access to resources inside an organization's network. To understand it better; remote access consists of a logical grouping of the following network access technologies:

- **DirectAccess**: Introduced in Windows Server 2008 R2 and uses IPsec to encrypt communication between the DirectAccess client and the DirectAccess server. It encapsulates IPv6 traffic over IPv4 to reach the intranet from the internet. Access to a corporate intranet is enabled without using a **Virtual Private Network (VPN)**.

- **Routing and Remote Access Service (RRAS)**: The successor to the **Remote Access Service (RAS)** in Windows NT, it was introduced in Windows 2000 and represents a combined service that establishes links between remote locations via VPN and dial-up, as well as traffic paths between the sub-networks.
- **Web Application Proxy**: Web Application Proxy in Windows Server 2016 replaced the **Microsoft Forefront Unified Access Gateway (UAG)** and acts as a recursive proxy. Web Application Proxy uses **Active Directory Federation Services (AD FS)** to authenticate corporate users so they can access web applications on the corporate intranet through an extranet.

To set up a remote access server in Windows Server 2016, you need to add **Remote Access** as a role to your server as shown in *Figure 5.12:*

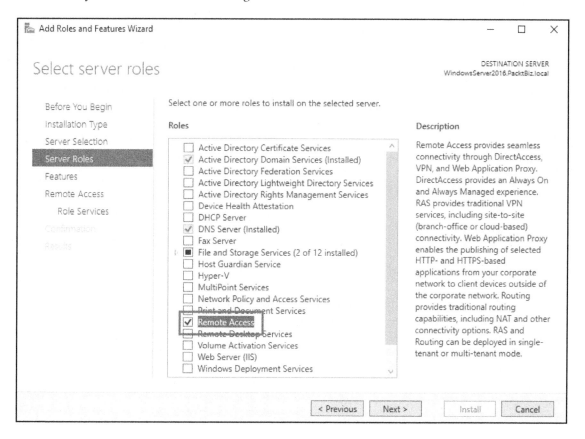

Figure 5.12. Adding the Remote Access (RA) role in Windows Server 2016

Remote Assistance (2.3.1)

Remote Assistance in Windows Server 2016 is a feature that enables a helper to access the host's desktop remotely for the purpose of assisting with the resolution of issues. That means you must use the **Add roles and features Wizard** to add the **Remote assistance** feature to your server as shown in *Figure 5.13*:

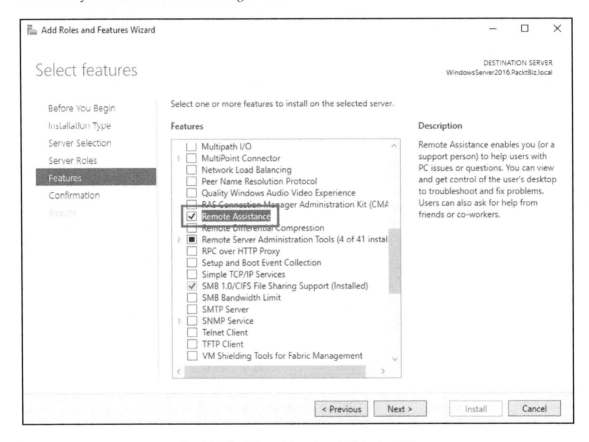

Figure 5.13. Adding the Remote Assistance feature in Windows Server 2016

Remote Server Administration Tools (2.3.2)

Remote Server Administration Tools (RSAT) in Windows Server 2016 is a feature that enables managing server roles and features of remote servers that run Windows Server 2016 (both in GUI and CLI modes). Additionally, RSAT is available for client computers running Windows 10 too. To enable the **Remote Server Administration Tools** feature in Windows Server 2016, use the **Add Roles and Features Wizard** as shown in *Figure 5.14:*

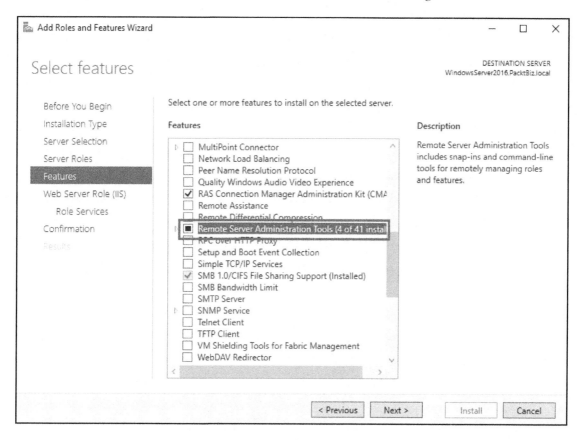

Figure 5.14. Adding the RSAT feature in Windows Server 2016

Remote Desktop Services (2.3.3)

Known as **Terminal Services (TS)** until Windows Server 2008, **Remote Desktop Services (RDS)** gained its name and identity with the release of Windows Server 2008 R2. This role set up a GUI with remote access to computers within an organization's network and over the internet. Additionally, RDS delivers individual, virtualized applications to user desktops. To set up an RDS server in Windows Server 2016, you need to add the RDS role to your server as in *Figure 5.15*:

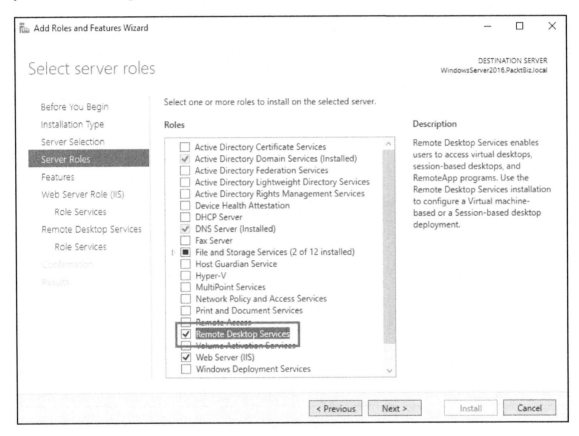

Figure 5.15. Adding the Remote Desktop Services role in Windows Server 2016

Licensing (2.3.4)

The RDS Licensing server manages RDS **Client Access Licenses (CAL)**. RDS CALs are used by users and computers to access a **Remote Desktop Session Host (RDSH)** server. By default, the RDS Licensing server provides two concurrent connections free of cost. If you need additional RDS CAL then you need to purchase them. To set up an RDS Licensing server in your organization's network with Windows Server 2016, you first add the **Remote Desktop Services** role and then add **Remote Desktop Licensing** role services as in *Figure 5.16*:

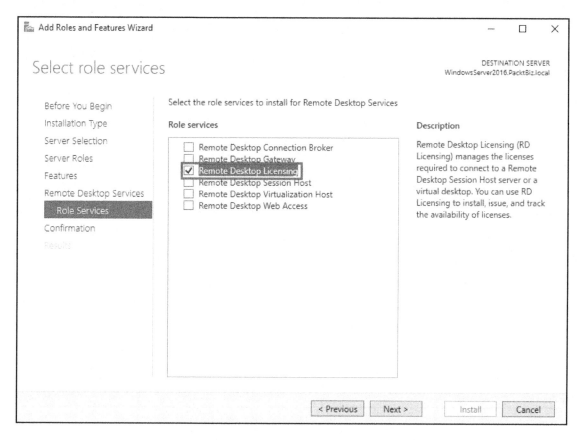

Figure 5.16. Adding Remote Desktop Licensing role services in Windows Server 2016

Remote Desktop Gateway (2.3.5)

A **Remote Desktop Gateway (RDG)** server, part of the RDS role, is a role service in Windows Server 2016 that enables authorized users to connect to computers within an organization's network and over the internet using a **Remote Desktop Connection (RDC)** client. To set up an RDG server in your organization's network with Windows Server 2016, you first add the **Remote Desktop Services** role and then add **Remote Desktop Gateway** role services as in *Figure 5.17*:

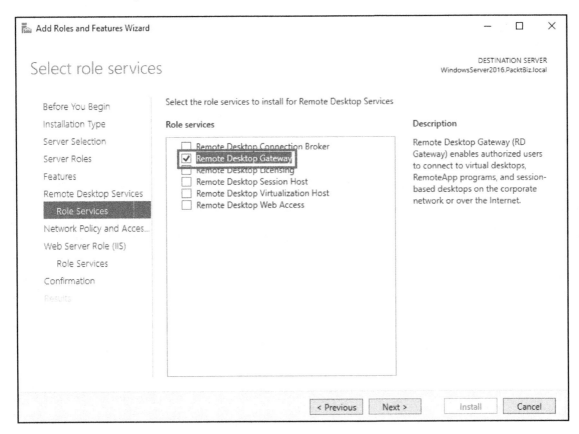

Figure 5.17. Adding Remote Desktop Gateway role services in Windows Server 2016

Virtual Private Network (2.3.6)

A **Virtual Private Network (VPN)** is a secure path within an organization's network, or on the internet, for transmitting sensitive data. A VPN, as its name suggests, creates a virtual private network on the public physical network. To better understand VPN, try to imagine that you are driving on the highway and in the far left lane you notice a tunnel made of glass in which there are other cars driving as well. Using tunneling and data encryption, VPN uses the internet infrastructure to connect remote users and remote offices. To set up a VPN server in Windows Server 2016, first add the **Remote Access** role and then add **DirectAccess and VPN (RAS)** role services as in *Figure 5.18*:

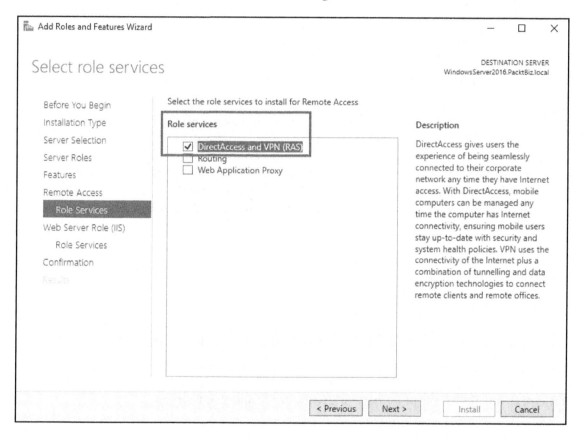

Figure 5.18. Adding DirectAccess and VPN (RAS) role services in Windows Server 2016

Application virtualization (2.3.7)

Microsoft Virtualization Application (App-V) delivers virtualized applications to users. These virtualized applications are installed on a server and are provided to users in the format of a service. From a user's perspective, users interact with the virtualized applications as if they were installed locally. To set up an *App-V server*, you should download the **Microsoft Desktop Optimization Pack (MDOP)** from Microsoft's website.

You can learn more about MDOP from: `https://technet.microsoft.com/en-us/windows/mdop.aspx?`.

Multiple ports (2.3.8)

As discussed earlier in the *Remote Desktop Services (2.3.3)* section, port `3389` is used by RDS to send and receive data. However, that is for accessing one computer at a time. What happens when you try to access more than one computer simultaneously with RDS? While the first computer is using port `3389`, sequential port numbers are assigned to other computers on the LAN starting with `3390`. That way, to access multiple computers simultaneously from a remote location over the internet, we use an IP socket. An IP socket is a combination of an IP address and a port number and tells the application where data should be delivered.

- Syntax: `Public_IP_address:Port_number`
- Example: `192.168.2.10:8080`

Understanding file and print services (2.4)

File and print services are considered core services of computer networks. Nowadays, every NOS on the market is capable of providing these services. For that reason, it is difficult to imagine a computer network without file and print servers.

The File Services role

In Windows Server 2016, the **File Services** role is automatically added upon completing the installation of an operating system. Perhaps that is a surprise to you? Maybe not, if you remember the fact that you have just installed a network operating system on your server (see *Figure 5.19*). As mentioned before, file services are must-have services in today's networks. From simple file sharing to work folders, or from DFS Namespaces to **BranchCache for Network Files**, it is all about the availability of the data and being able to access it anytime, anywhere:

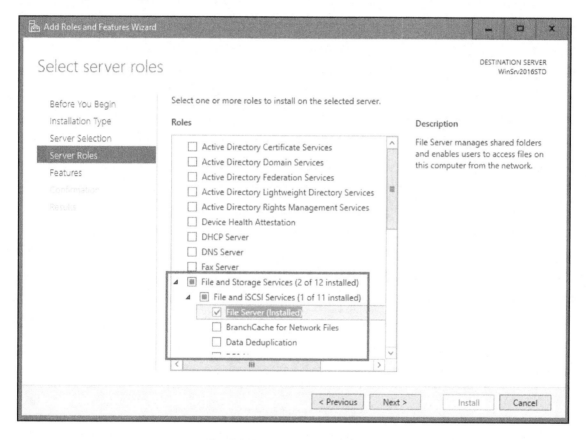

Figure 5.19. File Services role in Windows Server 2016

The Print and Document Services role

Print and Document Services (PDS) is a service that enables centralized printing on the network. Of course, PDS offers more than just the network printing service, such as services for document scanning. With the scanning service, users receive scanned documents from the network scanner and send them to the network shared resources. Usually, PDS is added as a role in Windows Server 2016 as in *Figure 5.20*:

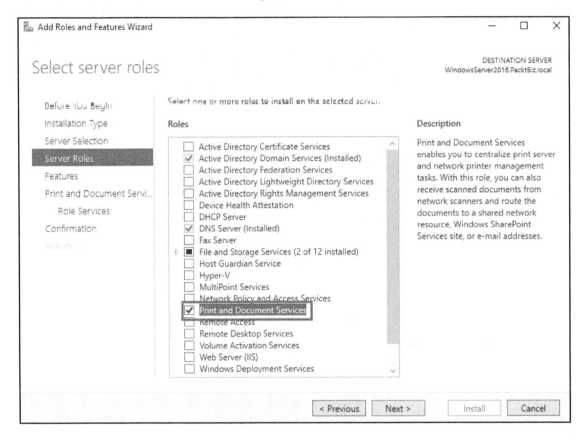

Figure 5.20. Adding Print and Document Services role in Windows Server 2016

The following role services can be installed as part of PDS (see *Figure 5.21*):

- **Print server**: Enables management of printing queues as well as the deployment and migration of print servers
- **Distributed scan server**: Enables configuration, management, and administration of scanners in a network, including scanned documents

- **Internet printing**: Enables setting up a website from where users, through **Internet Client Printing (ICP)**, can print
- **LPD service**: Enables Unix-based computers and other non-Windows OSes to use **Line Printer Remote (LPR)** to print

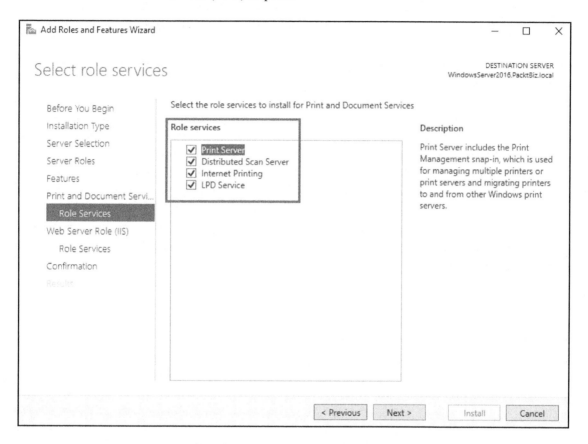

Figure 5.21. Adding PDS role services in Windows Server 2016

Local printers (2.4.1)

A local printer, as the name implies, is a printer that is physically connected to the computer through the parallel port (known as the printer port) or USB port. This printer primarily serves the computer to which it is connected. However, if the printer is shared by a host computer then it also serves other computers on the network.

Network printers (2.4.2)

Network printers, unlike local printers, are dedicated printers on the computer network that provide printing services. Depending on the type of network interface that they own, these printers can be connected to a wired or wireless network. To set up a print server in Windows Server 2016, select the **Print and Document Services (PDS)** role and add **Print Server** role services as shown in *Figure 5.22*:

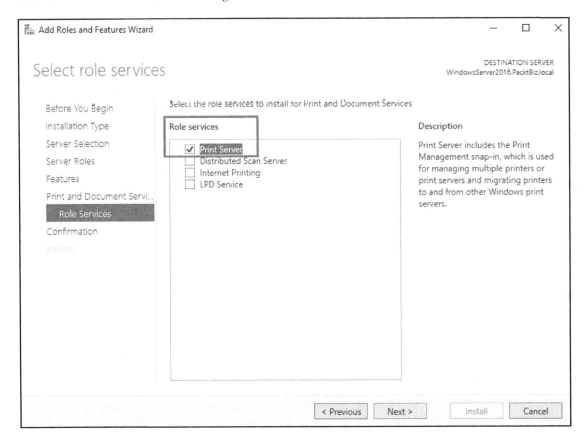

Figure 5.22. Adding Print Server role services in Windows Server 2016

Printer pooling (2.4.3)

Printer pooling in Windows Server 2016 is an option that helps configure two or more physical printers into one logical printer. To do that, printers installed on the print server are required to be almost identical or be able to use the same driver. From the client's perspective, though there are several physical network printers available, it seems to be a single printer. This logical connection of printers balances their load thus increasing their usability, and at the same time providing users with rational printing. You will set up printer pooling in Windows Server 2016 by adding the **Print and Document Services (PDS)** role and **Print Server** role services, then by installing printers and configure printer pooling through the **Print Management** console as in *Figure 5.23*:

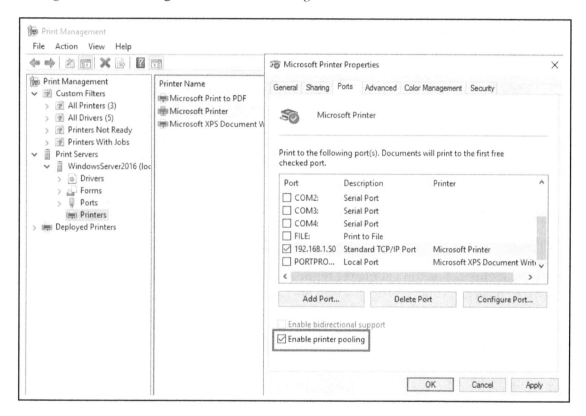

Figure 5.23. Setting up printer pooling in Windows Server 2016

Web printing (2.4.4)

Web printing enables users to print files to network printers through a web browser. To set up web printing in your organization's network, prior to adding the **Print and Document Services (PDS)** role and Internet Printing as a role service, you need to add the **Web Server (IIS) role** (see *Figure 5.24*). To access available printers through a web browser, enter `http://servername/printers` in the browser's web address bar:

Figure 5.24. Web printing in Windows Server 2016

Web management (2.4.5)

In addition to printing, web printing (or Internet Printing role services) enables web printing management. Through the web browser, users can manage print jobs in a similar way to the traditional method of managing print jobs (for example, the See what's printing option). To manage printers through a web interface, enter `http://servername/printers` in your browser's address bar and then select the printer. The next page lists the print jobs as shown in *Figure 5.25*:

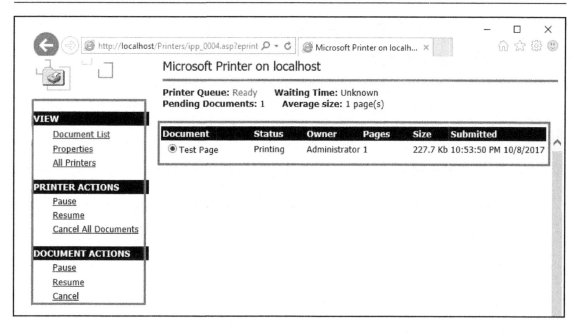

Figure 5.25. Web printing management in Windows Server 2016

Driver deployment (2.4.6)

When it comes to managing printers, we use the **Print Management** console to take care of this task. Everything from driver deployment to adding printers can be accomplished with **Print Management** as shown in *Figure 5.26*:

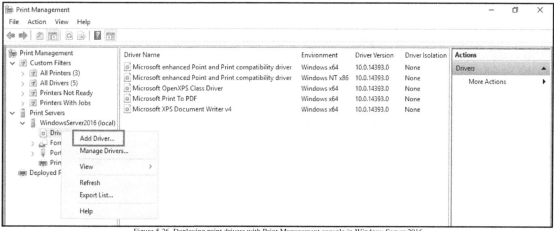

Figure 5.26. Deploying print drivers with Print Management console in Windows Server 2016

User rights, NTFS permissions, and share permissions (2.4.7)

First, let us try to understand what user rights and permissions are. If you open the *Properties* of a folder in any Windows OS and then click on the *Security* tab, you will notice that under the *Group and Usernames* section you can see the *Permissions for the* `<user>` section. That section lists the following permission types:

- **Full control**: Allows reading, writing, modifying, executing, changing attributes and permissions, and deleting files and subfolders
- **Modify**: Allows viewing, modifying, adding and deleting files and subfolders
- **Read and Execute**: Allows running and executing files
- **List folder contents**: Allows viewing data files and a list of a folder's content
- **Read**: Allows viewing files and file properties
- **Write**: Allows writing in a file
- **Special permissions**: Additionally advanced permissions

However, from the same section, we note that each permission may be allowed or denied (see *Figure 5.27*). In the broader context, users can be allowed or denied access to the objects and this can be said to be related to user rights. While in the narrower context, each allowance or denial has certain permissions that determine the type of access to the objects:

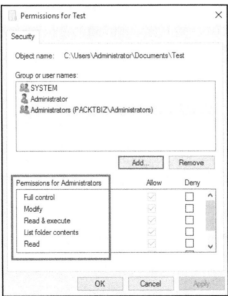

Figure 5.27. NTFS permissions in Windows Server 2016

Another consideration is the comparison of **NTFS permissions** with **share permissions**. NTFS permissions are actually about user access to files and folders at the local and network level. On the other hand, share permissions have to do with user access to the shared folders and drives on the network. Since NTFS permissions were previously mentioned, shared permissions are listed as follows (see *Figure 5.2*):

- **Full control**: Allows reading, modifying, and editing permissions, and taking ownership
- **Change**: Allows reading, executing, writing, and deleting files and subfolders
- **Read**: Allows listing and viewing the content

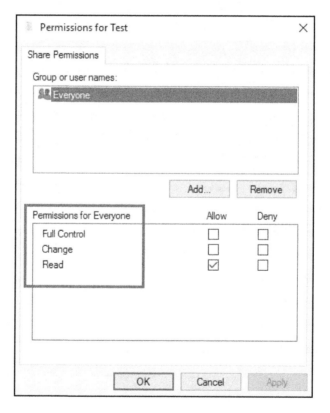

Figure 5.28. Share permissions in Windows Server 2016

Another perspective on user rights has to do with their assignment through the **Local Group Policy Editor** (gpedit.msc), Local Security Policy, or Default Domain Policy, and navigating to the ...\Security Settings\Policies\User Rights Assignment path. If your computer is part of a domain, then you will notice that some *Policies* are already configured (see *Figure 5.29*). From what we have already said in this section, we can conclude that there is an association between user rights and permissions:

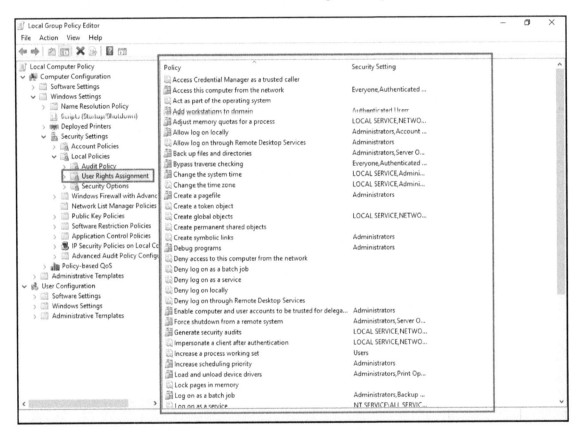

Figure 5.29. User Rights assignment in Windows Server 2016

Auditing file servers (2.4.8)

Given the fact that a file server holds very important and sensitive data for an organization, then auditing is an activity that you would not want to neglect. For that reason, file server auditing is a necessary measure to keep track of who has done what and when with the data. To configure auditing in Windows Server 2016, open Local Group Policy Editor (`gpedit.msc`), Local Security Policy, or Default Domain Policy and navigate to the `...\Security Settings\Local Policies\Audit Policy` path as shown in *Figure 5.30*:

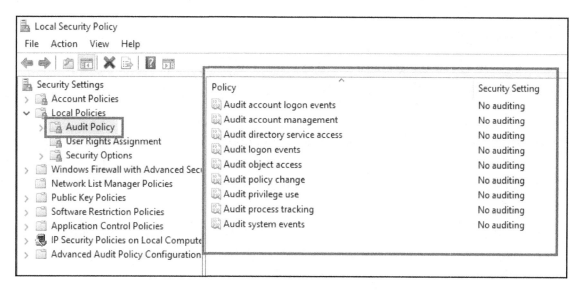

Figure 5.30. Auditing in Windows Server 2016

References from Windows IT Pro Center

1. Remote Server Administration Tools (`https://docs.microsoft.com/en-us/windows-server/remote/remote-server-administration-tools`)
2. Get started with Remote Desktop Services in Windows Server 2016 (`https://docs.microsoft.com/en-us/windows-server/remote/remote-desktop-services/rds-get-started`)

3. Remote Access in Windows Server 2016 (`https://docs.microsoft.com/en-us/windows-server/remote/remote-access/remote-access`)

4. Install or Uninstall Roles, Role Services, or Features in Windows Server 2016 (`https://docs.microsoft.com/en-us/windows-server/administration/server-manager/install-or-uninstall-roles-role-services-or-features`)

5. Enable or Disable Windows Features Using DISM (`https://technet.microsoft.com/library/hh824822.aspx`)

Summary

- A server role is a primary task that a server should perform
- While adding a role to your server you will encounter situations when you should add role services too
- Features are added to the server to support the given role
- To add roles in Windows Server 2016, you need to use Server Manager
- Application servers are servers that offer usable services to a network
- A mail server is a server that sends and receives emails
- A database server is a server that provides database services
- A collaboration server is a server that brings people together for a common project
- A monitoring server's functions include everything from monitoring a server's health to monitoring its performance
- A threat management server is a server that acts as a router, firewall, antivirus program, VPN server, proxy server, and other threat management roles
- A web service is a communication between two devices based on the request/response methodology using the HTTP protocol
- IIS is Microsoft's web server
- IIS Manager is a console that is used to manage a web server
- WWW, too, is an internet service that is accessed through the HTTP protocol and consists of electronic documents compiled with HTML
- FTP transfers files from computer to computer, computer to server, or vice-versa both on a LAN and WAN
- Each application in the application pool is supported by the same worker process

- A site is a collection of web pages whose purpose is to publish content on the intranet or the internet through web services
- A hardware port is any physical interface in a computer, peripheral device, or network device that allows interconnection for communication purposes
- A software port (often known as an application port) is any logical endpoint where applications from your computer communicate with other applications on other computers, both on a LAN and WAN
- SSL is a communication technology that encrypts the communication channel between a website on a web server and a browser on a computer
- A certificate is responsible for securing the communication channel between a website and browser
- The Remote Access role in Windows Server 2016 enables remote access to resources inside an organization's network
- Remote Assistance is a feature that enables a helper to access the host's desktop remotely to assist in resolving issues
- RSAT is a feature that enables managing server roles and features of remote servers that run Windows Server 2016
- RDS enables remote access with a GUI, to computers within an organization's network and over the internet
- RDS CALs are used by users and computers to access an RDSH server
- An RDG server is a role service in Windows Server 2016 that enables authorized users to connect to computers within an organization's network and over the internet using a Remote Desktop Connection (RDC) client
- VPN is a secure path within an organization's network or on the internet for transmitting sensitive data
- App-V stands for Microsoft Virtualization Application and delivers virtualized applications to users
- An IP socket is a combination of an IP address and a port number and tells the application where data should be delivered
- The File Services role is automatically added upon completing the installation of an operating system
- PDS is a service that enables centralized printing on the network
- The local printer, as the name implies, is a printer that is physically connected to the computer through the parallel port (known as the printer port) or USB port
- Network printers, unlike local printers, are dedicated printers on the computer network that provide printing services

- Printer pooling in Windows Server 2016 is an option that helps configure two or more physical printers into one logical printer
- Install printers and configure printer pooling through the Print Management console
- Web printing enables users to print files to network printers through a web browser instead of the traditional way of adding printers
- Users can be allowed or denied access to objects and this can be said to be related to user rights
- Each allowance or denial has certain permissions that determine the type of access to the objects
- Share permissions have to do with user access to the shared folders and drives on the network
- File server auditing is a necessary measure to keep track of who has done what and when with data

Questions

1. A server role is a primary task that a server should perform. (True | False)
2. _____ transfers files from computer to computer, computer to server, or vice-versa both on a LAN and WAN.
3. Which of the following are NTFS permissions in Windows Server 2016? (Choose three)
    1. Modify
    2. Write
    3. Change
    4. Read
4. A web service is a communication between two devices based on the request/response methodology using the File Transfer Protocol (FTP) protocol. (True | False)
5. _____ is any logical endpoint where applications from your computer communicate with other applications on other computers both on a LAN and WAN.

6. Which of the following protocols are utilized by mail servers? (Choose two)
    1. File Transfer Protocol (FTP)
    2. Hypertext Transfer Protocol (HTTP)
    3. Simple Mail Transfer Protocol (SMTP)
    4. Post Office Protocol (POP)

7. Remote Assistance is a feature that enables a helper to access the host's desktop remotely to assist with resolving issues. (True | False)

8. _____ is responsible for securing the communication channel between a website and browser.

9. Which of the following ports is used by Remote Desktop Services?
    1. 25
    2. 110
    3. 443
    4. 3389

10. Web printing enables users to print files to network printers through Windows Explorer. (True | False)

11. _____ have to do with user access to shared folders and drives on the network.

12. Which of the following are share permissions? (Choose two)
    1. Read
    2. Change
    3. Write
    4. Modify

13. Discuss the Remote Access and Remote Desktop Services (RDS) roles.

14. Discuss user rights, NTFS permissions, and share permissions.

6
Group Policy in Windows Server

So far, you have learned a lot about setting up Windows Server 2016 from the perspectives of installation, post-installation tasks, adding roles and features, and virtualizing your infrastructure. Also, by adding **Group Policy** (**GP**) in this chapter, it can be said that real administration has reached its peak. Other than gaining an understanding of GP in Windows Server, you will learn about GP processing, become familiar with the GP Management Console, find out about both computer and user policies, and get to know local policies for when your server is not part of a domain. At the same time, you will learn to configure computer and user policies in a domain-based network. That way, you will be able to understand what GPOs are and how you can configure the computer to use GPOs.

In this chapter, we will cover:

- Understanding **Group Policy** (**GP**)
- Understanding GP processing
- Becoming familiar with the **GP Management Console** (**GPMC**)
- Getting to know computer policies
- Getting to know user policies
- Understanding local policies

Understanding Group Policy (GP) (3.4)

To understand Group Policy easily let us recall the definitions for groups and objects in Chapter 4, *Directory Services in Windows Server*. As you know, from an administration point of view, domain-based networks are centralized environments. In the AD, a group is a collection of AD objects. AD objects typically represent users, computers, peripheral devices, and network services. In such a complex environment there is a need to set up configurations that will limit the user's ability to change options both on local computers and on the network. So, the GP is the best option offered by Microsoft to set up these restrictions at the computer account and user account level. So, it can be concluded that GPs are templates that enable system administrators to control what users can and cannot do on computers, peripheral devices, and network applications across the organization's network. By default, GPs are stored in the following path in your domain controller: `C:\Windows\SYSVOL\sysvol\<domain>\Policies` as shown in *Figure 7.1*:

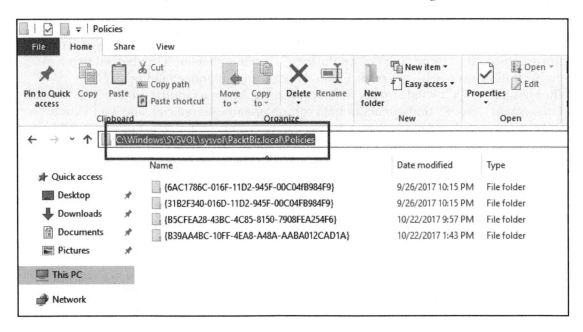

Figure 7.1. Group Policiey (GP) default store in Windows Server 2016

Group Policy processing (3.4.1)

As mentioned previously, GP settings are administrative templates that are configured by system administrators. Thus, **Group Policy Objects (GPOs)** are a collection of configured parameters that show how computers will look and behave for a certain group of users. Each GPO contains three possible settings as shown in Figure 7.2.

- **Not configured**: This is the default setting for the GPOs
- **Enabled**: This indicates that a GPO is enabled
- **Disabled**: This indicates that a GPO is disabled:

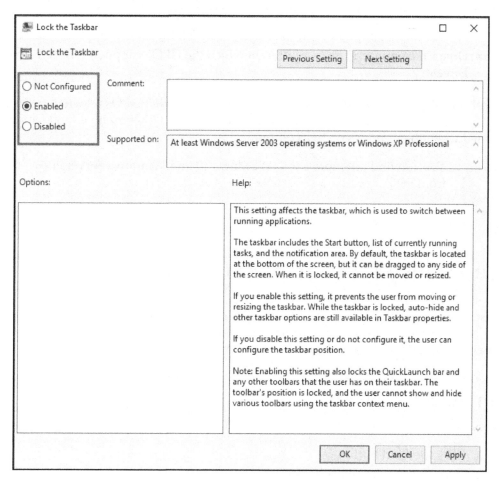

Figure 7.2. Group Policy Objects (GPOs) settings in Windows Server 2016

As you now know, GPOs apply to both computer and user accounts. The processing of GPOs takes place in the following (Local | Site | Domain | OU):

1. **Local**: GPOs that are applied to the computer's local policy for each user
2. **Site**: GPOs that are applied to the site of which the computer is a member
3. **Domain**: GPOs that are applied to the domain of which the computer is a member
4. **OUs**: GPOs that are applied to the OUs on which the computer is placed

Regardless of whether the computer for which GPOs are applied is or is not a member of the domain, we encounter the following two ways to apply GPOs:

- **Non-domain computer**: The computer on which the GPO is applied locally
- **Domain computer:** The computer on which the GPO is applied through Active Directory

As we continue to talk about GPOs, we should bear in mind that GPOs assigned to *computer accounts* are applied when computers are turned on, whereas GPOs assigned to *user accounts* are applied when the user logs on to a computer.

 You can find out more about Windows 10 and Windows Server 2016 GP from `http://getadmx.com/?Category=Windows_10_2016#`.

Group Policy Management Console (3.4.2)

The **Group Policy Management Console** (**GPMC**), as shown in *Figure 7.3*, is a system administrator's favorite tool for **Group Policy Objects** (**GPOs**) management. It is a console that helps create and deploy GPOs across the organization. To access the GPMC in Windows Server 2016, complete the following steps:

From the Start menu

To access the GPMC from the Start menu, complete the following steps:

1. Click the **Start** button.
2. Select **Windows Administrative Tools** from the **Start** menu.
3. Select **Group Policy Management**.

From the Run dialog box

To access the GPMC from the Run window, complete the following steps:

1. Press the combination of *Windows key + R*.
2. Enter `gpmc.msc` in the text box, and press **OK**.

> Typing `gpmc.msc` also works in the Cortana/Search box (**Start** menu), Windows PowerShell, and Command Prompt (`cmd.exe`).

From Server Manager

To access the GPMC from Server Manager, complete the following steps:

1. Click the **Start** menu.
2. Select **Server Manager** from the **Start** menu.
3. Click **Tools** and select **Group Policy Management**:

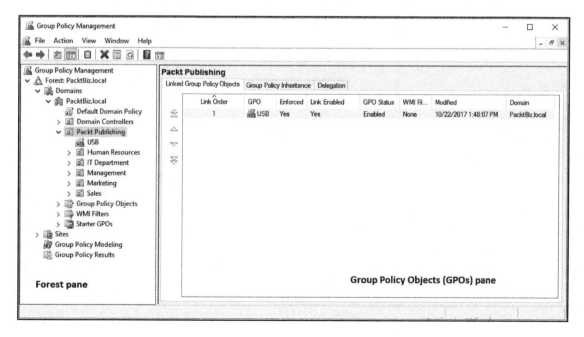

Figure 7.3. Group Policy Management Console (GPMC) in Windows Server 2016

Computer policies (3.4.3)

As explained in the *Group policy processing* section, GPOs assigned to computer accounts are applied when computers are turned on. So, computer configuration policies are bound to computers regardless of the user that is logged on to the computer. This applies both to computers in the domain and to non-domain computers. To set up GPOs for computer accounts, complete the following steps:

1. Open **Group Policy Management**.
2. Right-click your domain and select **Create a GPO in this domain and Link it here...**
3. In the **New GPO** window, enter the **name for the new GPO**, and click **OK**.
4. Right-click the newly created GPO and select **Edit**.
5. From the **Group Policy Management Editor** window, expand **Policies** under **Computer Configuration**, and select the desired template to configure as shown in *Figure 7.4*.
6. Close the **Group Policy Management Editor** window
7. Right-click the GPO and select **Enforced**.
8. In the **Group Policy Management Editor** window, click **OK**:

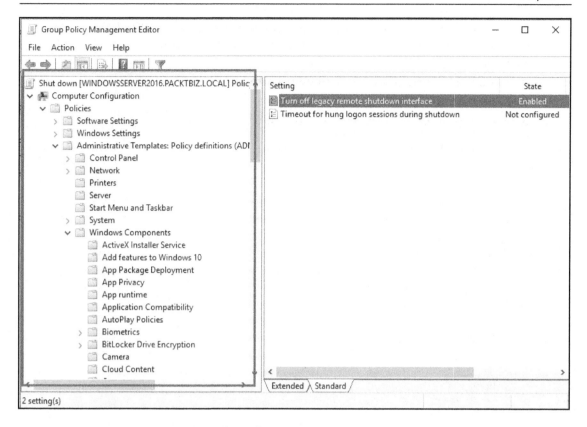

Figure 7.4. Computer Configuration Policies in Windows Server 2016

User policies (3.4.4)

Well, user configuration policies are the opposite of computer configuration policies. GPOs assigned to user accounts are applied when the user logs on to a computer regardless of the computer they log on to. To set up GPOs for user accounts, complete the following steps:

1. Open **Group Policy Management**.
2. Right-click your domain and select **Create a GPO in this domain and Link it here...**
3. In the **New GPO** window, enter the name for the new GPO, and click **OK**.
4. Right-click the newly created GPO and select **Edit**.

5. From the **Group Policy Management Editor** window, expand **Policies** under **User Configuration**, and select the desired template to configure as shown in *Figure 7.5*.

6. Close the **Group Policy Management Editor** window.

7. Right-click the GPO and select **Enforced**.

8. In the **Group Policy Management Editor** window, click **OK**:

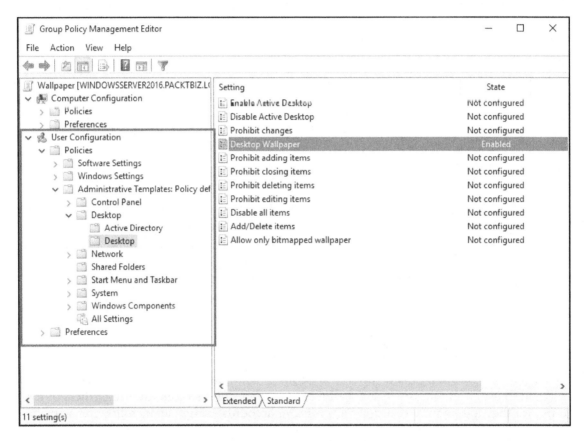

Figure 7.5. User Configuration Policies in Windows Server 2016

Local policies (3.4.5)

So far, what we've explained about GPOs applies to computer and user accounts for both domain-based networks, and standalone, non-domain computers. Unlike GPMC, which we are using to set up GPOs in an AD environment, to configure **Local Group Policies (Local GPOs)** you should use the **Local Group Policy Editor**. You can access the **Local Group Policy Editor** and configure **Local GPOs** as follows:

1. Press the combination of *Windows key + R*.
2. Enter `gpedit.msc` in the text box, and press **OK**.
3. The **Local Group Policy Editor** is displayed as in *Figure 7.6*:

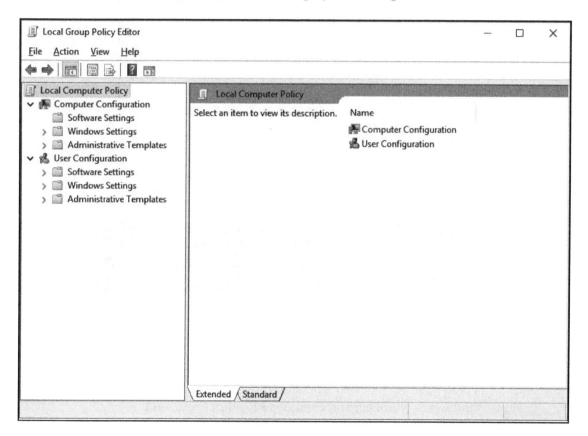

Figure 7.6. Local Group Policy Editor in Windows 10

4. Configure the desired templates for computer configuration and user configuration.

5. Close the **Local Group Policy Editor**.

6. Press the combination of *Windows key + R.*

7. Enter **gpupdate /force** as in *Figure 7.7*, and press **OK**:

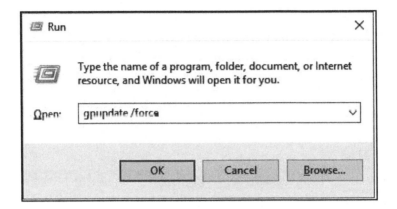

Figure 7.7. Running the **gpupdate /force** command to apply Local GPOs

8. You will see **Updating policy...** as in *Figure 7.8*:

Figure 7.8. Updating policy...

9. The window closes automatically when the **Computer Policy update has completed successfully**.

Typing gpedit.msc also works in the Cortana/Search box (**Start** menu), Windows PowerShell, and Command Prompt (cmd.exe).

References from Windows IT Pro Center

1. Create a Group Policy Object in Windows Server 2016 (`https://docs.microsoft.com/en-us/windows/access-protection/windows-firewall/create-a-group-policy-object`).
2. Copy a GPO to Create a New GPO in Windows Server 2016 (`https://docs.microsoft.com/en-us/windows/access-protection/windows-firewall/copy-a-gpo-to-create-a-new-gpo`).
3. Link the GPO to the Domain in Windows Server 2016 (`https://docs.microsoft.com/en-us/windows/access-protection/windows-firewall/link-the-gpo-to-the-domain`).

Summary

- GPs are templates that enable system administrators to control what users can and cannot do on computers, peripheral devices, and network applications across the organization's network
- GPs are stored in `C:\Windows\SYSVOL\sysvol\<domain>\Policies`
- GPOs are a collection of configured parameters that show how computers will look and behave for a certain group of users
- Each GPO contains three possible settings:
  - Not configured setting is the default for GPOs
  - Enabled setting indicates that a GPO is enabled
  - Disabled setting indicates that a GPO is disabled
- GPOs are processed in this order: Local, Site, Domain, Organizational Units
- GPOs assigned to computer accounts are applied when computers are turned on
- GPOs assigned to user accounts are applied when users are logged on to computers
- GPMC is a system administrator's favorite tool for GPOs management
- Computer configuration policies are bound to computers regardless of the users that are logged on to the computers
- User configuration policies are the opposite of computer configuration policies
- To configure Local GPOs you should use the Local Group Policy Editor

Questions

1. Processing GPOs takes place in this order: Local, Site, Domain, Organizational Units (OUs). (True | False)

2. _____ is a system administrator's favorite tool for Group Policy Objects (GPOs) management.

3. Which of the following are GPO settings? (Choose two)
    1. Enabled
    2. Disabled
    3. Allow
    4. Deny

4. Group Policy Objects (GPOs) are a collection of configured parameters that show how computers will look and behave for a certain group of users. (True | False)

5. _____ are templates that enable system administrators to control what users can and cannot do on computers, peripheral devices, and network applications across the organization's network.

6. In which order are GPOs processed?
    1. OUs, Domain, Site, Local
    2. Site, Domain, OUs, Local
    3. Domain, OUs, Local, Site
    4. Local, Site, Domain, OUs

7. To configure Local Group Policies (Local GPOs) you should use the Group Policy Management Console. (True | False)

8. _____ setting is a default for GPOs.

9. Which command would you use to enforce GPOs?
    1. gpupdate /enforce
    2. gpupdate /setup
    3. gpupdate /run
    4. gpupdate /force

10. Discuss computer configuration and user configuration policies.

7
Virtualization with Windows Server

You've probably heard the term *cloud services* but have not thought about the infrastructure that enables cloud services. Regardless, know that it is a complex infrastructure that is completely virtualized. In a data center that provides cloud services, a large number of servers have been grouped to form a cluster. On top of that cluster, there are hundreds or thousands of virtual machines running to make up the cloud's infrastructure. So, in this chapter, you will get to know the virtualization concept, as well as become familiar with the Hyper-V software, which enables the virtualization of Windows-based servers. You will find out the steps it takes to add the Hyper-V role to your server, familiarize yourself with Hyper-V Manager, and learn to create virtual machines. That way, you will be able to understand what virtualization is, how you can enable the Hyper-V role, and how to create virtual machines.

In this chapter, we will cover:

- Understanding virtualization
- Adding the Hyper-V role to your server
- Getting to know Hyper-V Manager
- Creating virtual machines
- Managing virtual machines

Understanding server virtualization (2.5)

According to the Merriam-Webster dictionary, the word *virtual* derives from the Latin word *virtus*, which in English is translated as *strength* or *virtue*. Furthermore, from the same dictionary, the definition of the word *virtual* is, *to exist in essence or in fact as far as it is not formally recognized or acknowledged.*

As the successor to Windows Virtual PC, Microsoft's Hypervisor Hyper-V was launched with Windows Server 2008. Since then, although younger than its competitors, Hyper-V has managed to gain the attention of system administrators around the globe, thus positioning itself strongly in second place in terms of virtualization platform market share. Hyper-V is a service that enables virtual environments. In specific terms, Hyper-V provides the services that you can use to create and manage virtual machines and their resources.

Virtualization modes (2.5.1)

Generally, the following two virtualized modes are the most used in today's virtualized environments:

- **Fully virtualized mode**: This enables an isolated and secure execution of one or more OSes in a single physical server where guest OSes use the host's OS resources (see *Figure 6.1*):

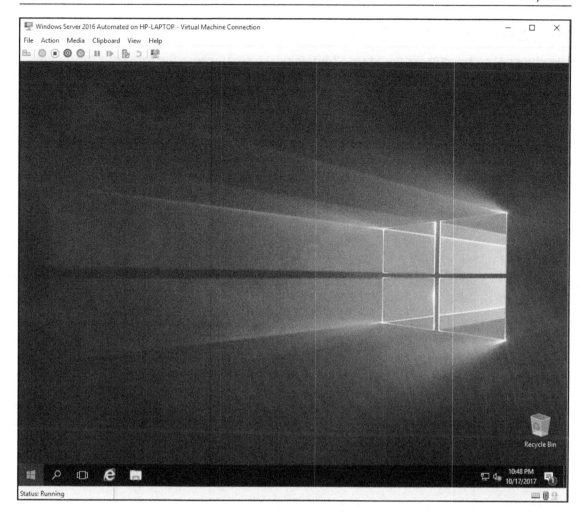

Figure 6.1. Windows Server 2016 running in an isolated and secure virtual environment

- **Paravirtualized mode**: This can be understood as a computer inside a computer that has an installed operating system that does not simulate the hardware. Rather, it offers a special **Application Program Interface** (**API**) to modify the guest OS.

 A host OS is the OS on a physical server, whereas a guest OS is the OS on a virtual machine. In my case, I am running Windows 10 Enterprise on a laptop as the host OS, and I am running Windows Server 2016 Standard as the guest OS.

Hyper-V architecture

The Hyper-V architecture is based on a hierarchical format where the first level represents the hypervisor as the main element that constitutes the Hyper-V virtual platform. Thus, a hypervisor is accommodated at the root and has direct access to hardware devices. The root component then creates branch OSes that represent isolated executable environments. Specifically, the branched OS represents a logical unit of isolation that has no access to hardware devices. Then, on these parts, it will be possible to run guest OSes. Components such as **Virtualization Service Providers (VSP)** and **Virtualization Service Consumers (VSC)**, through logical channels for communication known as VMBus, enable communication between the root portion and the branch OSes (see *Figure 6.2*):

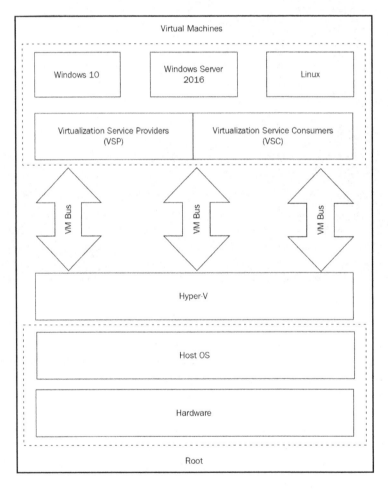

Figure 6.2. Hyper-V architecture

Hyper-V installation requirements

First things first. To accommodate the hypervisor, the server must support virtualization. To fulfill this requirement, it must be based on an Intel or AMD processor with **Intel Virtualization Technology (VT)** or **AMD Virtualization** enabled. To add the Hyper-V role in Windows Server 2016, complete the following steps:

1. Click **Add Roles and Features Wizard** in the Server Manager's **Welcome to Server Manager** section.
2. In the **Before You Begin** option, click **Next**.
3. Click **Next** in the **Installation Type** option.
4. In the **Server Selection** option, click **Next**.
5. Select the **Hyper-V** role as in *Figure 6.3*:

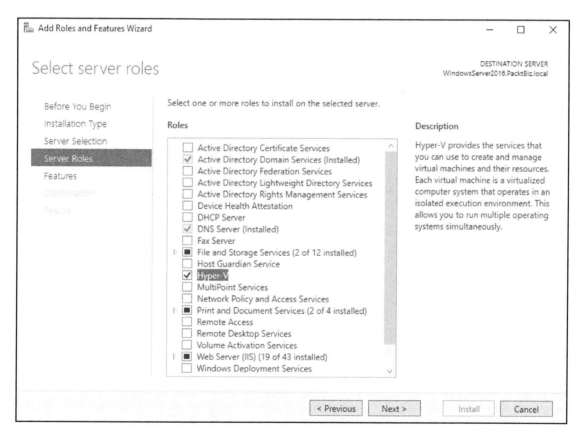

Figure 6.3. Adding the Hyper-V role in Windows Server 2016

6. Click the **Add Features** button to **Add features that are required for Hyper-V**.

7. There is no feature to add, so click **Next**.

8. Click **Next** in the Hyper-V definition option.

9. Select your available network adapter, and click **Next**.

10. Select **Allow this server to send and receive live migrations of virtual machines** and click **Next**.

11. Set up the path where you will store the virtual machines and click **Next**.

12. Confirm installation selections for the Hyper-V role by clicking **Install**.

13. When the installation process completes, click **Close**. The server will restart automatically.

 You can download Microsoft Hyper-V Server 2016 from the following URL: https://www.microsoft.com/en-us/evalcenter/evaluate-hyper-v-server-2016.

Hyper-V Manager

Hyper-V Manager is an administration tool that you will use to manage virtual machines. Operations such as creating, importing, and deleting virtual machines; creating a virtual switch; creating the SAN manager; inspecting and editing disks; stopping services; and much more are done with Hyper-V Manager. The Hyper-V Manager user interface consists of a servers pane, virtual machines pane, checkpoints pane, selected virtual machine details, and **Actions** pane (see *Figure 6.4*):

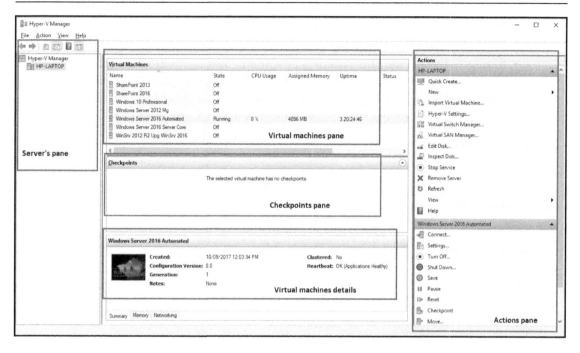

Figure 6.4. Hyper-V the Manager user interface in Windows Server 2016

Configuring Hyper-V settings

Now that you have added the Hyper-V role to your server, it is recommended that you spend a little time setting up the Hyper-V settings. To set up Hyper-V settings, open **Hyper-V Manager** and then click **Hyper-V Settings...** in the **Actions** pane. Among the settings (see *Figure 6.5*) that you can set up are the following:

- **Virtual Hard Disks**: This specifies the location on your server to store virtual hard disk files
- **Virtual Machines**: This specifies the location on your server to store virtual machine configuration files
- **Physical GPUs**: This specifies the **Graphical Processing Unit (GPU)** to be used by virtual machines

- **NUMA Spanning**: This provides virtual machines with additional computing resources, thus allowing you to run more virtual machines at the same time
- **Storage Migrations:** This specifies how many storage migrations can be performed at the same time on your server
- **Enhanced Session Mode Policy**: This allows redirection of local devices and resources from servers running **Virtual Machine Connection** (**VMC**):

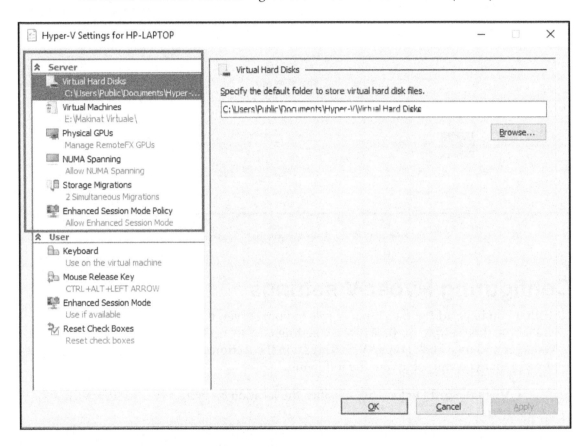

Figure 6.5. Hyper-V Settings in Windows Server 2016

Creating and configuring virtual hard disks (VHDs) (2.5.2)

To create a **virtual hard disk** (**VHD**) with Hyper-V Manager in Windows Server 2016, complete the following steps:

1. In the **Actions** pane, click **New**, and then click **Hard Disk** as shown in *Figure 6.6*:

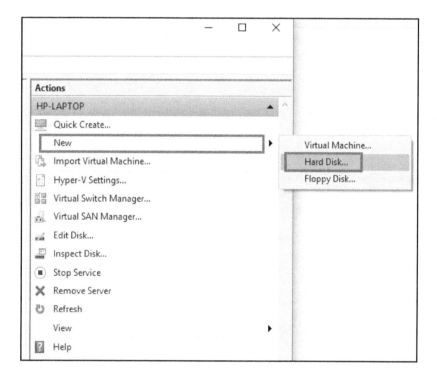

Figure 6.6. Creating the Virtual Hard Disk (VHD) with Windows Server's 2016 Hyper-V

2. Click **Next** in the **Before You Begin** option of the **New Virtual Hard Disk Wizard**.
3. Select the format that you want to use for the virtual hard disk, and then click **Next**.
4. Select the type of virtual hard disk that you want to create, and then click **Next**.
5. Specify the name and location of the virtual hard disk file, and then click **Next**.
6. Create a blank virtual hard disk or copy the contents of an existing physical disk, and then click **Next**.
7. To create the virtual hard disk and close the wizard, click **Finish**.

Managing virtual memory (2.5.3)

Keep in mind that virtual memory management is performed for every virtual machine, thus it is required that VMs be turned off prior to setting up memory settings. To manage virtual memory with Hyper-V Manager in Windows Server 2016, complete the following steps:

1. Right-click the inactive virtual machine, and then select **Settings** as shown in *Figure 6.7*:

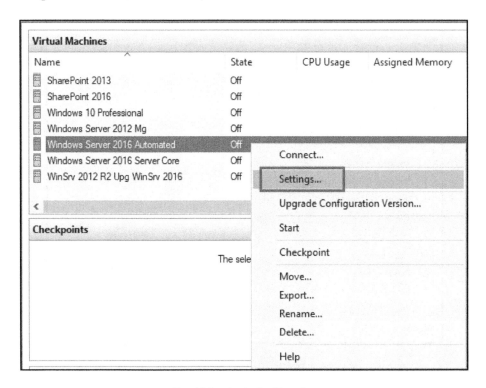

Figure 6.7. Accessing virtual machine settings

2. In the left pane, under Hardware, click **Memory**.
3. You have the option to set a fixed or dynamic amount of memory (see *Figure 6.8*):
    1. To set a fixed amount of memory enter the amount in MB within the RAM text box.
    2. To set a dynamic amount of memory, **Enable Dynamic Memory**, and then set the amount of memory for **Minimum RAM** and **Maximum RAM**:

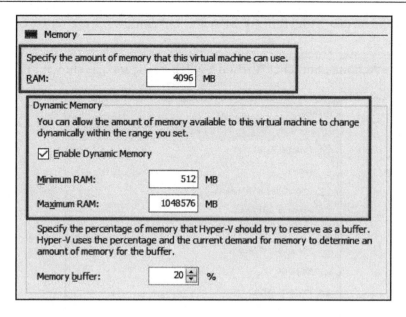

Figure 6.8. Setting up the fixed or dynamic amount of memory

4. Click **OK** to close the **VM Settings** window.

Setting up virtual networks (2.5.4)

In an attempt to establish an infrastructure in a virtual environment prior to creating virtual machines, virtual switches are required. There are three types of virtual switch available in Hyper-V:

- **External switch**: This binds the physical network adapter so that the virtual machines can access the physical network
- **Internal switch**: This can be used only by the virtual machines that run on the physical server, and between virtual machines and the physical server
- **Private switch**: This can be used only by the virtual machines that run on the physical server

To create a virtual switch with Hyper-V Manager in Windows Server 2016, complete the following steps:

1. In the **Actions** pane, click **Virtual Switch Manager...** as shown in *Figure 6.9*:

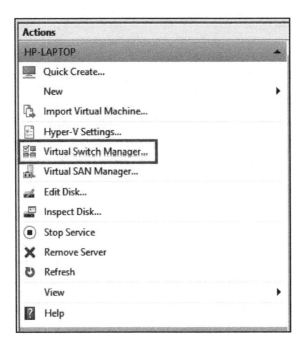

Figure 6.9. Creating a virtual switch with Windows Server's 2016 Hyper-V Manager

2. Select the type of virtual switch that you want to create, and then click **Create Virtual Switch**:
   1. Enter the **Name** for the new virtual switch (see *Figure 6.10*).
   2. Enter **Notes** for the new virtual switch.
   3. Select the **Connection type** that you want the virtual switch to connect to.
   4. Enable virtual LAN identification:

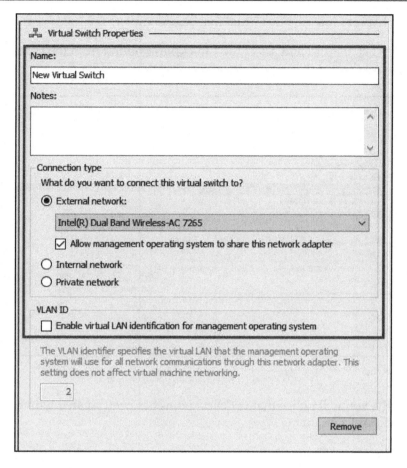

Figure 6.10. Virtual Switch properties

3. Click **OK** to close the **Virtual Switch Manager** window.

Checkpoints (2.5.5)

In order to ease administration of virtual environments, Hyper-V offers a variety of options and capabilities. Among them are **Checkpoints** (formerly **Snapshots**). I am not mistaken if I call it the Hyper-V's Restore Point. Whenever you want to install a new app on your virtual machine and want to avoid unwanted post-installation situations, then you have the checkpoint option available to you. This option enables you to make a copy of the disk image at a specific time so that, when unexpected situations occur you can revert your virtual machine to a previous state. However, checkpoints are not recommended for production use, only for development and test environments.

To create a checkpoint for a specific virtual machine, complete the following steps:

1. Right-click the VM and select the **Checkpoint** option from the context menu as shown in *Figure 6.11*:

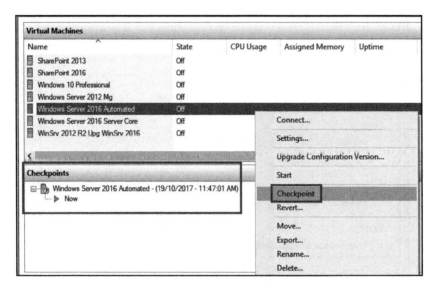

Figure 6.11. Creating a checkpoint with Windows Server's 2016 Hyper-V

2. Shortly, you will notice that the checkpoint has been created within the **Checkpoints** section.

 Note that, if your VM is turned off, the checkpoint will take less time compared to when your VM is up-and-running. Additionally, when creating a checkpoint for a running VM, you will receive confirmation that the checkpoint has been created as in *Figure 6.12*.

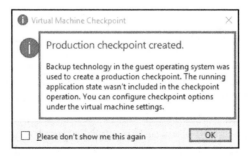

Figure 6.12. Production checkpoint created confirmation

In Windows Server 2016, unlike previous versions, two types of checkpoints are available (see *Figure 6.13*):

- **Production checkpoints:** This does not include information about running applications
- **Standard checkpoints**: This captures the current state of applications

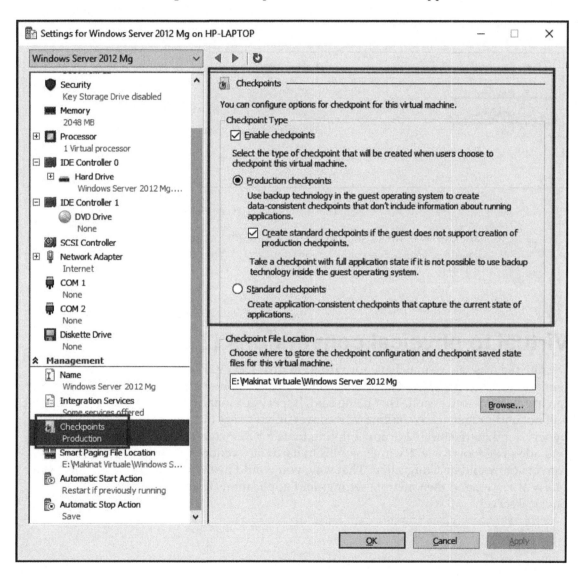

Figure 6.13. Checkpoint types in Windows Server's 2016 Hyper-V

Physical to virtual (P2V) conversions (2.5.6)

Nowadays, virtualization has become the major network service driver and organizations are migrating their **physical servers to virtual servers** (**P2V**) for reasons such as cost, ease of management, and future expansion. Thus, knowing that VMs are using VHDs, Microsoft engineers have developed the **Disk2vhd** app (see Figure 6.14) to convert a physical disk drive (PHD) to a **virtual hard disk** (**VHD**). Then, with Hyper-V Manager, you can create a VM using the converted VHD:

Name		Date modified	Type	Size
☐	Disk2vhd	17/12/2013 11:46 ...	Compiled HTML ...	40 KB
☑	disk2vhd	20/01/2014 2:16 PM	Application	6,968 KB
	Eula	28/07/2006 8:32 AM	Text Document	7 KB

Figure 6.14. Physical hard disk (PHD) to virtual hard disk (VHD) conversion with the Disk2Vhd app

 You can download the Disk2Vhd app from `https://docs.microsoft.com/en-us/sysinternals/downloads/disk2vhd` to do the P2V conversion.

Virtual to physical conversions (2.5.7)

Despite the reasons we may have for **virtual to physical** (**V2P**) conversion, it is good to remind ourselves that, because of the technological era that we live in, the trend is physical to virtual (P2V) conversion. That being said, hypervisor manufacturers including Microsoft will not encourage you to conduct V2P conversion. I guess that might be the reason why hypervisor manufacturers are now offering tools for V2P conversion. However, you might find adequate tools for V2P conversion from hardware vendors. Another option for V2P conversion would be a migration. That way, you would install Windows Server 2016 on a physical server, and then migrate settings and applications from a virtual server to a physical server.

You can download EZ Gig IV Cloning Software from `https://www.apricorn.com/upgrades/ezgig` to perform the V2P conversion. It works in three simple steps: select your source drive, select your destination drive, and press the **Start Clone** button.

Configuring virtual machine settings

To set up **virtual machine (VM)** settings, right-click the desired VM and select **Settings** from the context menu. Among the VM settings (see *Figure 6.15*) that you can set are the following:

- **Add Hardware**: This enables adding devices to your virtual machine
- **BIOS**: This enables setting the boot order
- **Security**: This enables encrypting state and virtual machine migration traffic
- **Memory**: This enables specifying the virtual machine memory
- **Processor**: This enables setting up the number of virtual processors
- **IDE Controller 0**: This enables adding hard drives and CD/DVD drives to the first IDE controller
- **IDE Controller 1**: This enables adding hard drives and CD/DVD drives to the second IDE controller
- **SCSI Controller**: This enables adding or removing hard drives to/from an SCSI controller
- **Network Adapter:** This enables specifying the configuration of the network adapter
- **COM 1**: This enables configuring the first virtual COM port
- **COM 2**: This enables configuring the second virtual COM port

- **Diskette Drive**: This enables specifying the virtual floppy disk file:

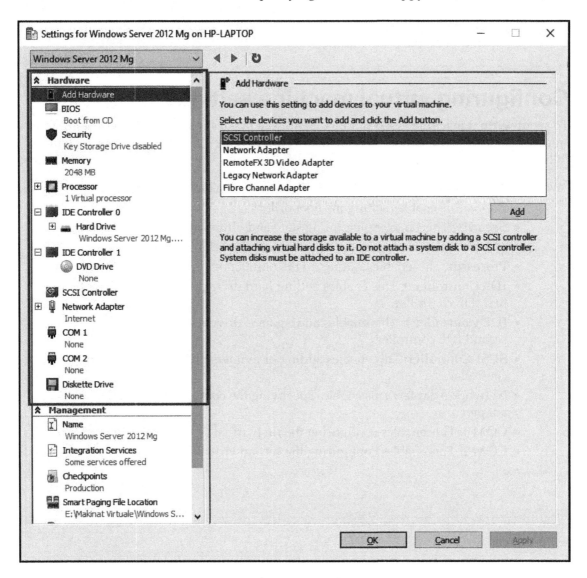

Figure 6.15. Virtual Machines (VM) settings in Windows Server's 2016 Hyper-V

Managing virtual machines

When it comes to managing virtual machines, the **Actions** pane and the *VM's context menu* offer plenty of options. From **Quick create** to **Help**, the **Actions** pane acts as a one-stop resource when it comes to creating VMs, setting up Hyper-V settings, creating virtual switches and virtual SANs, editing and inspecting disks, stopping services, removing servers, and refreshing as shown in *Figure 6.16*:

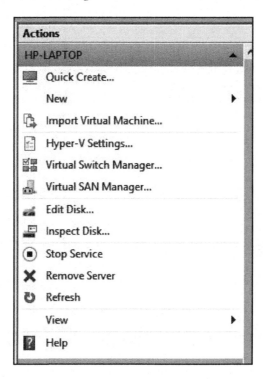

Figure 6.16. Hyper-V's Action pane in Windows Server 2016

Unlike the **Actions** pane, options from the *VM's context menu* are focused only on VMs. From **Connect** to **Rename**, you can select options to manage the specified VM as in *Figure 6.17*:

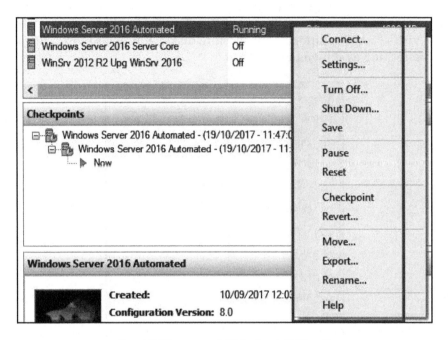

Figure 6.17. VMs context menu in Windows Server's 2016 Hyper-V

References from Windows IT Pro Center

1. Hyper-V on Windows Server 2016 (`https://docs.microsoft.com/en-us/windows-server/get-started/migrate-roles-and-features#windows-server-2016`).

2. Get started with Hyper-V on Windows Server 2016 (`https://docs.microsoft.com/en-us/windows-server/virtualization/hyper-v/get-started/get-started-with-hyper-v-on-windows`).

3. Manage Hyper-V on Windows Server 2016 (`https://docs.microsoft.com/en-us/windows-server/virtualization/hyper-v/manage/manage-hyper-v-on-windows-server`).

Summary

- Hyper-V provides services that you can use to create and manage virtual machines and their resources
- Fully virtualized mode enables an isolated and secure execution of one or more OSes in a single physical server where guest OSs use the host's OS resources
- Paravirtualized mode does not simulate hardware, rather it offers a special API to modify the guest OS
- Hyper-V architecture is based on a hierarchical format where the first level represents the hypervisor as the main element that constitutes the Hyper-V virtual platform
- Components such as VSP and VSC, through logical channels for communication known as VMBus, enable communication between the root portion and the branch OSs
- The server is required to support virtualization by enabling Intel Virtualization Technology (VT) or AMD Virtualization
- Hyper-V Manager is an administration tool that you can use to manage virtual machines
- Keep in mind that virtual memory management is performed for each individual virtual machine
- Prior to creating virtual machines, it is required to create virtual switches
- Checkpoints enable you to make a copy of the disk image at a specific time so that, when unexpected situations arise, you can revert your virtual machine to a previous state
- Production checkpoints do not include information about running applications
- Standard checkpoints capture the current state of applications
- Organizations migrate their P2V for reasons such as cost and development
- Microsoft's engineers have developed the Disk2vhd app to convert a physical disk drive to a virtual hard disk

Questions

1. Hyper-V provides services that you can use to create and manage virtual machines and their resources. (True | False)

2. _____ is based on a hierarchical format where the first level represents the hypervisor as the main element that constitutes the Hyper-V virtual platform.

3. Which of the following are virtualization modes in Hyper-V? (Choose two)
    1. Fully virtualized mode
    2. Paravirtualized mode
    3. Production checkpoints
    4. Standard checkpoints

4. Checkpoints enable you to make a backup of the disk image at a specific time so that when unexpected situations arise you can revert your virtual machine to a previous state. (True | False)

5. Components such as _____ and _____ , through logical channels for communication known as VMBus, enable communication between the root portion and the branch OSes.

6. Which of the following are checkpoint types in Hyper-V? (Choose two)
    1. Production checkpoints
    2. Standard checkpoints
    3. Inspect disk
    4. Edit disk

7. Organizations are migrating their physical servers to virtual servers (P2V) for reasons such as cost, ease of management, and future expansion. (True | False)

8. _____ is an administration tool that you can use to manage the virtual machines.

9. Which of the following are elements of the Hyper-V architecture? (Choose two)
    1. Hypervisor
    2. Root
    3. Branch
    4. Snapshot

10. Discuss physical to virtual (P2V) conversion.

11. Discuss virtual to physical (V2P) conversion.

8
Storing Data in Windows Server

Storage technologies are a broad topic for which a whole book could be written. That shows how important these devices are in the computer world. However, since these technologies are meant to be part of this book too, then a whole chapter has been reserved in order to highlight the importance of these technologies. That said, in this chapter, you will learn about storage technologies. Other than understanding storage technologies in general, you will learn about a variety of related topics. These include physical interfaces and disk controllers. We will also explore how data is stored in a medium, storage system types used in network environments, and various storage protocols. Readers will also learn how to manage server storage using both Server Manager and Windows PowerShell. And finally, they will get to know the concepts and types of RAID. Also, this chapter covers new concepts such as data deduplication, Storage Spaces Direct, and software-defined storage. At the same time, you will learn about primary and secondary storage in general, respectively RAM, ROM, HDDs, SSDs, and optical discs in particular. That way, the chapter is concluded with the steps for mounting a VHD disk and installing a DFS on your server.

In this chapter, we will cover:

- Understanding storage technologies
- Understanding storage architectures
- Understanding storage protocols
- Managing data with Server Manager and Windows PowerShell
- Understanding RAID
- Getting to know types of RAID
- Understanding primary storage

Understanding storage technologies (4)

Can you imagine what a file server would be without its data? Or, try thinking about the internet without data? Perhaps these questions may sound a little inappropriate given the fact that both the file server and the internet are intended to provide access to data. However, instantly the answers to these and related questions show how important data is to storage technologies that have been made to store data. So, besides the fact that storage technologies are an objective of the certification exams, their importance is absolute in the world of **information and communications technologies (ICT)**, and that is why these technologies have a whole chapter in this book.

Identifying storage technologies (4.1)

Besides high processing power, a sufficient amount of RAM memory, and several network connections, most likely your server will require a large amount of storage space too. Regardless of whether it is a single server or a cluster of servers, technologies such as IDE, SAS, SCSI, DAS, NAS, SAN, and RAID represent the wide range of storage technology options at your disposal.

Advantages and Disadvantages of different storage types (4.1.1)

Storage technologies are numerous, as there are numerous opportunities too. As such they offer many advantages and disadvantages at the same time. So let us look at some of these devices:

- **Optical discs:** They offer large capacities and read-and-write accepted speeds. However, they continue to play the role of data backup media.
- **HDDs:** They offer large capacities and high read-and-write speeds. Continue to maintain number one spot in secondary storage category.
- **SSDs:** With their growing capacities and extraordinary read-and-write speeds are becoming a convincing storage technology. Time will tell if they will take the first spot from HDDs.

ATA, PATA, SATA, and SCSI interfaces (4.1.2)

When acronyms such as ATA, PATA, SATA, and SCSI are mentioned, that is actually a discussion about the interfaces used to connect the storage devices and peripherals to computers. The **Advanced Technology Attachment (ATA)**, also known as **Integrated Drive Electronics (IDE)**, is a legacy interface that is used to connect hard disk drives, optical disc drives, floppy disk drives, and related storage technologies to computers. The two most popular types of ATA interface are (see *Figure 8.1*):

- **Parallel ATA** uses a 40-pin connector and cable for data transfer to connect the storage device to the computer's motherboard, and Molex as a power connector to connect the storage device to the computer's power supply. The disk controller resides on a drive itself.

- **Serial ATA** represents a replacement for the PATA interface and is used widely in personal computers. It uses a 7-pin cable for data transfer to connect the storage device to the computer's motherboard, and a 15-pin power supply connector to connect the storage device to the computer's power supply. As with PATA, in SATA too the disk controller is located on a drive.

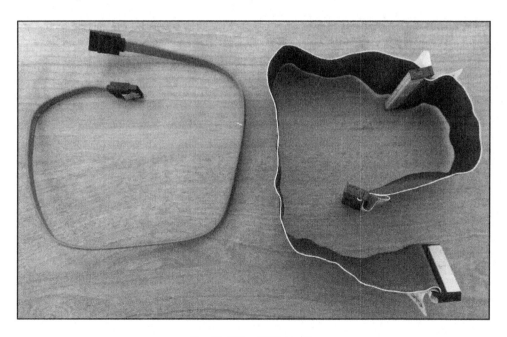

Figure 8.1. PATA and SATA data cables

The **Small Computer System Interface (SCSI)**, pronounced *scuzzy*, is another interface that connects storage devices and peripheral devices to computers. The two most popular types of SCSI are SPI and SAS. The SPI is the early version of SCSI, whereas the SAS is the modern version of SCSI that provides high data transfer rates, and is widely used in servers.

PCI and PCI Express (PCIe)

In the mid-90s, the **Peripheral Component Interconnect** (PCI) replaced IBM's **Industry Standard Architecture (ISA)**, a 16-bit built-in expansion slot on the motherboard. Unlike the ISA, Intel's PCI is a 32-bit and 64-bit built-in slot on the motherboard that enables the expansion of computer capabilities. Later on, with the increase in demand for faster speeds, the PCI has been replaced by the **PCI Express (PCIe)**. The PCIe is a serial expansion bus standard that comes with four connections, PCIe x1, PCIe x4, PCIEx8, and PCIe x16. It transmits the data in full-duplex mode (sending and receiving at the same time) over wires known as **lanes**.

Direct-attached storage

As the name suggests, **direct-attached storage (DAS)** is a group of disks that are directly connected to computers or servers. You are not wrong if you think of your computer's **hard disk drive (HDD)** as a DAS. However, in addition to internal storage devices, even external storage devices that are connected to computers or servers with any of the previously mentioned interfaces are considered as DAS, as shown in *Figure 8.2*:

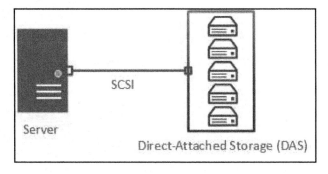

Figure 8.2. Direct-attached storage (DAS) system

Network attached storage (4.1.3)

As the name implies, **network-attached storage** (**NAS**) is a network appliance that connects to computers and servers through the switch and acts as dedicated storage in an organization's network (see *Figure 8.3*). There are manufacturers that build NAS as a file server. It brings flexibility so organizations can rely completely on NAS for file sharing services without the need to use other servers.

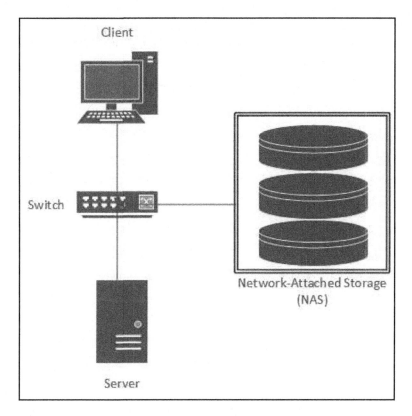

Figure 8.3. Network-Attached Storage (NAS) system

Storage area networks (4.1.4)

As you can see from the explanations for DAS and NAS, we are talking about storage technologies that are distinguished by their details. So **storage area networks (SANs)**, like DAS and NAS, are a storage technology too. However, unlike DAS and NAS, a SAN is a stand-alone infrastructure. If we refer to the designation, then the SAN is the same as a LAN. While on a LAN there are local computers that comprise a computer network, in a SAN there are storage devices and servers that comprise a storage network. As such, a SAN cannot be accessed by other LAN devices. Just because of that, proprietary protocols or SNMPs provide management for a SAN (see *Figure 8.4*). Usually, Ethernet or Fibre Channel is used to connect storage to servers.

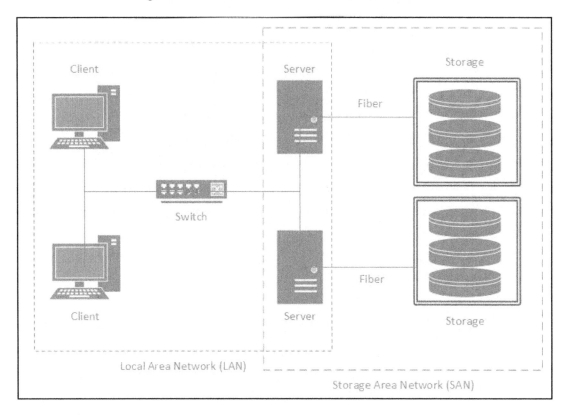

Figure 8.4. Storage area network (SAN) system

Block-level storage versus file-level storage

Comparing **block-level storage** to **file-level storage** is like comparing SAN systems to NAS systems. A reason for that is that block-level storage is used in SAN systems, while file-level storage is used in NAS systems. From here, the data on NAS systems is stored and accessed in the form of files and folders. Unlike NAS systems, data in the SAN systems is stored in blocks that represent volumes that are managed by the server operating system.

Adapter and controller types

The disk controller is an electronic circuit that resides on a hard disk, as shown in *Figure 8.5*. It performs operations such as spinning disks, moving heads for reading and writing, and transferring data from and to RAM. Unlike the disk controller, the **host bus adapter** (**HBA**) controller is an electronic board that is integrated with or attached to the motherboard of the server so it can connect the storage system to the server.

Figure 8.5. Disk controller in HDD

Serial bus technologies (4.1.7)

For data transmission, parallel and serial transmission is used. In parallel transmissions, a string of eight bits is usually transmitted that is equal to one byte at a time. In contrast, in serial transmissions, only one bit is usually transmitted at a given time. Even though more bits are transmitted through parallel transmission, serial transmission is most widely used in storage technologies. That is because disks tend to handle only one bit at a given time, meaning that the disk's read-and-write head reads and writes one bit within the given time. Thus, the serial method of transmission has been proven to be more pragmatic by eliminating overhead processing, signal skewing, and crosstalk. That said, today's most used serial interfaces in storage technologies, such as SATA, SAS, **Fibre Channel (FC)**, and USB, utilize serial buses.

Storage protocols (4.1.5)

Storage protocols enable storing and retrieving data in/from storage systems. The most used storage protocols are as follows:

- **Small Computer System Interface (SCSI)** is a storage protocol that is used heavily in block-level storage systems. The server operating system uses the SCSI protocol to read and write data on an SCSI controller that manages storage devices.
- **Internet Small Computer System Interface (iSCSI)** places the standard SCSI protocol into an IP packet, thus extending its functionalities throughout the organization's network.
- **Fibre Channel (FC)** is another way of extending the functionalities of the standard SCSI protocol, enabling storage consolidations and longer distances.
- **Fibre Channel over Ethernet (FCoE)** does the same for the FC protocol as iSCSI does for the SCSI protocol. That said, FCoE extends the functionalities of the FC protocol across Ethernet networks.

 You can learn more about SCSI at `https://www.lifewire.com/small-computer-system-interface-scsi-2626002`.

File sharing protocols (4.1.6)

File sharing protocols enable data sharing over LANs, WANs, and the internet. The most used file sharing protocols are as follows:

- **Server Message Block (SMB)**, known also as **Common Internet File Service (CIFS)**, is a file sharing protocol used mostly by Windows OSes
- **Network File Service (NFS)** is a file sharing protocol used mostly by Unix and Linux
- **File Transfer Protocol (FTP)** enables file sharing by transferring files from site to site
- **Hypertext Transfer Protocol (HTTP)** enables file sharing over a **World Wide Web (WWW)** service
- **Secure Shell (SSH)** enables remote file sharing over a secure connection

 You can learn more about SSH at `https://www.ssh.com/ssh/`.

FC, HBA, and FC switches (4.1.9)

The **Host Bus Adapter (HBA)** is an interface standard, whereas the **Fibre Channel (FC) switch** is a network switch. Both components are compatible with FC, a high-speed network technology that is used to connect the two, thus creating the FC fabric. FC fabric consists of one or more FC switches, and as such it establishes the SAN topology.

iSCSI hardware (4.1.8)

iSCSI, a block-level storage, uses an IP to send the SCSI commands over TCP/IP networks. iSCSI works in such a way that the clients, known as **initiators,** use the IP protocol to send SCSI commands called **Command Descriptor Blocks (CDBs)** to storage devices known as **targets**. In SANs, the **logical unit number (LUN)** represents a logical disk. In an iSCSI, TCP port 860 is reserved for the iSCSI system port, whereas TCP port 3260 represents iSCSI's default port.

Storage Spaces Direct

Storage Spaces Direct (S2D) is a new feature in Windows Server 2016 that enables you to group disks into storage pools (see *Figure 8.6*), thus creating software-defined storage called **storage spaces**.

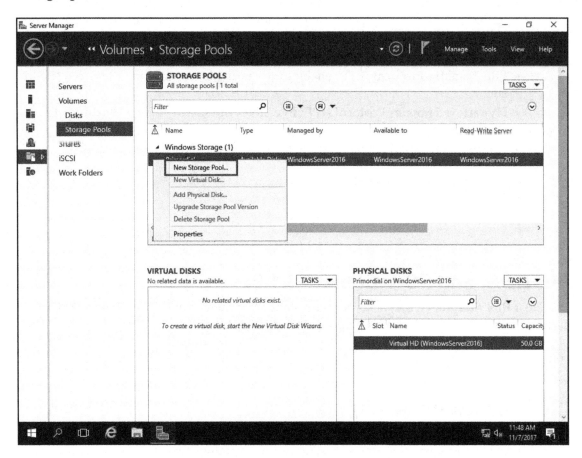

Figure 8.6. Creating a new storage pool in Windows Server 2016

Data deduplication

The idea behind the concept of **data deduplication (dedup)** is to provide disk space savings. Data deduplication is a technique for removing duplicated data from a dataset, thus storing a single copy of identical data on a disk. It first analyzes data to identify duplicated data in the dataset, then the original file is stored in the storage media while the duplicated files are replaced with a reference that points to the original file.

In contrast to Windows Server 2012 R2, Windows Server 2016 has further enhanced data deduplication by providing the following:

- Up to 64 TB support for large volumes
- Up to 1 TB support for large files
- It is available on Nano Server
- Seamless backup support
- Support for cluster rolling upgrades

To enable deduplication in Windows Server 2016, complete the following steps:

1. Click **Add Roles and Features Wizard** within the **Server Manager, Welcome to Server Manager** section.
2. In the **Before You Begin** option, click **Next**.
3. Click **Next** in the **Installation Type** option.
4. In the **Server Selection** option, click **Next**.
5. In the **Server Roles** option, expand **File and Storage Services**.
6. Then, expand **File and iSCSI Services**.

7. Select **Data Deduplication,** as in *Figure 8.7:*

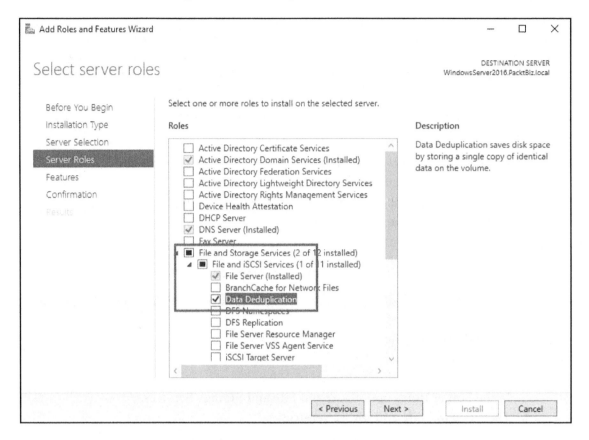

Figure 8.7. Adding data deduplication in Windows Server 2016

8. In the **Features** option, click **Next.**
9. In the **Confirmation** option, click **Install.**
10. When **Installation completes,** click **Close.**

 Cluster rolling upgrades let you upgrade the Oses of servers in a cluster without the need to stop Hyper-V.

Storage tiering

Another interesting built-in feature in Microsoft's Windows Server is storage tiering, which enables the automatic transfer of the most frequently accessed files to faster storage. That is, it lets you combine high-performing storage with low-performing storage (for example, the HDD and the SSD) to reduce the storage cost. Thus, the storage tiering agents will place the most accessed files on the faster storage, while rarely accessed files are placed into slower storage.

Managing storage with Server Manager and Windows PowerShell

Prior to managing storage with Server Manager (`servermanager.exe`), ensure that the **File and Storage Services** role is added to your server. *Figure 8.8* shows storage management with Server Manager on the local server:

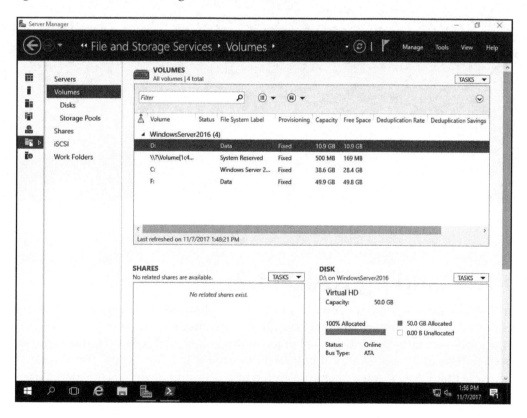

Figure 8.8. Managing storage with Server Manager

Other than Server Manager, you can manage storage with Windows PowerShell too. *Figure 8.9* shows the Windows PowerShell in action (`powershell.exe`):

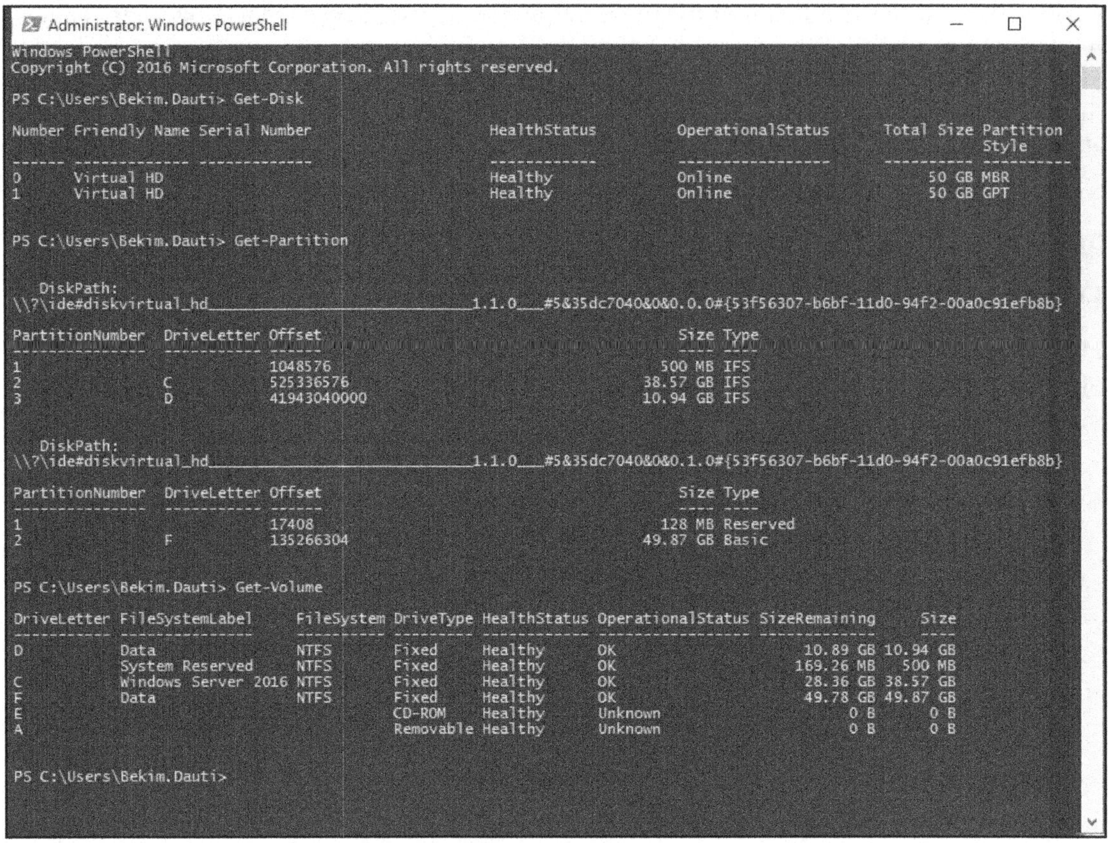

Figure 8.9. Managing storage with Windows PowerShell

Understanding RAID (4.2)

Regardless of whether you have come across the term **Redundant Array of Independent Disks** or **Redundant Array of Inexpensive Disks**, you should know that you are dealing with the fault-tolerance concept. RAID is a technology that combines a considerable number of physical disks into a single logical unit so it can protect the data in the case of disk failure. Note that RAID is not a backup solution and it should never be considered as such.

Types of RAID (4.2.1)

Well-known RAID types are as follows:

- **RAID 0**: This is known as disk striping, offers higher read and write performance, but it is not fault-tolerant. On Windows Server 2016, you can create a striped volume if you convert the disk from basic to dynamic.
- **RAID 1**: This is known as disk mirroring, requires at least two disks, and offers excellent read and write performance. It works in such a way that all the data that resides on disk A is mirrored on disk B. In the case of disk failure, the RAID controller uses any of the available disks.
- **RAID 5**: This is known as disk striping with parity, requires at least three disks, and represents the most fault-tolerant RAID available. The parity data is spread across all disks, meaning that RAID 5 can withstand the failure of a single disk.
- **RAID 10**: This is known as the stripe of mirrors and combines RAID 1 with RAID 0, thus offering disk mirroring and striping. It requires at least four disks; in the case of disk failure, the rebuild time is very fast since the striping is spread across all drives.

Hardware versus software RAID (4.2.2)

When it comes to implementing RAID, there are two types of RAID:

- **Hardware RAID**: This is an expensive solution and requires configuration prior to installing the OS. It is an electronic board that either the manufacturer of your server or yourself will plug into an adequate slot on the server's motherboard.
- **Software RAID**: This is a cheaper solution and is configured after the installation of an OS. It is an application that you will end up buying from a specific vendor.

Software-defined storage

If an organization, due to budget constraints, cannot afford to own NAS or SAN storage systems, then it can select the cheapest alternative that has to do with **software-defined storage (SDS)**. With Windows Server 2016, by using S2D, organizations can create virtualized networks with local storage. That way, they are able to build SDS that helps separate the software that manages the storage from the storage hardware. That then offers great diversity in the use of various storage technologies.

Redundancy using S2D

The fault-tolerance approach in S2D is called **resiliency**. It offers mirroring with parity, thus in terms of implementation, it is similar to RAID software. However, in Windows Server 2016, S2D offers fault tolerance and storage efficiency.

High availability

High availability (HA) is a characteristic of a system that never fails, thus being available at all times. However, that is possible only in an *ideal* world. In our world, the high availability standard is 99.999%. Lately, the standard of 99.9999% has taken its place too (see *Table 8.1*) in business continuity. To achieve such a standard, it is required to have numerous parameters in place. Thus, from backup to fault tolerance, from resilience to reliability, all storage medias are required to be operational so that the system as a whole is highly available.

Table 8.1. High availability standards

Availability (%)	Downtime per month	Downtime per year
99 %	7.20 hours	3.65 days
99.9 %	43.2 minutes	8.76 hours
99.99 %	4.32 minutes	52.6 minutes
99.999 %	25.9 seconds	5.26 minutes
99.9999 %	2.59 seconds	31.5 seconds

Understanding disk types (4.3)

One reason why you should know about disk types is to find about their benefits. In turn, that will help you understand the real storage potential of any disk types.

Hard disk drive

The **hard disk drive** (HDD) is a secondary storage type. As such, it is a computer component that uses the motor to spin the disc, has a magnetic read-and-write head, and has metal platters that permanently store data. Each platter contains tracks and sectors. The starting point for storing data in HDDs is the outer track. In the case of an HDD with one disc platter, the read-and-write head is located above the platter at a distance of microns, thus never touching the disc. If it does, then physical damage occurs. The data storage capacity is measured in bytes (nowadays it is GB), while the disc spinning speed is measured in **rotations per minute** (RPM). Most common RPM rates for PCs and laptops are from 5400 RPM to 7200 RPM, while for servers the most common RPM rates are from 10,000 RPM to 15,000 RPM. Usually, the HDD is located inside the computer's case and is mounted in drive bays. However, there are also external HDDs, mainly used for installing the operating system and applications, as well as for storing data. In the event of HDD disposal, it is recommended to perform disk shredding.

 You can learn more about HDDs at `https://www.computerhope.com/jargon/h/harddriv.htm`.

Solid-state drive

The **solid-state drive** (SSD) is another storage technology that is considered to be secondary storage. Unlike HDDs, SSDs are memory chips with no moving parts. They use less voltage (5V) than HDDs (12V for spinning the platters), are noiseless, are more physically reliable, and provide faster data access. SSDs are behind HDDs in capacity and cost. However, based on current development trends in storage technologies, things might turn in favor of SSDs over HDDs. These days, many manufacturers offer their PCs and laptops with SSD disks that hold the operating system and applications, as well as HDD disks to be used for data storage. Additionally, SSD drives are also encountered on servers, including NAS and SAN devices too.

 You can learn more about SSDs at `https://www.lifewire.com/solid-state-drive-833448`.

Optical disks (4.3.7)

Unlike HDDs that use the electromagnetic field to read and write data from/to disk platters, optical discs utilize laser beams with a specific wavelength to read and write data from/to **compact discs (CDs)**. Always try to differentiate between the **optical disk drives (ODDs)** and optical discs, such as a CDs or DVDs. The first is the device where the CD or DVD is inserted. CDs contain tracks in the form of a spiral. The starting point for storing data on CDs is the inner track. As is the case with HDDs, optical discs too are measured by capacity in **bytes (B)**. Usually, the capacity of common CDs is between 650 MB and 700 MB, while common DVDs range from 4.7 GB to 8.5 GB. In contrast to HDDs, the speed of optical discs is measured in KB/s and is determined by an x symbol that is equal to 150 KB/s. That said, if your optical drive has a speed of 24x, then its speed is *24 x 150 KB/s = 3600 KB/s = 3.6 MB/s*. There are three recording types of optical disks:

- **CD-ROM and DVD-RAM** are read-only optical discs
- **CD-R and DVD-R/DVD+R** are write-once optical discs
- **CD-RW and DVD-RW/DVD+RW** are rewritable optical discs

The most common forms of optical media at present are DVDs and Blu-ray discs. The latter has been designed to supersede DVD technologies, thus achieving tremendous capacities where a single layer holds 25 GB, a dual-layer holds 50 GB, 100 GB for triple-layer discs, and 128 GB for quadruple-layers.

 You can learn more about optical disc types at `https://www.ifixit.com/Wiki/Optical_Disc_Types`.

Basic disk (4.3.1)

Once you have installed the operating system on your server's hard disk, the hard disk is in its basic configuration. That means that the basic disk configuration is organized into partitions. As you now know (see the section *Understanding partition schemes* in `Chapter 2,` *Installing Windows Server*), the basic disk is based on the MBR and GPT partition schemes, and as such, one partition cannot be extended on one or more physical disks. Instead, a partition can be extended by adding unallocated space from the same physical disk.

Dynamic disk (4.3.2)

To overcome the limitations of the basic disk, to be able to increase the read-and-write performance with disk striping, and to operate with volumes instead of partitions, dynamic disk configuration has been introduced. That means that volumes in dynamic disk configuration can be extended to more than one physical disk, thus letting us create five types of volumes: simple, mirrored, striped, spanned, and RAID-5 volumes.

In Windows Server 2016, to convert a basic disk to a dynamic disk, complete the following steps:

1. Right-click the **Start** button.
2. Select **Disk Management.**
3. Right-click the preferred disk, and from the context menu select **Convert to Dynamic Disk...** (see *Figure 8.10*):

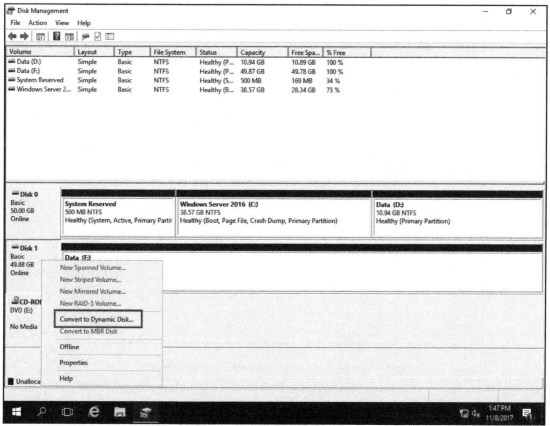

Figure 8.10. Converting basic disk to dynamic disk

4. If you have more than one disk, from the **Convert to Dynamic Disk** window select the disks and click **OK.**

5. Click **Convert** in the **Disks to Convert** window.

6. After you have read the information in the **Disk Management** dialog box, click **Yes.**

7. Shortly, the conversion is completed.

Mount points (4.3.3)

When you attach an unallocated partition to a blank folder, you have a mount point. This helps you to increase the size of your folder if the partition where you have created the folder is running out of space. In Windows Server 2016, you can use Disk Management (diskmgmt.msc) to create a mount point, as shown in *Figure 8.11:*

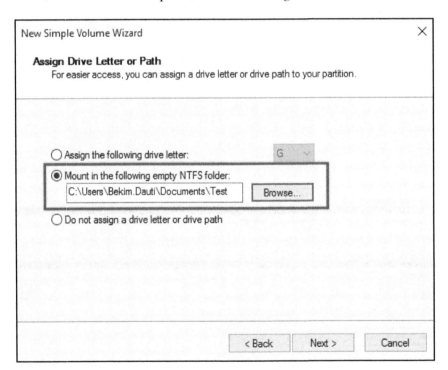

Figure 8.11. Creating a mount point with Disk Management in Windows Server 2016

Filesystems (4.3.4)

It often happens that, when Windows is mentioned, the listener immediately thinks of Windows Explorer. Does this happen to you? If so, then it has to do with the fact that Windows is very easy when storing and organizing data on the computer, on the computer's hard disk to be precise. All that is the result of the filesystem that Windows is using. With the following list, you will become familiar with the well-known filesystems used by Windows.

- **File Allocation Table (FAT)**: This is the earliest filesystem and was used by both MS-DOS and Windows. As the name implies, it is based on a table that contains a map of clusters. The cluster is the unit of logical storage on the hard disk. FAT32 is the latest version of FAT.
- **New Technology File System (NTFS)**: This was introduced in the 1990s with Windows NT 3.1, and is still in use. Among the features that NTFS offers are disk quotas, **Encrypting File System (EFS)**, journaling, and **Volume Shadow Copy Service (VSS)**. NTFS is a native filesystem on Windows Server 2016.
- **Resilient File System (ReFS)**: This was introduced in Windows Server 2012 and is supposed to be the successor to NTFS. Among the new features that ReFS offers are resiliency, performance, and scalability. ReFS is available as a disk format option in Windows Server 2016.
- **Extended File Allocation Table (exFAT)**: This is a new version of FAT, developed to be used primarily with USB flash drives and SD cards. It is interesting that exFAT is platform-independent, thus enabling drives formatted with this filesystem to be supported by Mac computers too.

 A journaling filesystem is an important feature that maintains data integrity by keeping track of changes to data in a separate log, thus making it possible to restore data whenever power outage or disk crashes occurs. Microsoft has removed `Journal.dll` from Windows Server 2016.

Mounting a virtual hard disk (VHD) (4.3.5)

On Windows Server 2016, you can attach a **virtual hard disk (VHD)** to your server using **Disk Management**. To do so, complete the following steps:

1. Press the *Windows key + R*.
2. In the **Run** window, enter `diskmgmt.msc` and hit *Enter*.
3. In the **Disk Management** window, click the **Action** menu and select **Attach VHD** (see *Figure 8.12*):

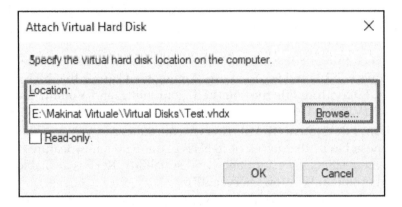

Figure 8.12. Attaching a VHD using Disk Management in Windows Server 2016

4. Shortly, the attached VHD is displayed in the **Disk Management** window

Distributed File System (4.3.6)

If you have ever wondered how to share data from your servers in an authorized and controlled way, then **Distributed File System (DFS)** will enable you to do so. With DFS, data that is stored in shared folders located on different servers can be grouped into logically structured namespaces. That makes it possible for users to access the data as if it was stored on local computers.

In Windows Server 2016, DFS is part of the **File and Storage Services** role. Thus, to install DFS on your server, you should expand the **File and Storage Services** role, expand **File and iSCSI Services**, and then select **DFS Namespace**, **DFS Replication**, and **File Server Resource Manager,** as shown in *Figure 8.13*:

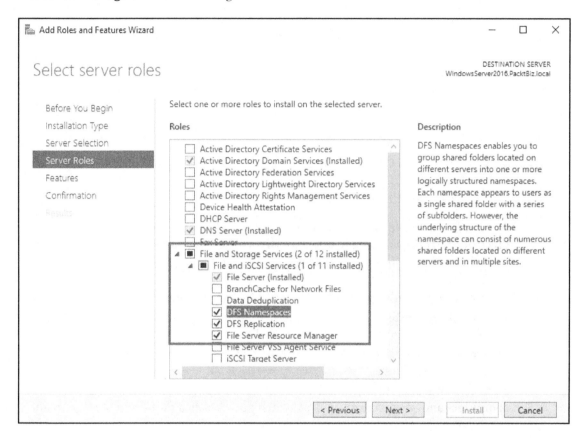

Figure 8.13. Installing DFS in Windows Server 2016

References from Windows IT Pro Center

1. Storage in Windows Server 2016 (`https://docs.microsoft.com/en-us/windows-server/storage/storage`)
2. Data Deduplication Overview in Windows Server 2016 (`https://docs.microsoft.com/en-us/windows-server/storage/data-deduplication/overview`)
3. Storage Spaces Direct in Windows Server 2016 (`https://docs.microsoft.com/en-us/windows-server/storage/storage-spaces/storage-spaces-direct-overview`)

Summary

In this chapter we discussed the following:

- **Advanced Technology Attachment (ATA)**, also known as **Integrated Drive Electronics (IDE)**, is a legacy interface that is used to connect hard disk drives, optical disc drives, floppy disk drives, and related storage technologies to computers
- The two most popular types of ATA interfaces are Parallel ATA and Serial ATA
- The **Small Computer System Interface (SCSI)**, pronounced *scuzzy*, is another interface that connects storage devices and peripheral devices to computers
- **Direct-attached storage (DAS)** is a group of disks that are directly connected to computers or servers
- **Network-attached storage (NAS)** is a network appliance that connects to computers and servers through the switch and acts as a dedicated storage in an organization's network
- A **storage area network (SAN)**, like DAS and NAS, is a storage technology
- File-level storage stores and accesses data in the form of files and folders
- Block-level storage stores data in blocks that represent volumes that are managed by the server operating system
- The disk controller is an electronic circuit that resides on a hard disk and performs operations such as spinning disks, moving heads for reading and writing, and transferring data from and to RAM
- The **host bus adapter (HBA)** controller is an electronic board that is integrated or attached to the computer's or server's motherboard so it can connect the storage system with computer, respectively server

- In parallel transmissions, a string of eight bits is usually transmitted that is equal to one byte at a given time
- In serial transmissions, one bit is usually transmitted for a given time
- The most used storage protocols are SCSI, iSCSI, FC, and FCoE
- The most used file sharing protocols are SMB, NFS, FTP, HTTP, and SSH
- **Storage Spaces Direct (S2D)** is a new feature in Windows Server 2016 that enables you to group disks into storage pools, thus creating software-defined storage called storage spaces
- The idea behind the concept of **data deduplication (dedup)** is to provide disk space savings
- Storage tiering enables automatic movement of the most accessed files to faster storage
- RAID is a technology that combines a considerable number of physical disks into a single logical unit so it can protect the data in the case of disk failure
- Well-known types of RAID are RAID 0, RAID 1, RAID 5, and RAID 10
- RAID can be implemented as hardware RAID and software RAID
- Software-defined storage helps separate the software that manages the storage from the storage hardware
- The fault-tolerance approach in **Storage Space Direct (S2D)** is called resiliency
- **High availability (HA)** is a characteristic of a system that never fails, thus being available at all times
- The **hard disk drive (HDD)** is a computer component that uses the motor to spin the disc, has a magnetic read-and-write head, and has metal platters that permanently store data
- A **solid-state drive (SSD)**, secondary storage, is a memory chip with no moving parts
- Optical discs utilize laser beams with a specific wavelength to read and write data from/to **compact discs (CDs)**
- Basic disk configuration is organized into partitions
- Dynamic disk configuration is organized into volumes
- When you attach an unallocated partition to a blank folder, you have a mount point
- Well-known filesystems used by Windows are FAT, NTFS, ReFS, and exFAT
- The **Distributed File System (DFS)** enables the sharing of data from your server in an authorized and controlled way

Questions

1. DFS enables the sharing of data from your server in an authorized and controlled way. (True | False)

2. _____ is a network appliance that connects with computers and servers through a switch and acts as a dedicated storage in an organization's network.

3. Which of the following are network storage technologies? (Choose two)
   1. DAS
   2. NAS
   3. RAM
   4. ROM

4. Block-level storage stores data in files and folders that represent volumes that are managed by the server operating system. (True | False)

5. _____ is an electronic circuit that resides on a hard disk and performs operations such as spinning discs, moving heads for reading and writing, and transferring data from and to RAM.

6. Which of the following are storage protocols? (Choose two)
   1. SCSI
   2. FC
   3. PATA
   4. SATA

7. The HDD is a computer component that uses the motor to spin the disc, has a magnetic read-and-write head, and has metal platters that permanently store data. (True | False)

8. _____ is a characteristic of a system that never fails, thus being available at all times.

9. Which of the following are RAID types? (Choose two)
   1. RAID 1
   2. RAID 5
   3. RAID 15
   4. RAID 20

10. The Small Computer System Interface (SCSI), pronounced "scuzzy", is another interface that connects storage devices and peripheral devices to computers. (True | False)

11. _____ is a legacy interface that is used to connect hard disk drives, optical disc drives, floppy disk drives, and related storage technologies to computers.

12. Which of the following are optical discs? (Choose two)
    1. CD-ROM
    2. DVD-RAM
    3. EPROM
    4. POST

13. Discuss data deduplication in Windows Server 2016

14. Discuss S2D in Windows Server 2016

15. Discuss the DFS in Windows Server 2016

9
Tuning and Maintaining Windows Server

This chapter is designed to teach you the best practices and considerations for server hardware. By understanding the importance of a server's role in a computer network, and possessing knowledge of each server component, we can be vigilant when selecting server hardware. In addition, this chapter teaches you server performance monitoring methodologies and procedures. Performance monitoring will help you to identify the cause of server performance issues at an early stage. In that way, you will be able to react in a timely manner to avoid further degradations of server performance. Lastly, the chapter concludes by uncovering the importance and purpose of logs and alerts in the server monitoring process.

In this chapter, we will cover:

- Understanding server hardware components
- Understanding the role that each component plays
- Understanding performance monitoring
- Becoming familiar with Performance Monitor, Resource Monitor, and Task Manager
- Understanding logs and alerts
- Learning how to log collected information and set up alerts

Identifying major server hardware components (5.1)

Apparently, the server is nothing but a big metal box. As we open this box, we notice various parts that make up the internals of the box. In computer jargon, these parts are called hardware component: in our case, the server's hardware components. Now the question arises, why should we pay that much attention to these hardware components? Does this sound like the right question? Let me remind you of something that you may already know: a server's primary task is not data processing, in fact, the server's role (see Chapter 5, *Adding Roles to Windows Server*) includes providing network services and handling user requests to access services. This is the reason why you should have some knowledge of the server hardware, and why you should pay attention when selecting that hardware. With that in mind, let us examine server hardware components, the roles they play, and the impacts they have on the performance of a server so as to strengthen further the assertion that there should be considerations taken into account when dealing with server hardware.

Processor (5.1.1)

There is no doubt that speed is one of the determining factors in choosing the right processor. The processor's speed is measured in **Hertz (Hz)**. Today's processor speeds are given in **gigaHertz (GHz)**. However, we would be making a mistake if we relied only on the speed factor. Therefore, the following factors should also be considered:

- **Cache**: The processor's memory. Modern processors have three types of cache: L1, L2, and L3. While L1 and L2 are inside the processor, L3 is located outside the processor. Obviously, their numbers determine the speed of each cache memory.
- **Cores**: The processor's processing unit. In the past, processors had just one core. Today, there are processors with two, four, and eight, or more cores. So, to understand the cores in a processor better, think about assembling two processors with a single core, each into a single package. Does that make sense? So, the more cores a processor has, the more multiprocessing is done.
- **Word size:** Word size has to do with the processor's internal architecture that defines the data bus size, the instruction size, and the address size. Today there are 32-bit and 64-bit processors. Obviously, these numbers determine the processor's word size: that is, the amount of data that the processor receives from the RAM to be processed and then sends back to the RAM.

- **Virtualization technology (VT)**: This refers to the processor's ability in relation to the virtualization concept: that is, whether the processor supports virtualization, where many operating systems simultaneously share processor resources efficiently.

Figure 9.1. Intel's Xeon quad-core processor

Memory (5.1.2)

The primary storage is a hardware component that is capable of temporarily storing data, allowing processors to access data faster and easier, as well as acting as a communication bridge between applications and peripheral devices to access the processor. Undoubtedly, all of these features belong to **random access memory (RAM)**. As with RAM, **read-only memory (ROM)** is also considered primary storage. Table 9.1 lists the differences between RAM and ROM.

Table 9.1. RAM versus ROM:

Random Access Memory (RAM)	Read-Only Memory (ROM)
Volatile	Non-volatile
The data is lost when the power goes off	The data is kept when the power goes off
Known as *working* memory as it loads the OS and apps	Known as *hardware initialization* memory as it runs **power-on-self-test** (POST)

When it comes to RAM for servers, the physical size is almost the same as that for PCs (see *Figure 9.2*), except that RAM modules for servers have one chip more. The other difference is in functionality, so servers use a type of RAM called **error correcting code** (ECC) memory. ECC RAM enables you to detect and correct memory faults. Other advanced types of RAM for servers include **Single Device Data Correction** (SDDC) and **Double Device Data Correction** (DDDC), that enable multiple memory faults to be detected and corrected. With all these advantages of RAM for servers, there is one disadvantage too and that is their price. In general, RAM for servers is expensive.

Figure 9.2. ECC RAM modules placed in memory banks

Disk (5.1.3)

As you already know, it is very important for servers to be up and running all the time. That is because the services and data stored on a disk (see *Figure 9.3*) should be available to users all the time. For the servers to be operational all the time, they must have hardware that enables such requirement. In that regard, *hot-swappable* technology enables the replacement of damaged disks with new disks while servers are running. All of that enables the high availability of data.

Figure 9.3. SAS HDDs

Network interfaces (5.1.4)

Servers usually have more than one network interface (see *Figure 9.4*). If they do not, then you have to consider adding **network interface cards** (**NICs**) to your server. That approach offers tremendous benefits. Some are as follows:

- **NIC teaming**: This enables you to increase bandwidth from/to the server
- **Network load balancing** (**NLB**): This enables you to distribute the network load across servers

- **Network separation**: This enables you to separate intranet traffic from internet traffic

Figure 9.4. Server network interfaces

32-bit and 64-bit architecture (5.1.5)

To understand the difference between 32-bit and 64-bit architecture, let's take the following example. Trucks A and B are delivering loads of 3200 kg and 6400 kg, respectively. Both trucks should carry these loads from city C to city D at identical traveling speeds over the same road. Which truck will bring more load to city D for the same distance traveled and time consumed? In computer jargon, that means a processor can exchange 64 bits of data with RAM memory in any communication. So, the recommendation is to consider 64-bit hardware for your server, without compromising 64-bit software such as the OS, applications, device drivers, and other utilities when available. All of that enables an increase in the overall performance of your server.

Removable drives (5.1.6)

First things first, the removable drive is a storage technology that can be plugged into, and unplugged from, the server while the server is running. Furthering the concept of hot-swapability explained earlier in the *Disk* section of this chapter, removable drives for your server can be attached using USB and IEEE 1394 ports. CDs, DVDs, HDDs, floppies (an obsolete technology), USB flash drives, and backup drives, are some of the types of removable drives, and some of these are shown in *Figure 9.5:*

Figure 9.5. Removable drive and USB flash drives

Graphic cards (5.1.7)

Generally speaking, servers are backend computing machines, thus they do not necessarily have advanced graphics cards. Regardless, everything depends on the purpose that the server serves. So, if it is a server that has to do with graphics and video processing, then it might require an advanced graphics card as shown in *Figure 9.6*:

Figure 9.6. AMD's Radeon video graphic adapter (VGA)

Cooling (5.1.8)

Without excluding other server components, processors and HDDs are the hardware components that generate the most thermal heat. In order to have optimal cooling, aside from processor coolers, servers are also equipped with multiple, additional coolers known as **case coolers,** as shown in *Figure 9.7*. Additionally, on top of the rack, there are extra coolers. There are often air conditioners in the server room too, which aid in the overall cooling of the environment.

Figure 9.7. Cooling system in a server's case

Power usage (5.1.9)

Several processors, multiple disks, several network interfaces, large motherboards, multiple ports, graphics cards, RAID cards, optical drives, backup tapes, and other server hardware make up a list of potential components that are eager to consume power. Because power supplies are considered to be a single point of failure, servers are equipped with a redundant power supply. Depending on a server's form factor, most servers are equipped with two or more **Power Supply Units** (**PSUs**) (see *Figure 9.7*):

Figure 9.8. Power Supply Units (PSUs)

Ports (5.1.10)

It is a characteristic of servers to have multiple ports. That is due to the role that the servers play in computer networks. Some of the ports (see *Figure 9.9*) we encounter at the back of servers are: AC power connectors, gigabit ethernet ports, PCIe ports, USB ports, HD-15 video connectors, management ports, and although rarely seen nowadays, legacy ports such as serial ports, parallel ports, and PS/2 ports.

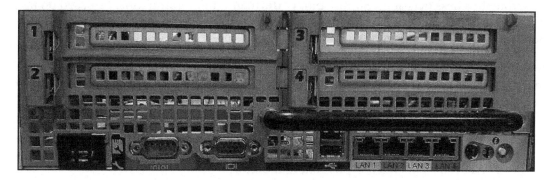

Figure 9.9. Various ports to connect various devices

Understanding performance monitoring (5.2)

There is a saying: *prevention is better than cure.* If we apply that to server administration, then we can understand how important performance monitoring is. Monitoring the server's performance helps identify server problems at an early stage of development, and we can then take the necessary steps to prevent them from turning into costly problems, in terms of both time and business. In order to have productive performance monitoring, a clear plan with the right tools is required. That also means setting up a metric by which performance monitoring will be measured. Such a metric needs baseline information. This will help to evaluate the actual performance of servers, determine when hardware and software upgrades are needed, and help to evaluate whether an upgraded system is working better than the previous one.

 Microsoft's TechNet website, `https://technet.microsoft.com/en-us/`, provides very useful information about Microsoft products, including monitoring.

Performance monitoring methodology (5.2.1)

In the previous section, we learned that the responsibility of performance monitoring is to maintain the server in a healthy state. But, if there is no clear plan for its implementation, then the results obtained from performance monitoring will be based on multiple assumptions. Viewed from a business perspective, that means that the wrong data results in the wrong business decisions. Simply put, performance monitoring must be based on facts and not assumptions. To avoid that from happening, an approach known as a performance monitoring methodology steps in.

In that regard, the methodology helps with the conduct of research. At that stage, a questionnaire is drawn up that helps us to understand the process and achieve a goal. For that reason, you need to make sure that your questionnaire contains questions such as:

- What is the purpose that the server serves?
- What are the services that the server is providing?
- What components do you want to monitor?
- What is the metric of component performance?
- Which tool will you use for systems analysis and data collection?

You can read more about monitoring and tuning your server at: `https://msdn.microsoft.com/en-us/library/bb742410.aspx`.

Performance monitoring procedures (5.2.2)

From what has been said previously, it can be understood that the methodology helps in the development of procedures. In this instance, we are talking about server performance monitoring procedures that are well-structured activities. In that regard, to monitor the performance of your servers, you may want to consider the following procedures:

- Document the server's hardware, software, and configuration
- Establish the server's baseline
- Upgrade the server's hardware and software
- Perform the server's baseline and compare that with previous baselines
- Identify server bottlenecks
- Take concrete steps to fine-tune the server's performance

Server baseline (5.2.3)

In general, a server's performance must be monitored. As a system administrator, you should ask yourself a few questions in regard to server performance monitoring. Questions such as the following:

- How do you know when servers are working under their load?
- Do you have a sample to compare their performance against?

Questions like these may encourage you to approach such an activity with more dedication. For that reason, before explaining how to establish a baseline, and what to consider when creating a baseline, it is good to know what a baseline is. In short, a server baseline represents a snapshot of your server's performance under a normal workload. It enables you to compile a detailed report on the performance of various server components in normal workload conditions. Without neglecting other server components, the main reason for a baseline is to collect the following performance information:

- Collecting processor utilization
- Collecting RAM utilization
- Collecting disk read-and-write operations
- Network connection utilization

This implies that performance monitoring is not confined solely to collecting information from the previously-mentioned hardware components. The fact that there are many computer networks that serve different purposes strengthens the opinion that the parameters that we are monitoring need to be different too.

Performance Monitor (5.2.4)

Simply, Performance Monitor is a Windows **Microsoft Management Console (MMC)** console that monitors server performance. It enables us to visualize performance information, either in real time or from a log file. The examined performance information is displayed in formats such as a line graph, histogram bar, or report. To access **Performance Monitor** in Windows Server 2016, complete the following steps:

1. Press Windows key + *R.*
2. Enter `perfmon.exe` and press *Enter.*
3. Shortly, **Performance Monitor** will be shown, as in *Figure 9.10*:

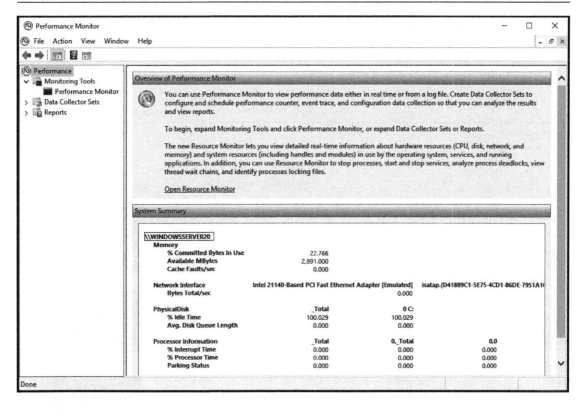

Figure 9.10. Performance Monitor in Windows Server 2016

You can open Resource Monitor from within the Performance Monitor.

Resource Monitor (5.2.5)

If you have owned a computer with a Windows OS for a while, you may have just recently started to feel that it now seems slower than when you first bought it. Regardless, you do not need to worry because you can use the Resource Monitor to determine the causes of your computer's slow performance. The same thing happens with servers too. So, whenever it is proven that server performance has decreased considerably, Resource Monitor is at your disposal to view the real-time usage of both hardware and software resources.

To access **Resource Monitor** in Windows Server 2016, complete the following steps:

1. Press Windows key + *R*.
2. Enter `resmon.exe` and press *Enter*.
3. Shortly, **Resource Monitor** will be shown, as in Figure 9.11:

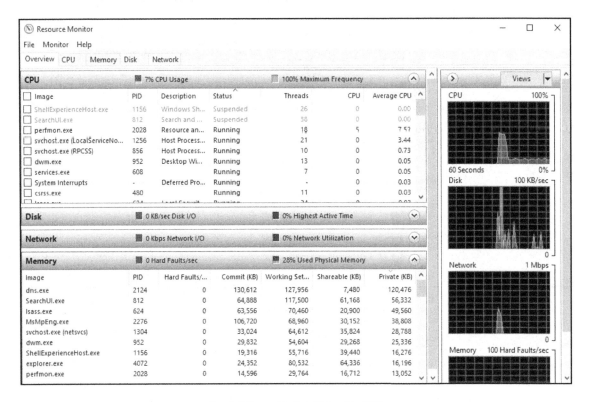

Figure 9.11. Resource Monitor in Windows Server 2016

Task Manager (5.2.6)

In addition to Performance Monitor and Resource Monitor, Task Manager enables you to monitor the processes, performance, and services currently running on your server. Other than that, Task Manager allows us to start/stop applications and background processes. Regarding the performance of your server, Task Manager offers a visual representation of this. Available views are a summary and graph.

To access Task Manager in Windows Server 2016, complete the following steps:

1. Right-click the Taskbar and from the context menu select **Task Manager**.
2. Shortly, **Task Manager** will be shown, as in *Figure 9.12*:

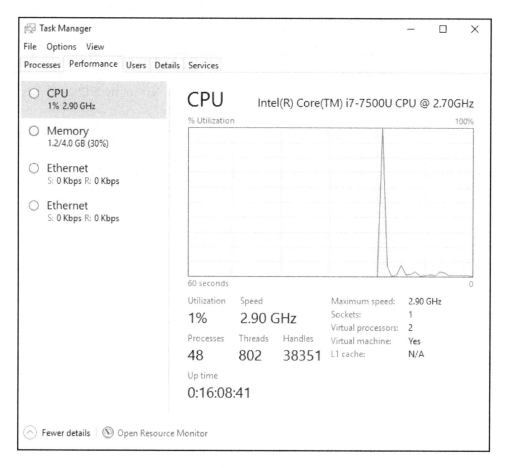

Figure 9.12. Task Manager in Windows Server 2016

 You can open Resource Monitor from within Task Manager.

Performance counters (5.2.7)

In Performance Monitor, you can use counters and instances of selected objects to collect data for the server hardware that you are keeping your eye on. Counters provide performance information on how well an operating system, application, service, or driver is working. Objects have counters to measure different aspects of performance, where each object has at least one instance that represents a unique copy of a particular type of object. That way you are able to determine your server's bottlenecks and are able to react in a timely manner to avoid further degradations of server performance. Then, by following the necessary steps, you can fine-tune your server's performance. To set up a Data Collector Set in Windows Server 2016, complete the following steps:

1. With the **Performance Monitor** open, expand **Monitoring Tools** and select **Performance Monitor**.
2. Right-click **Performance Monitor** and select **New | Data Collector Set**.
3. Enter the name for your **Data Collector Set** and click **Next**.
4. Specify the location where you want to save it by clicking **Browse**, and click **Next**.
5. Set the user in **Run as**, and select either **Start this data collector set now**, or **Save and close**.
6. Click **Finish**.
7. Right-click **Graph** and select **Add Counters...**
8. Select counters from the **Available counters** section and click the **Add** button to add them to the list in the **Added counters** section.
9. Repeat *step 8* to add more counters, as shown in *Figure 9.13.*

10. Click **OK** to close the window:

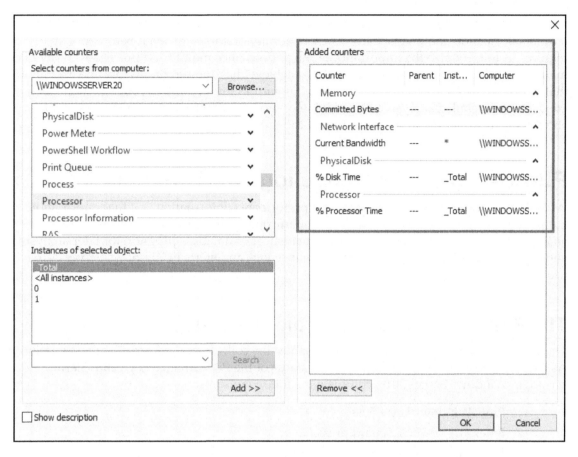

Figure 9.13. Performance Monitor counters in Windows Server 2016

 You can find information about performance monitoring thresholds and other useful monitoring information for various technologies at: `https://www.manageengine.com/network-monitoring/network-performance-monitoring.html`

Understanding logs and alerts (5.3)

As you know, the performance monitoring activity is a continuous activity. As such, it requires dedication and patience from system administrators. However, before that, it requires us to recognize the importance of the performance monitoring process as a way of maintaining the server's continuous work. To achieve that, the right tools must be used. For that reason, tools such as logs and alerts play an important role in that process. While logs are useful for detailed analysis and archiving of records, alerts enable you to be vigilant about the performance and configuration of the servers.

Purpose of performance logs and alerts (5.3.1)

With Performance Monitor, you can collect performance information, log that information automatically, and set up alerts. The logged performance information can be used for analysis, or it can be exported to either a spreadsheet or database program for later analysis and report generation. To configure performance logs and alerts in Windows Server 2016, use the following approach.

The Performance logs and alerts service

The Performance Logs and Alerts service enables the collection of performance information. As such, it should be running. To check the status of the Performance Logs and Alerts service in Windows Server 2016, complete the following steps:

1. Press Windows key + R.
2. Enter services.msc and press *Enter.*
3. From the list of services, locate the **Performance Logs & Alerts** (see *Figure 9.14*) service to check its status.
4. If it is stopped, then right-click and select **Start**.
5. Close the **Services** window.

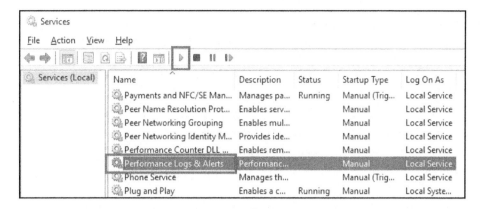

Figure 9.14. Performance Logs and Alerts service in Windows Server 2016

The Performance Monitor Logs folder

The collected performance information from Performance Monitor is logged in the
`PerfLogs` folder. As such, it is a system folder. To check for the existence of the `PerfLogs`
folder in Windows Server 2016, complete the following steps:

1. Press *Windows key + R.*
2. Enter `C:` and press *Enter.*
3. The `PerfLogs` folder is shown as in *Figure 9.15:*

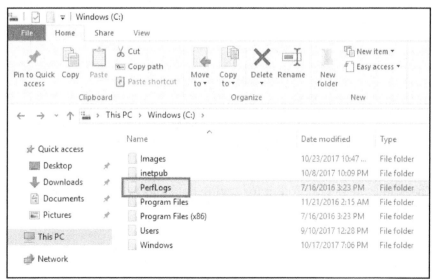

Figure 9.15. PerfLogs folder in Windows Server 2016

Performance data logs

To create data logs in Windows Server 2016, complete the following steps:

1. With **Performance Monitor** open, expand **Data Collector Sets** and select **User Defined**.
2. Right-click **User Defined** and select **New | Data Collector Set**.
3. Enter the name for your **Data Collector Set**.
4. Choose the **Create manually (Advanced)** option and click **Next**.
5. Choose the **Create data logs** option and the **Performance counter** sub-option, and then click **Next**.
6. Click the **Add** button to add counters, as in *Figure 9.16*, specify the time interval, and then click **Next**:

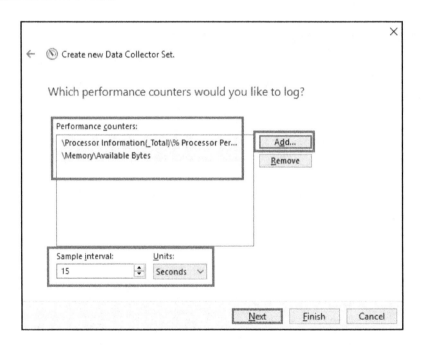

Figure 9.16. Adding performance counters

7. Check that the default folder for saving data logs is the PerfLogs folder, and then click **Next**.

8. Set the user in **Run as**, and select the **Start this data collector set now** option.
9. Click **Finish**.

Performance counter alerts

To set up a performance counter alert in Windows Server 2016, complete the following steps:

1. Repeat *steps 1 to 4* from the *Performance data logs* section.
2. Choose **Performance Counter Alert**, and then click **Next**.
3. Click the **Add** button to add counters as in *Figure 9.17*, specify an Alert Limit, and then click **Next**:

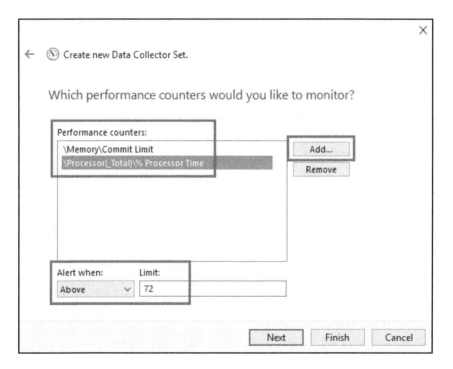

Figure 9.17. Setting up the performance counter alert

4. Set the user in **Run as**, and select the **Start this data collector set now** option.
5. Click **Finish**.

References from Windows IT Pro Center

1. Performance Tuning Guidelines for Windows Server 2016 (`https://docs.microsoft.com/en-us/windows-server/administration/performance-tuning/`)
2. Microsoft Server Performance Advisor (`https://docs.microsoft.com/en-us/windows-server/administration/server-performance-advisor/microsoft-server-performance-advisor`)

Summary

- Servers provide network services and handle user requests to access services
- Cache is a processor's memory
- Cores are a processor's processing units
- Word size has to do with the processor's internal architecture and defines the data bus size, the instructions size, and the address size
- VT refers to the processor's ability in relation to the virtualization concept
- RAM and ROM are considered to be primary storage
- ECC memory enables you to detect and correct memory faults
- SDDC and DDDC enable multiple memory faults to be detected and corrected
- Hot-swapablility is the technology that enables the replacement of damaged disks with new disks while servers are running
- Servers usually have more than one network interface
- NIC teaming enables you to increase bandwidth from/to the server
- NLB enables you to distribute the network load across servers
- Network separation enables you to separate intranet traffic from internet traffic
- The recommendations are to consider 64-bit hardware for your server, without compromising 64-bit software such as the OS, applications, device drivers, and other utilities when available
- The removable drive is a storage technology that can be plugged into, and unplugged from, the server while the server is running
- Servers are backend computing machines, thus they do not necessarily have advanced graphics cards

- Processors and HDDs are the hardware that generates the most thermal heat
- Because power supplies are considered to be a single point of failure, servers are equipped with a redundant power supply
- It is a characteristic of servers to have multiple ports
- Monitoring the server's performance helps identify server problems at an early stage of development, and helps us to take the necessary steps to prevent them turning into costly problems in terms of both time and business
- A methodology helps in the development of procedures
- A server baseline represents a snapshot of your server's performance under normal workload
- Performance Monitor is a Windows MMC that monitors server performance
- Resource Monitor is at your disposal to view the real-time usage of both hardware and software resources
- Task Manager enables you to monitor the processes, performance, and services currently running on your server
- Counters provide performance information on how well an operating system, application, service, or driver works
- Objects have counters to measure different aspects of performance, where each object has at least one instance that represents a unique copy of a particular type of object
- Logs are useful for the detailed analysis and archiving of records
- Alerts enable you to be vigilant about performance and configuration of the servers

Questions

1. Servers provide network services and handle user requests to access services. (True | False)
2. _____ represents a snapshot of your server's performance under normal workload.
3. Which of the following is related to processors? (Choose two)
   1. Cache
   2. Cores
   3. NIC Teaming
   4. Hot-swapablility

4. Task Manager enables you to monitor the processes, performance, and services currently running on your server. (True | False)

5. _____ are the hardware that generate the most thermal heat.

6. Which of the following are the benefits of having multiple NICs on the server? (Choose two)
   1. Network load balancing (NLB)
   2. Network separation
   3. Word size
   4. Virtualization technology (VT)

7. Because power supplies are not considered to be a single point of failure, servers are not equipped with a redundant power supply. (True | False)

8. _____ has to do with the processor's internal architecture and defines the data bus size, the instructions size, and the address size.

9. Which of the following Windows MMCs are used for performance and resource monitoring? (Choose two)
   1. Performance Monitor
   2. Resource Monitor
   3. Server Manager
   4. Device Manager

10. Counters provide performance information on how well an operating system, application, service, or driver works. (True | False)

11. _____ helps to identify server problems at an early stage of development, and take the necessary steps to prevent them turning into costly problems in terms of both time and business.

12. Which of the following are considered to be a server's primary storage? (Choose two.)
    1. RAM
    2. ROM
    3. HDD
    4. USB Flash Drive

13. Discuss Performance Monitor and Resource Monitor.

14. Discuss Performance Logs and Alerts.

10
Updating and Troubleshooting Windows Server

This chapter is designed to teach you the hardest part of working with servers. Yes, this is true! And trust me, it is not easy. However, if you are willing to learn and practice at the same time, then no work is difficult. Thus, by understanding the importance of troubleshooting, updating, and maintaining servers, it increases the potential to have a high standard of business continuity. Along the same lines, this chapter teaches you the server startup process, advanced boot options and Safe Mode, backup and restore, disaster recovery plan, updating the OS, hardware, and software. We also mention Event Viewer, which helps you monitor different logs on your system, thus helping you to troubleshoot and solve the problem. In that way, you will be able to minimize the downtime that, from a business point of view, is expressed in money loss. The chapter concludes with a step-by-step explanation of using Event Viewer in monitoring and managing logs.

In this chapter, we will cover:

- Understanding the startup process
- Becoming familiar with recovery tools and Safe Mode
- Understanding business continuity
- Getting to know how to maintain business continuity
- Understanding updates
- Learning how to update the OS, drivers, and applications
- Understanding the troubleshooting process
- Getting to know Event Viewer

Identifying steps in the startup process (6.1)

Although it is completely technical compared to the usual work of a system administrator, understanding the hardware components in general, and being able to identify the steps in the **startup process** in particular, have tremendous benefits. This is because it helps you in troubleshooting hardware-related problems, and so keeps downtime to a minimum.

The Basic Input/Output System (6.1.1)

The **Basic Input/Output System** (BIOS), is a program that controls the functionality of the server hardware components. Along with the task of controlling the functionality of the server hardware components, the other important tasks of the BIOS are to identify and configure the hardware in a server and to identify the boot devices. Unlike computers in the past, modern computers do not have legacy BIOS; instead, they are equipped with a **Unified Extensible Firmware Interface** (UEFI). Unlike the BIOS, UEFI is easily updated by downloading updates from the manufacturer's website, supports 32-bit and 64-bit modes, and boots from disks with capacities far larger than the BIOS.

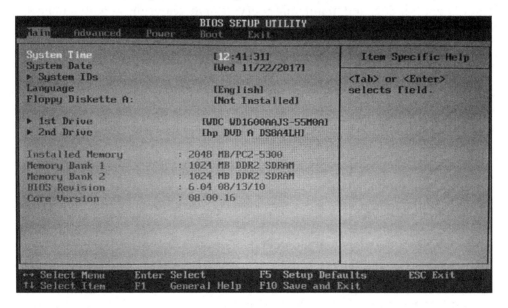

Figure 10.1. The BIOS Setup Utility

In the Understanding boot options section of `Chapter 2`, *Installing Windows Server*, you can find additional information about the BIOS including boot options.

Boot sector (6.1.2)

In the **Hard Disk Drive (HDD)** section of `Chapter 8`, *Storing Data in Windows Server*, tracks and sectors are mentioned. **Tracks** look like concentric circles and there are thousands of them on a disk. **Sectors** are the tracks' divisions and their size depends on the file system that the server's OS uses. I guess, you now understand what a **boot sector** is (see *Figure 10.2*). Obviously, it is the sector on a server's disk that contains the information to boot your server. Physically, the boot sector is located in the first sector of the first disk track. Usually, a boot sector contains the MBR.

```
Administrator: Command Prompt

Microsoft Windows [Version 10.0.16299.64]
(c) 2017 Microsoft Corporation. All rights reserved.

C:\WINDOWS\system32>bootsect

bootsect {/help|/nt60|/nt52} {SYS|ALL|<DriveLetter>:} [/force] [/mbr]

Boot sector restoration tool

Bootsect.exe updates the master boot code for hard disk partitions in order to
switch between BOOTMGR and NTLDR.  You can use this tool to restore the boot
sector on your computer.

Run "bootsect /help" for detailed usage instructions.

C:\WINDOWS\system32>
```

Figure 10.2. Running bootsect.exe in Windows 10

Boot loader (6.1.3)

Boot loader is a program that loads the OS kernel into RAM and is located in the MBR. In Windows OSs, there are two types of boot loaders: NTLDR and BOOTMGR. **NT Loader (NTLDR)** is the old Windows boot loader used in Windows NT to Windows Server 2003, while **Boot Manager (BOOTMGR)** and is the newest Windows boot loader. It is used in Windows Vista to Windows Server 2016.

Master Boot Record (MBR) (6.1.4)

Once POST finishes verifying that the server hardware is working correctly, the BIOS then hands over control to the first boot device. That is because the BIOS looks after the boot device that contains the **Master Boot Record** (**MBR**). The MBR is created when disk partitions are created; however, the MBR resides outside the disk partitions. More precisely, the MBR is located in the first disk sector. As we learned earlier, the MBR contains either NTLDR, BOOTMGR, or both depending on the Windows OS installed on the server's disk. That then determines the progress of the programs (see *Table 10.1*) that will get executed with the purpose of loading the OS into RAM.

Table 10.1. NTLDR versus BOOTMGR:

NTLDR (Windows NT to Windows Server 2003)	BOOTMGR (Windows Vista to Windows Server 2016)
BOOT.INI	BCD
NTDETECT.COM	WinLoad.exe
NTOSKRNL.EXE	NTOSKRNL.EXE
HAL.DLL	Boot-class device drivers

 In the *Understanding partition schemes* section of `Chapter 2`, *Installing Windows Server*, you can find additional information about the MBR, including information on GPT.

Boot menu (6.1.5)

If you have multiple Windows OSes on your computer, known as **multi-booting**, then every time you turn on your computer you will see a boot menu that lists multiple OSes. If you did not know, this is the `boot.ini` (see *Figure 10.3*), a text file that enables the boot menu display. It works with OSes from Windows NT to Windows Server 2003. Unlike the MBR, boot.ini is located inside the disk partitions. The path to boot.ini is `C:\boot.ini`. `boot.ini` consists of two parts: the `bootloader` and the operating system.

The former includes a timeout value of 30 seconds and the default OS location, while the latter consists of the OSes and their respective boot entries:

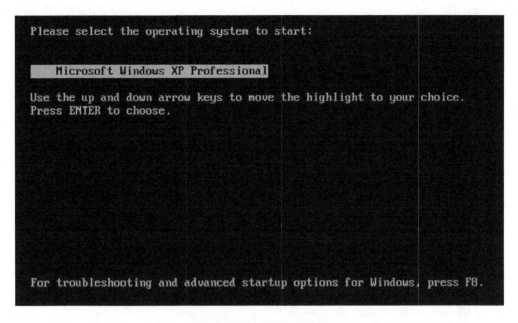

Figure 10.3. Boot.ini displays the list of OSs

Boot Configuration Data (6.1.6)

Boot Configuration Data (BCD) and represents a store consisting of specific files that enables control over what should happen when an OS boots. Bcdedit.exe (see *Figure 10.4*) is a file that is used to manage the BCD data store. In a similar fashion to boot.ini, bcdedit.exe is located inside the disk partitions. It works with OSes from Windows Vista to Windows Server 2016.

In a multiple boot scenario, the MBR contains both NTLDR and BOOTMGR. This means that both `boot.ini` and `bcdedit.exe` are also present to display the respective OS's list. As mentioned earlier, you can use `bootsect.exe` (see *Figure 10.2*) to update the MBR for hard disk partitions in order to switch between NTLDR and BOOTMGR.

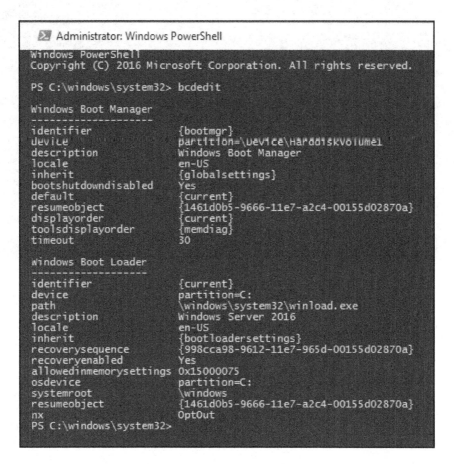

Figure 10.4. Running bcdedit.exe in Windows Server 2016

Power-On Self-Test (6.1.7)

When a server is booted, the BIOS performs a hardware test known as a **Power-On Self-Test (POST)**. The POST is a diagnostic test that verifies that the server hardware is working correctly. Regardless of the BIOS manufacturer, it is good practice to learn the beeps that the POST produces during server hardware initialization. It is recommended to keep an eye on components, such as processors, RAM, and graphics cards, as these are the first three components to be examined by a POST. If any of these are faulty, then your server boot fails.

 You can learn more about various beep codes from different BIOS manufacturers at: https://www.computerhope.com/beep.htm.

Safe Mode (6.1.8)

At some point, you may have experienced your OS not starting when you've tried to turn on your computer. Without thinking too much about it, you might have turned your computer off and on again, and then by pressing the *F8* key, accessed the Windows Advanced Options menu from where you select the **Safe Mode** option. The reason we do this is that **Safe Mode** is Windows, diagnostic mode and uses a minimal set of drivers and services. The *F8* (see *Figure 10.5*) option can be used in the OSes, Windows NT to Windows Server 2003. For Windows Vista to Windows Server 2016, Microsoft offers **Advanced Startup Options** to recover OSes. Regardless, you can access **Safe Mode** with them too, but in other ways.

One of them is explained as follows:

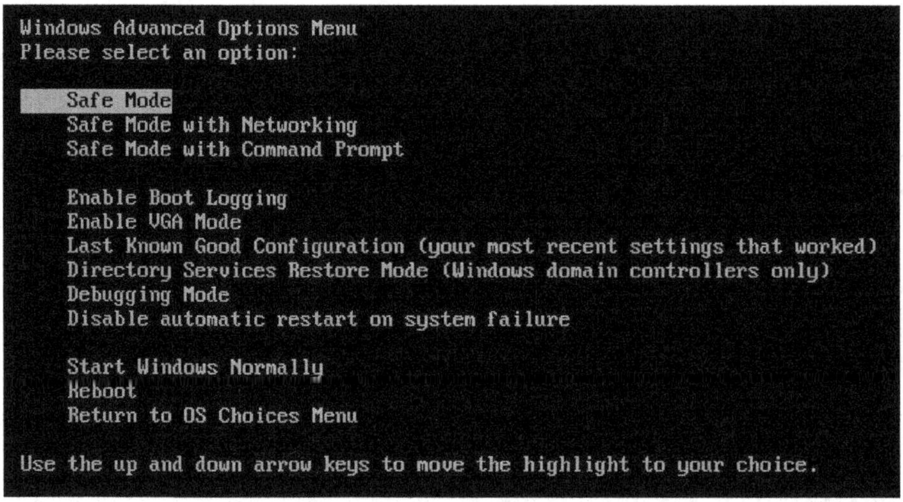

```
Windows Advanced Options Menu
Please select an option:

    Safe Mode
    Safe Mode with Networking
    Safe Mode with Command Prompt

    Enable Boot Logging
    Enable VGA Mode
    Last Known Good Configuration (your most recent settings that worked)
    Directory Services Restore Mode (Windows domain controllers only)
    Debugging Mode
    Disable automatic restart on system failure

    Start Windows Normally
    Reboot
    Return to OS Choices Menu

Use the up and down arrow keys to move the highlight to your choice.
```

Figure 10.5. Windows Advanced Options menu in Windows XP Professional

In Windows Server 2016, complete the following steps to access the **Safe Mode** option from the **Advanced Boot Options** menu:

1. While holding down the *Shift* key, restart Windows Server 2016 by clicking **Restart** from the **Power** option.
2. On the **Choose an option** screen, select **Troubleshooting**.
3. On the **Advanced options** screen, select **Startup Settings**.
4. Click the **Restart** button on the **Startup Settings** screen.

5. Shortly, the **Advanced Boot Options** screen will be displayed as in *Figure 10.6*:

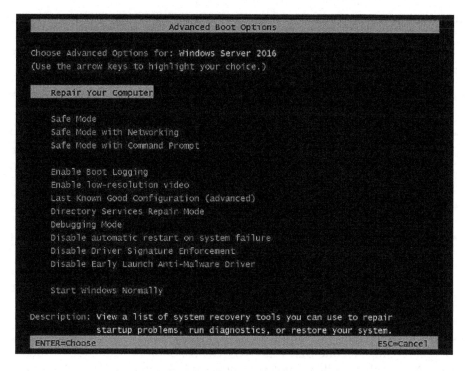

Figure 10.6. Advanced Boot Options menu in Windows Server 2016

In the Advanced startup options section of Chapter 2, *Installing Windows Server*, you can find additional information on how you can access **Safe Mode** in OSes from Windows Vista to Windows Server 2016.

Understanding business continuity (6.2)

In this digital age, as a system administrator, you must understand the fact that all downtime means a loss of profit for the company. So, it is your primary responsibility to minimize downtime as much as possible. That is achieved through proper assessment of the components that have the potential to fail and undertaking the appropriate measures to avoid that.

Backup and restore (6.2.1)

It is hard to think of a server with lost data. To avoid such situations, backups are usually made for making a copy of data in case the original data is lost. In addition to a backup, a restore is the process of data recovery whenever data on a server is lost or corrupted. The following types of backups can be made:

- **Full backup**: It makes a copy of all of the data. To restore data, you need only the last set of full backups.
- **Incremental backup**: It makes a copy of the data that has changed since the last backup, regardless of the type. Usually, from Monday to Thursday, incremental backups are done, and on Friday, the full backup takes place. To restore data, you need the last set of full backups and all of the sets of incremental backups between the full backup and the day you want to restore the data from. Because of that, it takes less time to do the backup, but more time to restore data.
- **Differential backup**: It makes a copy of the data that has changed since the last full backup. The same as incremental, differential backup is done Monday to Thursday, and on Friday the full backup takes place. To restore data, you need the last set of full backups and the last set of incremental backups. Because of that, it takes more time doing a backup, and less time restoring the data.

When it comes to choosing a backup media, usually it depends on the importance and the quantity of data. Storage technologies such as CDs, DVDs, removable HDDs, backup tapes, NASs, and SANs are all considered potential storage technologies for backing up. These days, organizations use online backup services too. Convenience, security, and cost are among the decisive factors for choosing online backup services. Last but not least, it is worth mentioning the most common backup rotation scheme, known as **Grandfather-Father-Son** (**GFS**). The son backup is done daily, the father backup is done weekly, and the grandfather backup is done monthly.

In Windows Server 2016, Windows Server Backup is a feature that can be added by using Server Manager. To add Windows Server Backup, complete the following steps:

1. Press Windows key + *R*, enter `servermanager.exe`, and press *Enter*.
2. From the **Server Manager** console, select **Add Roles and Features**.
3. In the **Before You Begin** option, click **Next**.
4. In the **Installation Type** step, make sure that **Role-based or feature-based installation** is selected, and then click **Next**.

5. In the **Server Selection** option, make sure that **Select a server from the server pool** is selected, and then click **Next**.

6. In the **Server Roles** option there is no need to add roles, thus click **Next**.

7. In the **Features** step, scroll down the list of features and select **Windows Server Backup** (see *Figure 10.7*), then click **Next**:

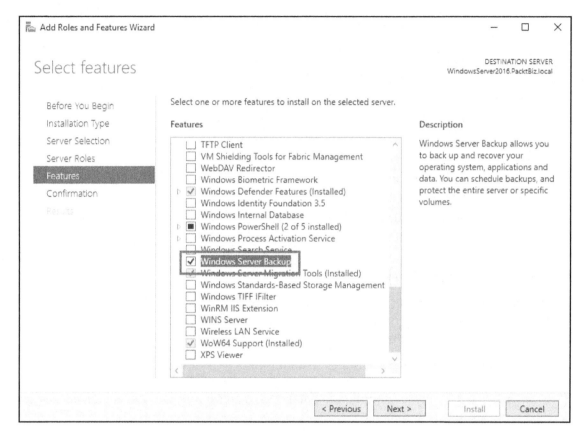

Figure 10.7. Adding the Windows Server Backup feature in Windows Server 2016

8. In the **Confirmation** option, click **Install**.

9. When the installation is complete, click **Close** to close the **Add Roles and Features Wizard**.

Disaster Recovery Planning (6.2.2)

The **Disaster Recovery Plan (DRP)** is a well-structured plan that ensures that the organization will continue to provide services, or soon recover from a disastrous situation. If you take into account the fact that you cannot prevent the unexpected from happening, you can at least minimize losses if you are always prepared. So, in such situations, DRP is known as a proactive method for maintaining business continuity. The following is a list of things that organizations should consider when compiling DRP:

- Make an inventory of hardware and software
- Analyze all potential threats and vulnerabilities
- Establish the organization's priorities
- Define the organization's tolerance in case of disaster
- Review how the disaster was handled in the past
- Acknowledge that staff matters more than data recovery and services
- Execute DRP DRY tests regularly
- Have management approve the DRP
- Never forget to update the DRP

Clustering (6.2.3)

Clustering refers to a group of servers that combine processor power, RAM, storage capacity, and network interfaces to achieve the high availability of services. Clustering recognizes the two most common practices:

- **Fail-over clustering**: It requires a minimum of two servers, and works on the active-passive principle, where one server is active and the other server is passive. Usually, it is applied to databases, mail servers, and in general, backend processing environments.

- **Load-balancing clustering**: It requires a minimum of two servers as well; however, servers are merged into one virtual server exchanging heartbeats. As far as users are concerned, they access a single server; as far as back-end processing is concerned, the loads are distributed between the servers. Usually, it is applied to web servers, and in general, frontend processing environments.

Active Directory restore (6.2.4)

Remember that during the process of adding the AD DS role (in the *Adding the Active Directory Domain Services role* section of `Chapter 4`, *Directory Services in Windows Server*), in one of the steps of the *Active Directory Domain Services Configuration Wizard* the **Directory Services Restore Mode** (**DSRM**) password is required (see *Figure 10.8*). That password is very important for AD restore, so you have to be careful. DSRM is to AD as **Safe Mode** is to the OS. It is a way of restoring AD when the latter has failed or requires restoring. Usually, there are two methods for restoring data that is replicated on a DC. The first method has to do with reinstalling the OS, reconfiguring the DC, and then through normal replication, it will get populated from the second DC on a network. The second method takes into consideration the backup as a way of restoring the DC's replicated data. From that, the replicated data from a backup medium can be restored in the following two ways:

- **Non-authoritative restore**: It is applied in cases where DC has failed because of hardware or software related problems. The AD structure is restored from a backup medium, and then it will get populated from the second DC on a network through normal replication.

- **Authoritative restore**: This takes place after a non-authoritative restore, thus helping to restore the entire system to a state before the AD objects were deleted. It uses the `Ntdsutil` command that enables an authoritative restore of the entire AD:

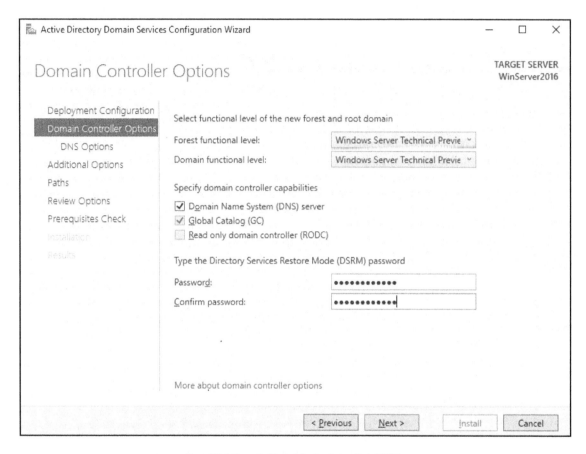

Figure 10.8. Setting up the Directory Services Restore Mode (DSRM)

Folder redirection (6.2.5)

System administrators can use Folder Redirection to redirect the folder on a local computer, or a shared folder on a network, to a new location. With Folder Redirection, the data that is stored on the server will be accessed by users in a similar fashion to how it would be if it was stored on a local computer.

In Windows Server 2016, you can create a GPO as in *Figure 10.9* to redirect a folder. The steps are as follows:

1. Press Windows key + *R* and enter `gpmc.msc` and press *Enter*.
2. Expand **User Configuration**.
3. Expand **Policies**.
4. Expand **Windows Settings**.
5. Expand **Folder Redirection**.
6. Right-click **Documents** and select **Properties**.
7. Select the **Basic - Redirect everyone's folder to the same location** setting.
8. In the **Target folder location** section, select **Redirect to the following location**.
9. Specify the **Root Path** to your redirected folder.
10. Click OK to close the **Document Properties** window:

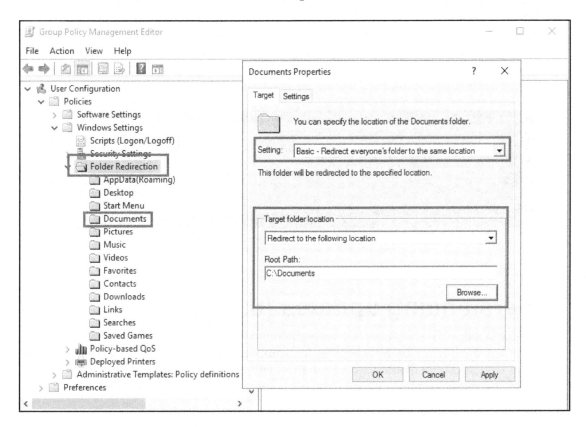

Figure 10.9. Creating a GPO for Folder Redirection in Windows Server 2016

Data Redundancy (6.2.6)

The idea behind Data Redundancy is to be able to store the same set of data in multiple locations and to be able to update them all automatically. But, what if data updates are not successfully implemented? Then, data inconsistency problems occur. That then leads to more problems, causing the problem of data integrity. That multiplies problems with the data and tends to develop into serious problems for organizations that have a large amount of data and multiple data storage locations.

Uninterruptible power supply (6.2.7)

Regardless of the processor power, RAM capacity, data storage space, and network interfaces that your server can have, all that is useless if you have no power supply. This means the power supply is very important for the server's overall well-being. That is why the **Uninterruptible power supply (UPS)** (see *Figure 10.10*) approach has an important place in the world of servers. The UPS is a device with a battery that continues to supply the server with power when a power outage occurs. Despite the capabilities offered by the UPS, it still does not offer a solution for long power outages. For that reason, electric generators represent an alternative solution to overcome such issues.

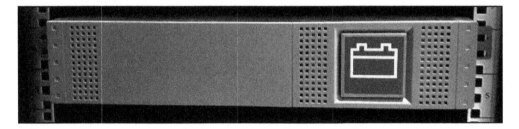

Figure 10.10. Rack-mountable uninterruptible power supply (UPS)

Understanding updates (6.3)

After every Windows installation, it is recommended that you check whether Microsoft Windows Update has any updates to offer for your newly-installed OS. Naturally, through Windows Update, you will add feature enhancements and more importantly - security. Therefore, it is not good at all to neglect or, for whatever reason, compromise the OS update process.

Software (6.3.1)

Regardless of whether your server is running a Microsoft OS, it is normal to use software from vendors other than Microsoft. Therefore, because of that, we must know the difference between the processes of updating Microsoft software and updating software from other vendors. If we assert that each software company is unique, then it can be concluded that updating software from vendors other than Microsoft has its own specific approach. Let us go back to the Microsoft software update process in order to find out what new things Windows Server 2016 has to offer. The steps are as follows:

1. Press Windows key + *I* to open **Windows Settings**.
2. In the **Windows Settings** window, click **Update & security**.
3. Under the **Update settings** section, click **Advanced options**.
4. Select the **Give me updates for other Microsoft products when I update Windows** option as in *Figure 10.11*:

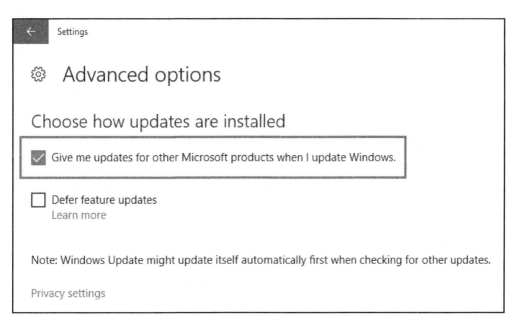

Figure 10.11. Configuring to receive updates for other Microsoft products

5. Close **Windows Settings**.

Drivers (6.3.2)

In the *Updating device drivers* section of `Chapter 3`, *Post-Installation Tasks in Windows Server*, we presented the steps to update your device drivers using **Device Manager**. That is why here, you will be shown how to configure **Windows Update** to check automatically for the latest drivers and updates for your server hardware. The steps are as follows:

1. Press Windows key + *R* and enter **Control Panel** and press **Enter**.
2. Click **Hardware**.
3. Click **Devices and Printers**.
4. From within the **Devices and Printers** window, right-click the name of your server, and then click **Device installation settings**.
5. Select the **Yes (recommended)** option as in *Figure 10.12*:

Figure 10.12. Configuring Device installation settings in Windows Server 2016

6. Click **Save Changes** to close the **Device installation settings** dialog box.

Operating systems (6.3.3)

To update the operating system (in our case, Windows Server 2016) using Windows Update, complete the following steps:

1. Press Windows key + *I* to open **Windows Settings**.
2. In the **Windows Settings** window, click **Update & security**.

3. Under **Update status**, click the **Check for updates** button.

4. **Checking for updates...** rolls on.

5. If Windows Update finds new updates, it will then prompt you to **Install** updates as in Figure 10.13:

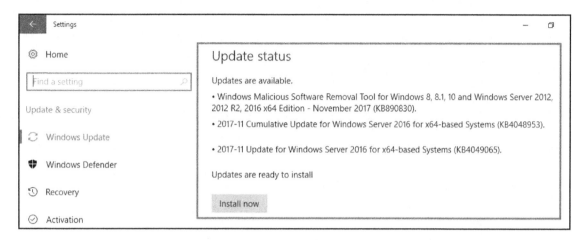

Figure 10.13. Updating Windows Server 2016 using Windows Update

6. In most cases, you need to **Restart** your server for the updates to take effect.

Applications (6.3.4)

Mostly, on Windows-based servers, Windows Update is responsible for updating Microsoft OSs, applications, and utilities. Also, earlier in this chapter, we have explained that software from vendors other than Microsoft is unique in the way it is updated. In that case, we will show you how to update a third-party application (Adobe Reader X) on Windows Server 2016. The steps are as follows:

1. Open **Adobe Reader** from the **Start** menu.

2. In the **Help** menu, select **Check for Updates...**

3. Shortly, the **Adobe Reader Updater** displays that an **update is available for download**.

4. Click the **Download** button.

5. The icon in the System Tray silently downloads the update.

6. Depending upon your internet connection speed, **Adobe Reader Updater** will notify you that the update is ready to install.

7. Click the **Install** button as in *Figure 10.14*:

Figure 10.14. Updating Adobe Reader app on Windows Server 2016

8. You need to close **Adobe Reader** when prompted to do so and click **Retry**.

9. Click **Yes** to confirm that you allow the app to install.

10. When the update is successfully installed, click **Close**.

Windows Update (6.3.5)

Every second Tuesday of each month, unofficially known as **Patch Tuesday**, Microsoft releases new updates, among which are cumulative updates, security patches, and other fixes for their operating systems and applications. Everything is distributed through **Windows Update**. That is the way, from time to time, a notification is displayed on the system tray saying: **You need some updates** as in *Figure 10.15*.

Figure 10.15. Notification in Windows Server 2016 when updates are available

In Windows Server 2016, Windows Update has undergone a slight change in interface and the way it accesses the updates. The following options are available (see *Figure 10.15*):

- **Update history**: It displays the list of updates and their statuses. In addition, you can uninstall updates and access recovery options.
- **Change active hour:** It enables you to set up active hours so Windows Update will not restart your server, even if it requires a restart of the server so that installation of the updates is completed.
- **Restart options**: This enables you to schedule a time to restart your server so that Windows Update finishes installing the updates.
- **Advanced options**: This enables you to choose how updates are installed. You have two choices: *Give me updates for other Microsoft products when I update Windows*, and *Defer feature updates:*

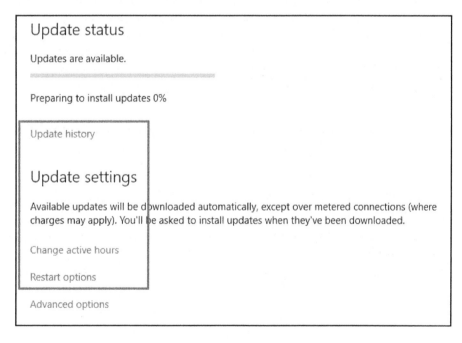

Figure 10.16. Windows Update interface in Windows Server 2016

As you might know, Windows 10 has introduced a new way of updates, known as **Windows as a service**. This means that Windows 10 will constantly evolve, and thus new releases will be delivered through Windows Update. But, what if you do not want to receive these new releases? The option offered by Microsoft is called **Defer feature updates**. You can learn more about this interesting feature at: `https://www.onmsft.com/news/mean-defer-feature-updates-windows-10`.

Windows Server Update Services (6.3.6)

As the successor to **Software Update Services (SUS)**, **Windows Server Update Services (WSUS)** enables system administrators to manage the distribution of Microsoft's product updates to their organization's computers. WSUS works in such a way that its infrastructure enables the downloading of updates, patches, and fixes to an organization's server, and then the server distributes the updates to other computers. Using WSUS, system administrators can approve or cancel the updates, set the installation of updates on a given date, and generate reports to determine which updates for each computer are needed. That way, the organization's computers do not need to refer to Microsoft Update anymore, since updates are provided by WSUS.

In Windows Server 2016, WSUS is a role that is added using Server Manager. Thus, to add the WSUS role, complete the following steps:

1. Press Windows key + *R*, enter `servermanager.exe`, and press *Enter*.
2. In the **Server Manager** console, select **Add Roles and Features**.
3. In the **Before You Begin** step click **Next**.
4. In the **Installation Type** step, make sure that **Role-based or feature-based installation** is selected, and then click **Next**.
5. In the **Server Selection** step, make sure that **Select a server from the server pool** is selected, and then click **Next**.

6. In the **Server Roles** step, select **Windows Server Update Services** as in *Figure 10.17*, and then click **Next**:

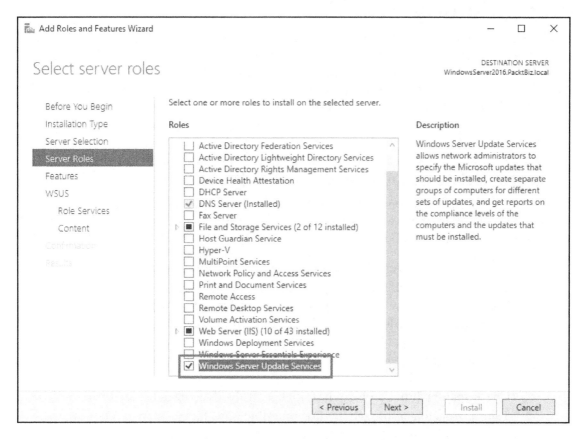

Figure 10.17. Adding Windows Server Update Services (WSUS) in Windows Server 2016

7. In the **Features** step there is no need to add features, thus click **Next**.
8. In the WSUS step, the definition and things to note regarding WSUS installation are presented; click **Next**.
9. In the **Role services** step, **WID Connectivity** and **WSUS Services** are selected by default; click **Next**.
10. In the **Content** step, enter the name of the local or network location where updates are gonna be stored; click **Next**.
11. In the **Confirmation** step, click **Install**.
12. When the installation is complete, click **Close** to close the **Add Roles and Features Wizard**.

Understanding the troubleshooting methodology (6.4)

Troubleshooting in IT is a skill that you are going to master with time, meaning, each time you solve a problem, you gain more confidence, become more experienced, and you establish a knowledge base. That is why learning and practicing means a lot in IT because, while learning how to troubleshoot, you practice troubleshooting at the same time. With that in mind, the more you refine your mastery, the bigger the chances that you will solve problems and overcome issues.

The troubleshooting process (6.4.1)

Among dozens of available methodologies, there exists a six-step troubleshooting model known as the **detect method**, which is used by Microsoft Product Support Services engineers. The steps are as follows:

1. **Discover the problem**: By gathering as much technical information as possible
2. **Evaluate system configuration**: By asking questions to determine if any hardware, software, or network changes have been made recently
3. **List or track possible solutions:** By isolating the problem through removing or disabling hardware or software components
4. **Execute a plan**: Through testing solutions, and at the same time, ensuring that you have a plan B too
5. **Check results**: If the problem has not been solved, go back to step three
6. **Take a proactive approach**: By documenting any changes that you have made while troubleshooting the problem

 You can learn more about the troubleshooting process in general, and the Detect Method in particular, at: https://technet.microsoft.com/en-us/library/bb457121.aspx.

Troubleshooting procedures (6.4.2)

No matter how skillful you might be, know that troubleshooting is a skill that relies on certain guidelines. It requires an organized and logical approach to problems with servers in particular, and computer networks in general. The procedures that you may want to consider when involved in troubleshooting are as follows:

- You may want to consider checking the documentation if the problem has happened in the past
- You may want to check any available logs including the Event Viewer
- You may want to consider searching the Microsoft **Knowledge Base** (**KB**) articles
- You may want to consider running a backup prior to testing solutions
- You may want to consider running diagnostics programs

The tools that you may want to consider when troubleshooting problems are as follows:

- Advance Boot Options menu including Safe Mode
- Windows Repair
- Memory Diagnostics
- System Information
- Device Manager
- Task Manager
- Performance Monitor
- Resource Monitor
- Event Viewer

Best practices (6.4.3)

In the world of IT, best practices are well-defined methods that are applied whenever problems occur. Best practices are basically based on past practices whenever a method has been shown to be successful in solving similar problems. However, the phrase best is relative as the problems are unique too. This means that while the same problem can be solved by the same method in a particular infrastructure, the same does not necessarily apply to another infrastructure. For that reason, in establishing good practices, practices are subject to a process that consists of a number of significant steps that are intended to filter the practices in such a way as to ascertain that they fulfill the criteria to be called best practices. Developing realistic expectations and *But, will it work here?* are two of the steps that are applied to practices in defining a best practice. This has made best practices a feature of well-known accredited management standards such as ISO 9000 and ISO 14001.

So, by following best practices, your servers will run more efficiently, your services will be more reliable, your applications will be more secure, and your infrastructure will be more scalable.

 You can learn more about the ISO 9000 standard at: `http://asq.org/learn-about-quality/iso-9000/overview/overview.html`, and the ISO 14001 standard at: `http://asq.org/learn-about-quality/learn-about-standards/iso-14001`.

Systematic versus specific approach (6.4.4)

In general, the troubleshooting process and problem-solving techniques recognize two methods:

1. **Systematic approach**: An effective troubleshooting methodology because it is based on structured steps toward solving the problem, regardless of the type of problem.
2. **Specific approach**: Based primarily on knowledge and preliminary experience of solving the same/similar problems. In this approach, guesswork comes into play.

Event Viewer (6.4.5)

The **Event Viewer**, as the name suggests, is an MMC snap-in that enables system administrators to monitor events in servers. This feature also makes the Event Viewer a good source of troubleshooting information whenever software, hardware, and network related issues knock on your server infrastructure. From **Application** to **Forwarded Events**, there are five types of logs that you can monitor with **Event Viewer**:

- **Application**: It contains applications or program events
- **Security:** It contains events that are triggered by security-related activities, such as an invalid logon attempt or trying to access a folder with denied permissions. Requires auditing enabled
- **Setup:** It contains applications setup events
- **System**: It contains events that are triggered by Windows system components
- **Forwarded Events**: It contains events that are triggered by remote computers. Requires creating an event subscription

In Windows Server 2016, **Event Viewer** (see *Figure 10.18*) is accessible from Administrative Tools. In addition, you can enter `eventvwr.msc` in the **Run** dialog box to open **Event Viewer**:

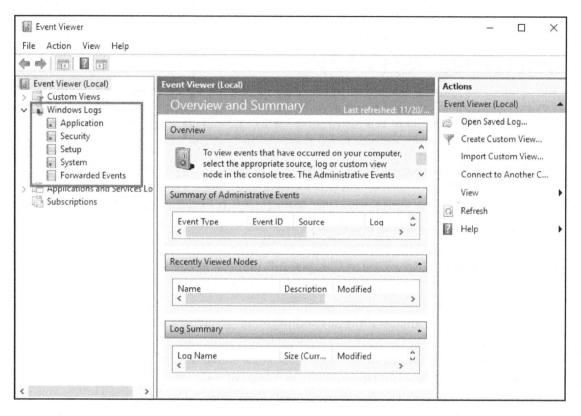

Figure 10.18. Event Viewer in Windows Server 2016

Information Technology Infrastructure Library (ITIL) (6.4.6)

Information Technology Infrastructure Library (ITIL) represents the foundation for IT service management. ITIL, a well-structured framework, consists of best practices that guide IT organizations in designing, implementing, operating, and managing IT services. All of these ITIL practices are presented in the form of publications. At the same time, these publications constitute the ITIL version 3 core books. In summary, ITIL enables you to tailor IT services to business needs, thus making IT an important driver in today's economy.

You can learn more about ITIL at: `https://www.axelos.com/best-practice-solutions/itil`.

Central logging (6.4.7)

One of the strongest reasons behind central logging is to set up the centralized monitoring of event logs. Instead of monitoring the different event logs of each server, you can set up central logging. To do that in Windows Server 2016, you can configure servers in your infrastructure to forward messages to a centralized server. The steps are as follows:

1. On a Remote Server, open **Command Prompt** with elevated admin rights, enter `winrm quickconfig`, and press **Enter**.
2. Right-click the **Start** button and select **Computer Management**.
3. Expand **Local Users and Groups** and click **Groups**.
4. Open the **Administrators** group and Add the Central Server.
5. On a Central Server, open **Command Prompt** with elevated admin rights, enter `wecutil qc`, and press *Enter*.
6. Press *Y* for (Yes) when prompted to do so.
7. From the **Command Prompt** window, enter `eventvwr.exe` to open **Event Viewer**.
8. Right-click **Subscriptions** and select **Create Subscription...**
9. Enter the **Subscription name** and its **Description**.
10. Select **Forwarded Events** as **Destination log**.
11. Select **Remote Server** by clicking **Select Computers...** button as in *Figure 10.19* and click **OK**:

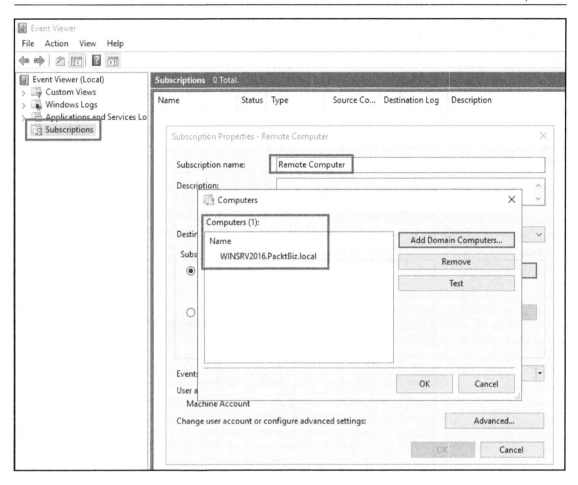

Figure 10.19. Adding Remote Server in order to collect events from

12. In the **Subscription Properties** window, click the **Select Events...** button, and select **Edit**.

13. In the **Query Filter** window, set the Event Logs filtering criteria that you want to collect and click **OK**.

14. Click the **Advanced...** button to make sure that **Machine Account** is the chosen option, and click **OK**.

15. Click **OK** to close the **Subscription Properties** window.

Event filtering (6.4.8)

As you might have noticed, the Event Viewer generates an enormous number of logs. Therefore, to be more pragmatic in finding the right information that would help in overcoming the issues, event filtering becomes part of best practices. However, you have to be very careful when setting Event Logs filtering criteria. Setting the wrong filtering criteria will cause you to get filtered results that will not help you find the right information to overcome the issues. To filter **Event Viewer** logs in Windows Server 2016, complete the following steps:

1. Press Windows key + *R*, enter `eventvwr.msc`, and press *Enter*.
2. Expand **Windows Logs** and select the **log type** that you want to filter.
3. In the **Actions** pane, click **Filter Current Log...** as in *Figure 10.20*.

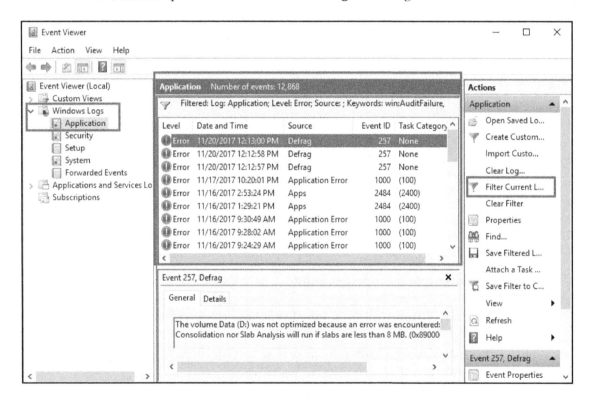

Figure 10.20. Filtering Event Viewer logs in Windows Server 2016

4. In the **Filter Current Log** window, set filtering criteria to get the desired results.
5. Click **OK** to close the **Filter Current Log** window.

Default logs (6.4.9)

The problem with Event Logs is that they consume storage space. Thus, to overcome this issue, you have the option of changing the default logs location. That way, you will be able to increase storage space by relocating the default logs location and avoid the issue of not being able to write event messages to any of the log files due to lack of storage space. To relocate the default logs location in Windows Server 2016, complete the following steps:

1. Press Windows key + *R*, enter `regedit`, and press *Enter*.

2. Locate the following path: `HKEY_LOCAL_MACHINE\System\CurrentControlSet\Services\EventLog\System`.

3. Within the `System` folder, open the `File` value, enter the new path in the **Value data** textbox as in *Figure 10.21*, and click **OK**:

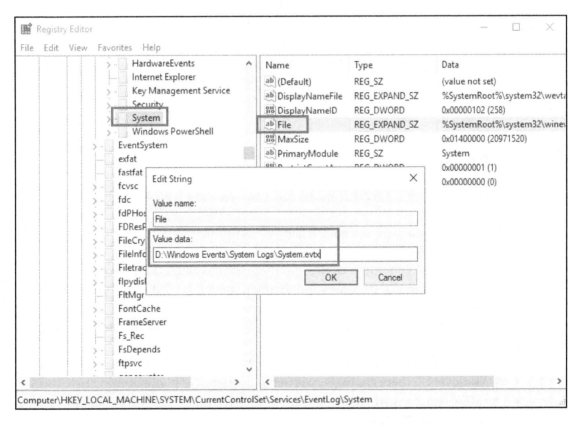

Figure 10.21. Changing the default logs location in Windows Server 2016

4. Locate `HKEY_LOCAL_`
   `MACHINE\System\CurrentControlSet\Services\EventLog\Application`
   to change the default location for Application logs.

5. Locate `HKEY_LOCAL_`
   `MACHINE\System\CurrentControlSet\Services\EventLog\Security` to
   change the default location for Security logs.

6. Close the **Registry Editor** window.

References from Windows IT Pro Center

1. AD DS Troubleshooting (`https://docs.microsoft.com/en-us/windows-server/` `identity/ad-ds/manage/ad-ds-troubleshooting`)

2. Top support solutions for Windows Server 2016 (`https://docs.microsoft.com/` `en-us/windows-server/troubleshoot/windows-server-support-solutions`)

3. WSUS Messages and Troubleshooting Tips (`https://docs.microsoft.com/en-` `us/windows-server/administration/windows-server-update-services/` `manage/wsus-messages-and-troubleshooting-tips`)

Summary

- BIOS is a program that controls the functionality of the server hardware components
- Modern computers do not have legacy BIOS residing in the ROM; instead, they are equipped with UEFI
- Tracks look like concentric circles and there are thousands of them on a disk
- Sectors are the tracks' divisions and their size depends on the file system that the server's OS uses
- A boot sector is the sector on a server's disk that contains the information to boot your server
- A boot loader is a program that loads the OS kernel into RAM
- In Windows OS there are two types of bootloaders: NTLDR and BOOTMGR
- The MBR is created when disk partitions are created too; however the MBR resides outside the disk partitions

- In Multi-booting, every time you turn on your computer, you will notice a boot menu that lists multiple OSes
- BCD represents a store consisting of specific files that enable control over what should happen when an OS boots
- A POST is a diagnostic test that verifies that the server hardware is working correctly
- Safe Mode is a Windows diagnostics mode that uses a minimal set of drivers and services
- A backup is made to take a copy of data in case the original data is lost
- Restoring is the process of data recovery when data on a server is lost or corrupted:
    - A full backup makes a copy of all of the data
    - An incremental backup makes a copy of the data that has changed since the last backup regardless of the type
    - A differential backup makes a copy of the data that has changed since the last full backup
- The most common backup rotation scheme is known as GFS
- The DRP is a well-structured plan that ensures that the organization will continue to provide services, or soon recover if a disaster occurs
- Clustering refers to a group of servers that combine processor power, RAM, storage capacity, and network interfaces to achieve the high availability of services:
    - Fail-over clustering requires a minimum of two servers, and works on the active-passive principle where one server is active and the other server is passive
    - Load-balancing clustering requires a minimum of two servers too; however, servers are merged into one virtual server exchanging heartbeats
- DSRM is a way of restoring AD when the latter has failed or requires restoring:
    - A non-authoritative restore is applied in cases when DC has failed because of hardware or software related problems
    - An authoritative restore takes place after a non-authoritative restore, thus helping restore the entire system to a state before the AD objects were deleted
- System administrators can use Folder Redirection to redirect the folder on a local computer, or a shared folder on a network, to a new location

- The idea behind Data Redundancy is to be able to store the same set of data in multiple locations, and to be able to update them all automatically
- UPS is a device with a battery that continues to supply the server with power when a power outage occurs
- Configure the Windows Update to check automatically for the latest drivers and updates for your server hardware
- Every second Tuesday of each month, unofficially known as Patch Tuesday, Microsoft release new updates among which are cumulative updates, security patches, and other fixes for their operating systems and applications
- WSUS enables system administrators to manage the distribution of Microsoft's product updates to an organization's computers
- The MPSS engineers use a six-step troubleshooting model known as the detect method
- Troubleshooting is a skill that relies on certain guidelines
- Best practices are well-defined methods that are applied whenever problems occur:
    - The systematic approach is an effective troubleshooting methodology because it is based on structured steps to solving the problem, regardless of the type of problem
    - The specific approach is based primarily on the knowledge and preliminary experience of solving the same/similar problems
- The Event Viewer, as the name suggests, is an MMC snap-in that enables system administrators to monitor events in servers
- ITIL represents the foundation for IT service management
- One of the strong reasons behind central logging is to set up the centralized monitoring of event logs
- To be more pragmatic when looking for the right information for overcoming an issue, event filtering becomes part of best practices

Questions

1. A boot sector is the sector on a server's ROM that contains the information to boot your server. (True | False)

2. _____ is an MMC snap-in that enables system administrators to monitor events in servers.

3. Which of the following are troubleshooting methods?
    1. Rational approach
    2. Pragmatic approach
    3. Systematic approach
    4. Specific approach

4. A six-step troubleshooting model known as the detect method is used by Apple Product Support Services engineers. (True | False)

5. _____ is a device with a battery that continues to supply the server with power when a power outage occurs.

6. Which of the following are Event Viewer types of logs?
    1. Application
    2. Security
    3. Software
    4. Driver

7. The DRP is a well-structured plan that ensures that the organization will continue to provide services or it will soon recover in situations when a disaster occurs. (True | False)

8. _____ is a diagnostic test that verifies that the server hardware is working correctly.

9. Which of the following are Windows boot loaders?
    1. NTLDR
    2. BOOTMGR
    3. `BOOT.INI`
    4. `BCDEDIT.EXE`

10. The Basic Input/Output System, known as the BIOS, is a program that controls the functionality of the server hardware components. (True | False)

11. _____ refers to a group of servers that combine processor power, RAM, storage capacity, and network interfaces to achieve the high availability of services.

12. Which of the following are backup types?
    1. Incremental
    2. Differential
    3. Arithmetic
    4. Geometric

13. Discuss the startup process.

14. Discuss the troubleshooting process.

15. Discuss Event Viewer filtering and central logging.

Studying and Passing the MTA 98-365 Exam

This appendix is designed to provide you with an overview of the Windows Server Administration Fundamentals MTA 98-365 exam objectives. However, this appendix does not contain any explanations as to what the MTA 98-365 exam is because, at the end of the appendix, you can find references so that you can learn about the exam. Also, this appendix does not contain suggestions on how to prepare for the exam, or motivational words on how to pass the exam, because we think that such information can also be found on the internet. Regardless, this appendix provides you with the detailed objectives of the MTA 98-365 exam, as well as the chapter reference for each and every objective so you can find more explanations in the book concerning the respective objectives. Last but not least, learn and practice as much as you can with the technology in general, and Windows Server 2016 in particular, because only by doing so will you be able to get the skills to administer Windows Server 2016, and pass the exam without hurdles.

Objective 1—Understanding Server installation (10 - 15%)

To accomplish this objective, the candidate is required to know how to install Windows Server in general, and Windows Server 2016 in particular. Clean installation, upgrade, migration, unattended installation, and installation over network are the installation options that you need to know. The best way to learn these is to practice as much as you can. Then, you must have good knowledge of operating with devices and device drivers, and you should know about the Windows Registry too. When you are confident that you have the skills that are required in this objective, then feel free to move on to the next objective.

Objective 1.1 - Understanding device drivers

This objective may include, but is not limited to:

- **Objective 1.1.1**: Adding devices and installing device drivers (Chapter 3, *Post-installation tasks in Windows Server*)
- **Objective 1.1.2**: Removing devices and uninstalling device drivers (Chapter 3, *Post-installation tasks in Windows Server*)
- **Objective 1.1.3**: Managing devices and disabling device drivers (Chapter 3, *Post-installation tasks in Windows Server*)
- **Objective 1.1.4**: Updating device drivers (Chapter 3, *Post-installation tasks in Windows Server*)
- **Objective 1.1.5**: Rolling back device drivers (Chapter 3, *Post-installation tasks in Windows Server*)
- **Objective 1.1.6**: Troubleshooting a device driver (Chapter 3, *Post-installation tasks in Windows Server*)
- **Objective 1.1.7**: Plug and play (Chapter 3, *Post-installation tasks in Windows Server*)
- **Objective 1.1.8**: **Interrupt request (IRQ)** and **direct memory access (DMA)** (Chapter 3, *Post-installation tasks in Windows Server*)
- **Objective 1.1.9**: Driver signing (Chapter 3, *Post-installation tasks in Windows Server*)

Objective 1.2 - Understanding services

This objective may include, but is not limited to:

- **Objective 1.2.1**: Windows services (Chapter 3, *Post-installation tasks in Windows Server*)
- **Objective 1.2.2**: Working with the registry and services (Chapter 3, *Post-installation tasks in Windows Server*)
- **Objective 1.2.3**: Service startup types (Chapter 3, *Post-installation tasks in Windows Server*)
- **Objective 1.2.4**: Service recovery options (Chapter 3, *Post-installation tasks in Windows Server*)

- **Objective 1.2.5**: Service delayed startup (Chapter 3, *Post-installation tasks in Windows Server*)
- **Objective 1.2.6**: Run As settings for a service (Chapter 3, *Post-installation tasks in Windows Server*)
- **Objective 1.2.7**: Starting, stopping, and restarting the service (Chapter 3, *Post-installation tasks in Windows Server*)
- **Objective 1.2.8**: Service accounts and dependencies (Chapter 3, *Post-installation tasks in Windows Server*)

Objective 1.3 - Understanding server installation options

This objective may include, but is not limited to:

- **Objective 1.3.1**: Windows Server 2016 editions (Chapter 1, *Introducing Windows Server*)
- **Objective 1.3.2**: Understanding partition schemes (Chapter 2, *Installing Windows Server*)
- **Objective 1.3.3**: Advanced startup options (Chapter 2, *Installing Windows Server*)
- **Objective 1.3.4**: Desktop Experience, Server Core, and Nano Server installation options (Chapter 2, *Installing Windows Server*)
- **Objective 1.3.5**: Performing a clean installation (Chapter 2, *Installing Windows Server*)
- **Objective 1.3.6**: Performing an unattended installation (Chapter 2, *Installing Windows Server*)
- **Objective 1.3.7**: Performing installation over a network using WDS (Chapter 2, *Installing Windows Server*)
- **Objective 1.3.8**: Upgrade and migration overview (Chapter 2, *Installing Windows Server*)
- **Objective 1.3.1**: Windows Server 2016 editions (Chapter 1, *Introducing Windows Server*)

Objective 2—Understanding server roles (25 - 30%)

To accomplish this objective, the candidate is required to be able to identify the application servers, to know about web services, understand Remote Access, to know the difference between NTFS and shared permissions, and understand the concept of virtualization in Windows Server. Specifically, you should have good knowledge of each and every role available in Windows Server 2016, and at the same time know how to add them to your server. This objective requires you to know about printers too. When you are confident that you have the skills that are required in this objective, then feel free to move on to the next objective.

Objective 2.1 - Identifying application servers

This objective may include, but is not limited to:

- **Objective 2.1.1**: Mail servers (Chapter 5, *Adding Roles to Windows Server*)
- **Objective 2.1.2**: Database servers (Chapter 5, *Adding Roles to Windows Server*)
- **Objective 2.1.3**: Collaboration servers (Chapter 5, *Adding Roles to Windows Server*)
- **Objective 2.1.4**: Monitoring servers (Chapter 5, *Adding Roles to Windows Server*)
- **Objective 2.1.5**: Threat management (Chapter 5, *Adding Roles to Windows Server*)

Objective 2.2 - Understanding web services

This objective may include, but is not limited to:

- **Objective 2.2.1**: What is IIS? (Chapter 5, *Adding Roles to Windows Server*)
- **Objective 2.2.2**: What is the WWW? (Chapter 5, *Adding Roles to Windows Server*)
- **Objective 2.3.2**: What is FTP? (Chapter 5, *Adding Roles to Windows Server*)
- **Objective 2.2.4**: Separate worker processes (Chapter 5, *Adding Roles to Windows Server*)
- **Objective 2.2.5**: Adding components (Chapter 5, *Adding Roles to Windows Server*)
- **Objective 2.2.6**: Sites (Chapter 5, *Adding Roles to Windows Server*)
- **Objective 2.2.7**: Ports (Chapter 5, *Adding Roles to Windows Server*)

- **Objective 2.2.8**: **Secure Sockets Layer (SSL)** (Chapter 5, *Adding Roles to Windows Server*)
- **Objective 2.2.9**: Certificates (Chapter 5, *Adding Roles to Windows Server*)

Objective 2.3 - Understanding Remote Access

This objective may include, but is not limited to:

- **Objective 2.3.1**: Remote Assistance (Chapter 5, *Adding Roles to Windows Server*)
- **Objective 2.3.2**: Remote Server Administration Tools (Chapter 5, *Adding Roles to Windows Server*)
- **Objective 2.3.3**: Remote Desktop Services (Chapter 5, *Adding Roles to Windows Server*)
- **Objective 2.3.4**: Licensing (Chapter 5, *Adding Roles to Windows Server*)
- **Objective 2.3.5**: Remote Desktop Gateway (Chapter 5, *Adding Roles to Windows Server*)
- **Objective 2.3.6**: Virtual Private Network (Chapter 5, *Adding Roles to Windows Server*)
- **Objective 2.3.7**: Application virtualization (Chapter 5, *Adding Roles to Windows Server*)
- **Objective 2.3.8**: Multiple ports (Chapter 5, *Adding Roles to Windows Server*)

Objective 2.4 - Understanding file and print services

This objective may include, but is not limited to:

- **Objective 2.4.1**: Local printers (Chapter 5, *Adding Roles to Windows Server*)
- **Objective 2.4.2**: Network printers (Chapter 5, *Adding Roles to Windows Server*)
- **Objective 2.4.3**: Printer pooling (Chapter 5, *Adding Roles to Windows Server*)
- **Objective 2.4.4**: Web printing (Chapter 5, *Adding Roles to Windows Server*)
- **Objective 2.4.5**: Web management (Chapter 5, *Adding Roles to Windows Server*)
- **Objective 2.4.6**: Driver deployment (Chapter 5, *Adding Roles to Windows Server*)

- **Objective 2.4.7**: User rights, NTFS permissions, and share permissions (Chapter 5, *Adding Roles to Windows Server*)
- **Objective 2.4.8**: Auditing file servers (Chapter 5, *Adding Roles to Windows Server*)

Objective 2.5 - Understanding server virtualization

This objective may include, but is not limited to:

- **Objective 2.5.1**: Virtualization modes (Chapter 6, *Group Policy in Windows Server*)
- **Objective 2.5.2**: Creating and configuring virtual hard disks (VHDs) (Chapter 6, *Group Policy in Windows Server*)
- **Objective 2.5.3**: Managing virtual memory (Chapter 6, *Group Policy in Windows Server*)
- **Objective 2.5.4**: Setting up virtual networks (Chapter 6, *Group Policy in Windows Server*)
- **Objective 2.5.5**: Checkpoints (Chapter 6, *Group Policy in Windows Server*)
- **Objective 2.5.6**: Physical to virtual (P2V) conversions (Chapter 6, *Group Policy in Windows Server*)
- **Objective 2.5.7**: Virtual to physical conversions (Chapter 6, *Group Policy in Windows Server*)

Objective 3—Understanding Active Directory (20 - 25%)

To accomplish this objective, the candidate is required to have a good knowledge of Directory Services and **Group Policy (GP)** in Windows Server. Specifically, you should be able to add **Active Directory Domain Services (AD DS)** and promote the server to a domain controller, add **Domain Name System (DNS)** roles and understand DNS zones, and know how to access the GPM console and how to enable GPOs in Windows Server 2016. When you are confident that you have the skills that are required in this objective, then feel free to move on to the next objective.

Objective 3.1 - Understanding accounts and groups

This objective may include, but is not limited to:

- **Objective 3.1.1**: Domain accounts (Chapter 4, *Directory Services in Windows Server*)
- **Objective 3.1.2**: Local accounts (Chapter 4, *Directory Services in Windows Server*)
- **Objective 3.1.3**: User profiles (Chapter 4, *Directory Services in Windows Server*)
- **Objective 3.1.4**: Group types (Chapter 4, *Directory Services in Windows Server*)
- **Objective 3.1.5**: Group scopes (Chapter 4, *Directory Services in Windows Server*)
- **Objective 3.1.6**: Group nesting (Chapter 4, *Directory Services in Windows Server*)

Objective 3.2 - Understanding organizational units (OUs) and containers

This objective may include, but is not limited to:

- **Objective 3.2.1**: The purpose of OUs (Chapter 4, *Directory Services in Windows Server*)
- **Objective 3.2.2**: Uses for different container objects (Chapter 4, *Directory Services in Windows Server*)
- **Objective 3.2.3**: Delegating control to an OU (Chapter 4, *Directory Services in Windows Server*)
- **Objective 3.2.4**: Default containers (Chapter 4, *Directory Services in Windows Server*)

Objective 3.3 - Understanding the Active Directory infrastructure

This objective may include, but is not limited to:

- **Objective 3.3.1**: Domain controller (Chapter 4, *Directory Services in Windows Server*)
- **Objective 3.3.2**: Forest (Chapter 4, *Directory Services in Windows Server*)

- **Objective 3.3.3**: Operations master roles (Chapter 4, *Directory Services in Windows Server*)
- **Objective 3.3.4**: Domain versus workgroup (Chapter 4, *Directory Services in Windows Server*)
- **Objective 3.3.5**: Child domain (Chapter 4, *Directory Services in Windows Server*)
- **Objective 3.3.6**: Trust relationship (Chapter 4, *Directory Services in Windows Server*)
- **Objective 3.3.7**: Functional level (Chapter 4, *Directory Services in Windows Server*)
- **Objective 3.3.8**: Namespace (Chapter 4, *Directory Services in Windows Server*)
- **Objective 3.3.9**: Site (Chapter 4, *Directory Services in Windows Server*)
- **Objective 3.3.10**: Replication (Chapter 4, *Directory Services in Windows Server*)

Objective 3.4 - Understanding Group Policy (GP)

This objective may include, but is not limited to:

- **Objective 3.4.1**: Group Policy processing (Chapter 7, *Virtualization with Windows Server*)
- **Objective 3.4.2**: Group Policy Management Console (Chapter 7, *Virtualization with Windows Server*)
- **Objective 3.4.3**: Computer policies (Chapter 7, *Virtualization with Windows Server*)
- **Objective 3.4.4**: User policies (Chapter 7, *Virtualization with Windows Server*)
- **Objective 3.4.5**: Local policies (Chapter 7, *Virtualization with Windows Server*)

Objective 4—Understanding storage (10 - 15%)

To accomplish this objective, the candidate is required to have a good knowledge of storage technologies in general, and each and every storage technology in particular. You should be able to identify different storage types, to understand the concept behind the RAID and know the RAID types, and have a good knowledge of disk types. In addition, you must have a good knowledge of filesystems, being able to perform disk formatting, disk conversion from basic to dynamic, mounting points and virtual disks, and adding DFS roles in Windows Server 2016. When you are confident that you have the skills that are required in this objective, then feel free to move on to the next objective.

Objective 4.1 - Identifying storage technologies

This objective may include, but is not limited to:

- Objective 4.1.1: Advantages and disadvantages of different storage types (Chapter 8, *Storing Data in Windows Server*)
- Objective 4.1.2: ATA, PATA, SATA, and SCSI interfaces (Chapter 8, *Storing Data in Windows Server*)
- Objective 4.1.3: Network-attached storage (Chapter 8, *Storing Data in Windows Server*)
- Objective 4.1.4: Storage area networks (Chapter 8, *Storing Data in Windows Server*)
- Objective 4.1.5: Storage protocols (Chapter 8, *Storing Data in Windows Server*)
- Objective 4.1.6: File-sharing protocols (Chapter 8, *Storing Data in Windows Server*)

Objective 4.2 - Understanding RAID

This objective may include, but is not limited to:

- **Objective 4.2.1**: Types of RAID (Chapter 8, *Storing Data in Windows Server*)
- **Objective 4.2.2**: Hardware versus software RAID (Chapter 8, *Storing Data in Windows Server*)

Objective 4.3 - Understanding disk types

This objective may include, but is not limited to:

- **Objective 4.3.1**: Basic disk (Chapter 8, *Storing Data in Windows Server*)
- **Objective 4.3.2**: Dynamic disk (Chapter 8, *Storing Data in Windows Server*)
- **Objective 4.3.3**: Mount points (Chapter 8, *Storing Data in Windows Server*)
- **Objective 4.3.4**: Filesystems (Chapter 8, *Storing Data in Windows Server*)
- **Objective 4.3.5**: Mounting a virtual hard disk (VHD) (Chapter 8, *Storing Data in Windows Server*)
- **Objective 4.3.6**: Distributed File System (Chapter 8, *Storing Data in Windows Server*)

Objective 5—Understanding server performance management (10 - 15%)

To accomplish this objective, the candidate is required to be able to identify major server hardware components, understand server performance monitoring, and have a good knowledge of logs and alerts. Specifically, you need to have good knowledge of each and every server hardware component in general, and redundant hardware in particular. In addition, you need to have good knowledge of operating with performance monitoring and resource monitoring consoles and understand the importance of logs and alerts in maintaining the servers' performance. When you are confident that you have the skills that are required in this objective, then feel free to move on to the next objective.

Objective 5.1 - Identifying major server hardware components

This objective may include, but is not limited to:

- **Objective 5.1.1**: Processor (Chapter 9, *Tuning and Maintaining Windows Server*)
- **Objective 5.1.2**: Memory (Chapter 9, *Tuning and Maintaining Windows Server*)
- **Objective 5.1.3**: Disk (Chapter 9, *Tuning and Maintaining Windows Server*)
- **Objective 5.1.4**: Network interfaces(Chapter 9, *Tuning and Maintaining Windows Server*)
- **Objective 5.1.5**: 32-bit and 64-bit architecture (Chapter 9, *Tuning and Maintaining Windows Server*)
- **Objective 5.1.6**: Removable drives (Chapter 9, *Tuning and Maintaining Windows Server*)
- **Objective 5.1.7**: Graphic cards (Chapter 9, *Tuning and Maintaining Windows Server*)
- **Objective 5.1.8**: Cooling (Chapter 9, *Tuning and Maintaining Windows Server*)
- **Objective 5.1.9**: Power usage (Chapter 9, *Tuning and Maintaining Windows Server*)
- **Objective 5.1.10**: Ports (Chapter 9, *Tuning and Maintaining Windows Server*)

Objective 5.2 - Understanding performance monitoring

This objective may include, but is not limited to:

- **Objective 5.2.1**: Performance monitoring methodology (Chapter 9, *Tuning and Maintaining Windows Server*)
- **Objective 5.2.2**: Performance monitoring procedures (Chapter 9, *Tuning and Maintaining Windows Server*)
- **Objective 5.2.3**: Server baseline (Chapter 9, *Tuning and Maintaining Windows Server*)
- **Objective 5.2.4**: Performance Monitor (Chapter 9, *Tuning and Maintaining Windows Server*)
- **Objective 5.2.5**: Resource Monitor (Chapter 9, *Tuning and Maintaining Windows Server*)
- **Objective 5.2.6**: Task Manager (Chapter 9, *Tuning and Maintaining Windows Server*)
- **Objective 5.2.7**: Performance counters (Chapter 9, *Tuning and Maintaining Windows Server*)

Objective 5.3 - Understanding logs and alerts

This objective may include, but is not limited to:

- **Objective 5.3.1**: Purpose of performance logs and alerts (Chapter 9, *Tuning and Maintaining Windows Server*)

Objective 6—Understanding server maintenance (15 - 20%)

To accomplish this objective, the candidate is required to be able to identify steps in the startup process, understand business continuity, understand the importance of updates, and have good knowledge of the troubleshooting process. Specifically, you should be able to identify and troubleshoot issues in the startup process, know how to perform backup and restore, understand that performing updates is a proactive approach that helps you to avoid issues, and have good knowledge of the troubleshooting process.

Additionally, you should be aware that downtime is the biggest enemy of servers' high availability, thus equip yourself with the right knowledge that will help you maintain the healthy status of servers. When you are confident that you have the skills that are required in this objective, we have no doubts that you will pass the MTA 98-365 certification exam. So, what are you waiting for? Yes, go and sit the exam and pass it proudly. Good luck!

Objective 6.1 - Identifying steps in the startup process

This objective may include, but is not limited to:

- **Objective 6.1.1: Basic Input/Output System (BIOS)** (Chapter 10, *Updating and Troubleshooting Windows Server*)
- **Objective 6.1.2**: Bootsector (Chapter 10, *Updating and Troubleshooting Windows Server*)
- **Objective 6.1.3**: Bootloader (Chapter 10, *Updating and Troubleshooting Windows Server*)
- **Objective 6.1.4**: Master Boot Record (MBR) (Chapter 10, *Updating and Troubleshooting Windows Server*)
- **Objective 6.1.5**: Boot menu (boot.ini) (Chapter 10, *Updating and Troubleshooting Windows Server*)
- **Objective 6.1.6**: Boot Configuration Data (bcdedit.exe) (Chapter 10, *Updating and Troubleshooting Windows Server*)
- **Objective 6.1.7**: Power-On Self-Test (POST) (Chapter 10, *Updating and Troubleshooting Windows Server*)
- **Objective 6.1.8**: Safe Mode (Chapter 10, *Updating and Troubleshooting Windows Server*)

Objective 6.2 - Understanding business continuity

This objective may include, but is not limited to:

- **Objective 6.2.1**: Backup and restore (Chapter 10, *Updating and Troubleshooting Windows Server*)
- **Objective 6.2.2: Disaster recovery planning (DRP)** (Chapter 10, *Updating and Troubleshooting Windows Server*)

- **Objective 6.2.3**: Clustering (Chapter 10, *Updating and Troubleshooting Windows Server*)
- **Objective 6.2.4**: Active Directory restore (Chapter 10, *Updating and Troubleshooting Windows Server*)
- **Objective 6.2.5**: Folder redirection (Chapter 10, *Updating and Troubleshooting Windows Server*)
- **Objective 6.2.6**: Data redundancy (Chapter 10, *Updating and Troubleshooting Windows Server*)
- **Objective 6.2.7**: **Uninterruptible power supply (UPS)** (Chapter 10, *Updating and Troubleshooting Windows Server*)

Objective 6.3 - Understanding updates

This objective may include, but is not limited to:

- Objective 6.3.1: Software (Chapter 10, *Updating and Troubleshooting Windows Server*)
- Objective 6.3.2: Driver (Chapter 10, *Updating and Troubleshooting Windows Server*)
- Objective 6.3.3: Operating systems (Chapter 10, *Updating and Troubleshooting Windows Server*)
- Objective 6.3.4: Applications (Chapter 10, *Updating and Troubleshooting Windows Server*)
- Objective 6.3.5: Windows Update (Chapter 10, *Updating and Troubleshooting Windows Server*)
- Objective 6.3.6: **Windows Server Update Services (WSUS)** (Chapter 10, *Updating and Troubleshooting Windows Server*)

Objective 6.4 - Understanding troubleshooting methodology

This objective may include, but is not limited to:

- **Objective 6.4.1**: Troubleshooting process (Chapter 10, *Updating and Troubleshooting Windows Server*)
- **Objective 6.4.2**: Troubleshooting procedures (Chapter 10, *Updating and Troubleshooting Windows Server*)

- **Objective 6.4.3**: Best practices (Chapter 10, *Updating and Troubleshooting Windows Server*)
- **Objective 6.4.4**: Systematic versus specific approach (Chapter 10, *Updating and Troubleshooting Windows Server*)
- **Objective 6.4.5**: Event viewer (Chapter 10, *Updating and Troubleshooting Windows Server*)
- **Objective 6.4.6**: **Information Technology Infrastructure Library (ITIL)** (Chapter 10, *Updating and Troubleshooting Windows Server*)
- **Objective 6.4.7**: Central logging (Chapter 10, *Updating and Troubleshooting Windows Server*)
- **Objective 6.4.8**: Event filtering (Chapter 10, *Updating and Troubleshooting Windows Server*)
- **Objective 6.4.9**: Default logs (Chapter 10, *Updating and Troubleshooting Windows Server*)

References for MTA 98-365 exam

1. Windows Server Administration Fundamentals MTA 98-365 Exam, https://www.microsoft.com/en-us/learning/exam-98-365.aspx
2. Windows Server Administration Fundamentals Course, https://mva.microsoft.com/en-US/training-courses/windows-server-administration-fundamentals-8477?l=LaRRbeXz_5004984382
3. Windows Server Administration Fundamentals Exam Profile, http://www.pearsonitcertification.com/articles/article.aspx?p=1713589
4. Windows Server Administration Fundamentals Exam Forum, https://borntolearn.mslearn.net/certification/server/f/512
5. PearsonVUE Microsoft, http://www.pearsonvue.com/microsoft/

B
Examples of GPOs for Sys Admins

There are thousands of policies in **Group Policy** (**GP**), whose main purpose is to configure and manage Windows-based computers. So the following are some of the most commonly used GPOs. Nonetheless, the other purpose of the following examples is to show how the work is done with GPOs.

GPOs of interest to Sys Admins

The following examples are different in content as they include GPOs that control the working environment of both user accounts and computer accounts.

Renaming the administrator account

The following things are set up to rename the administrator account:

1. **Path:** `Computer Configuration\Policies\Windows Settings\Security Settings\Local Policies\Security Options`
2. **Policy: Accounts: Rename administrator account**

3. **Policy Setting:** Define this policy setting by providing new entry

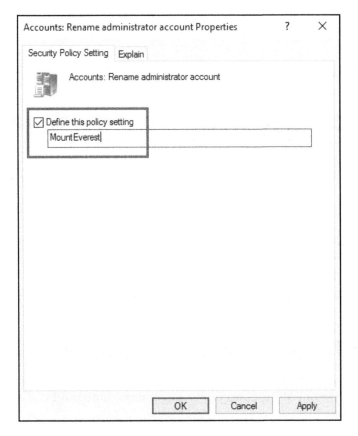

Figure C.1. Renaming administrator account policy

Disabling the Guest Account

The following things are set up to disable the guest account:

1. **Path:** Computer Configuration\Policies\Windows Settings\Security Settings\Local Policies\Security Options

2. **Policy:** Disable the Guest Account

3. **Policy Setting: Disabled**

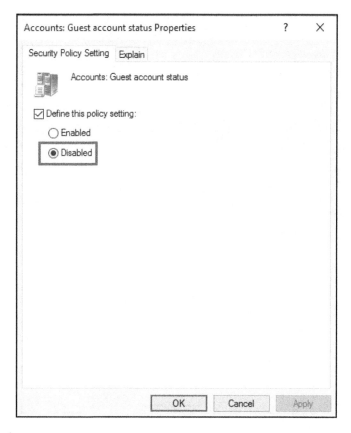

Figure C.2. Disabling Guest Account status policy

LAN Manager authentication level

The following steps can be carried out for LAN Manager Authentication:

1. **Path:** `Computer Configuration\Policies\Windows Settings\Security Settings\Local Policies\Security Options`
2. **Policy: Network Security: LAN Manager authentication level**

3. **Policy Setting: Send NTLMv2 response only\refuse LM**

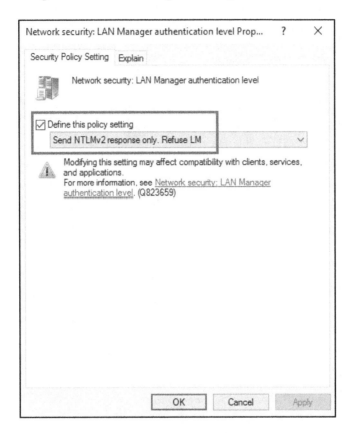

Figure C.3. Disabling LM and NTLM v2 policy

Do not store LAN Manager hash value on next password change

If you are not willing to store the hash value of LAN Manager on next password change, the following can be done:

1. **Path:** `Computer Configuration\Policies\Windows Settings\Security Settings\Local Policies\Security Options`

2. **Policy: Network Security: Do not store LAN Manager hash value on next password change**

3. **Policy Setting: Disabled**

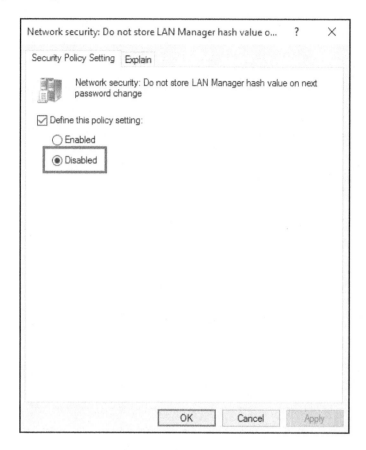

Figure C.4. Disabling LM hash storage policy

Minimum password length

Set the policy for minimum password change using the following steps:

1. **Path:** `Computer Configuration\Policies\Windows Settings\Security Settings\Account Policies\Password Policy`

2. **Policy: Minimum password length**

3. **Policy Setting:** Define this policy setting by specifying the length of password

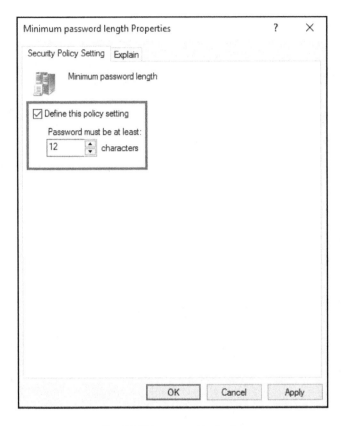

Figure C.5. Minimum password length policy

Maximum password age

1. **Path:** Computer Configuration\Policies\Windows Settings\Security Settings\Account Policies\Password Policy
2. **Policy: Maximum password age**

3. **Policy Setting:** Define this policy setting by specifying the maximum age of password

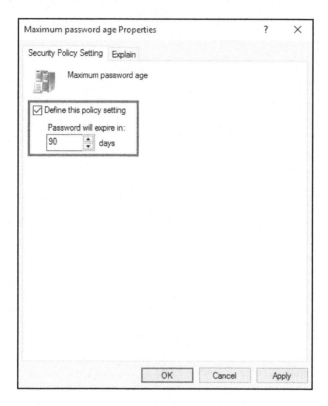

Figure C.6. Maximum password age policy

Blocking Microsoft accounts

To block any Microsoft accounts, go through the following:

1. **Path:** `Computer Configuration\Policies\Windows Settings\Security Settings\Local Policies\Security Options`

2. **Policy: Accounts: Block Microsoft accounts**

3. Policy **Setting: Users can't add or log on with Microsoft accounts**

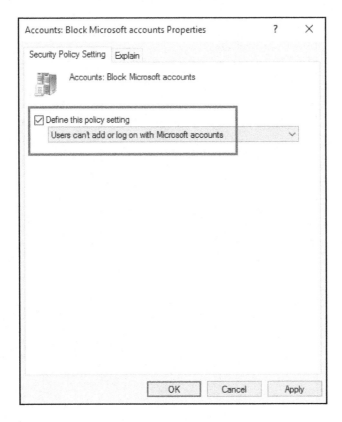

Figure C.7. Block Microsoft accounts

Disabling anonymous SID

To disable anonymous SID do the following:

1. **Path:** `Computer Configuration\Policies\Windows Settings\Security Settings\Local Policies\Security Options`

2. **Policy: Network Access: Allow anonymous SID/name translation**

3. Policy **Setting: Disabled**

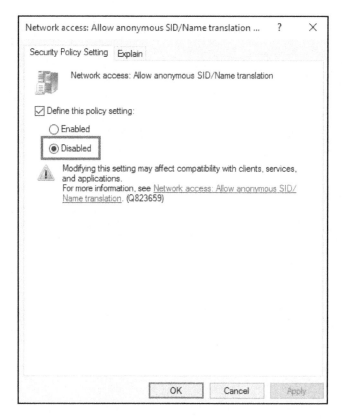

Figure C.8. Disabled: Allow anonymous SID/name translation

Disabling Everyone permissions to apply to anonymous users

To disable Everyone permission follow the steps:

1. **Path:** `Computer Configuration\Policies\Windows Settings\Security Settings\Local Policies\Security Options`

2. **Policy: Network Access: Let Everyone permissions apply to anonymous users**

3. Policy **Setting: Disabled**

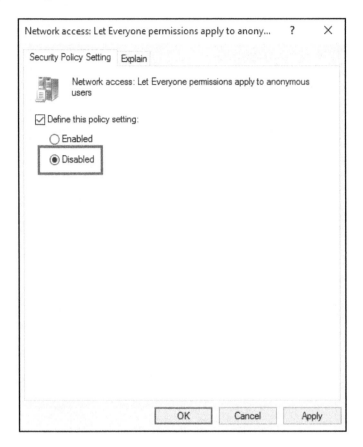

Figure C.9. Disabled: Let Everyone permissions apply to anonymous users

Machine account threshold

To set a machine account threshold, perform the following steps:

1. **Path:** `Computer Configuration\Policies\Windows Settings\Security Settings\Local Policies\Security Options`

2. **Policy: Interactive logon: Machine account lockout threshold**

3. **Policy Setting:** Define this policy setting by specifying the invalid logon attempts

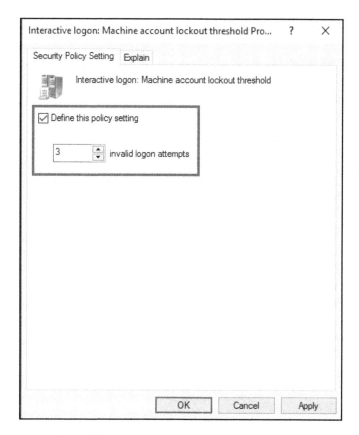

Figure C.10. Machine account threshold

Prohibiting access to Control Panel and PC Settings

To prohibit access to Control Panel settings and PC setting, perform the following steps:

1. **Path:** User Configuration\Policies\Administrative Templates\Control Panel

2. **Policy: Prohibit access to Control Panel and PC Settings**

3. **Policy Setting: Enabled**

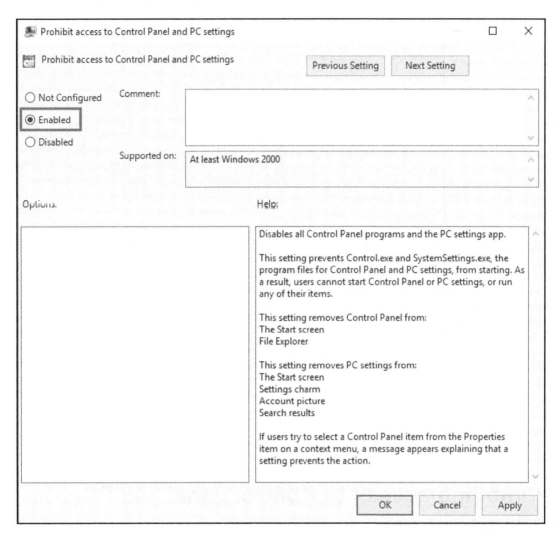

Figure C.11. Prohibit access to Control Panel and PC Settings

Preventing access to the Command Prompt

To prevent access to command prompt, perform the following steps:

1. **Path:** `User Configuration\Policies\Administrative Templates\System`
2. **Policy: Prevent access to the command prompt**
3. **Policy Setting: Enabled**

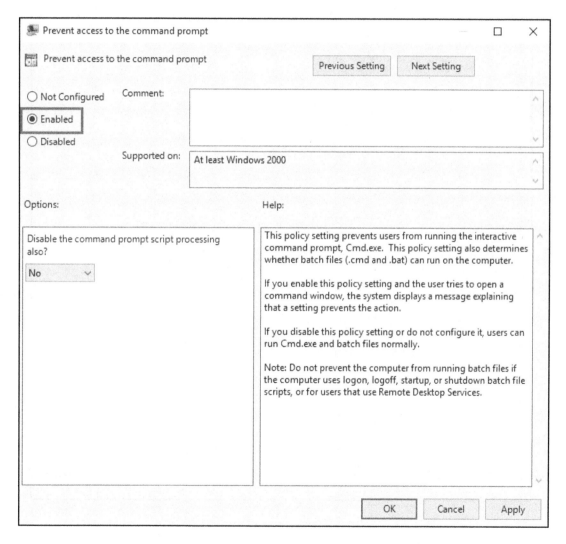

Figure C.12. Prevent access to Command Prompt

Preventing access to Registry editing tools

To prevent access to Registry editing tools, perform the following steps:

1. **Path:** `User Configuration\Policies\Administrative Templates\System`
2. **Policy: Prevent access to registry editing tools**
3. **Policy Setting: Enabled**

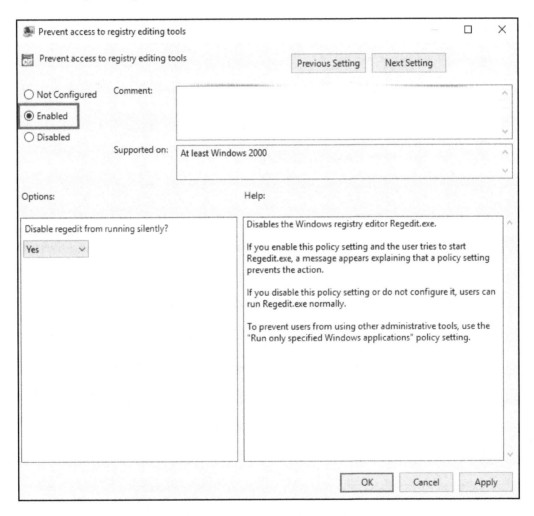

Figure C.13. Prevent access to Registry editing tools

Preventing adding features to Windows 10

To prevent someone from adding features to Windows 10, perform the following steps:

1. **Path:** `Computer Configuration\Policies\Administrative Templates\Windows Components\Add features to Windows 10`
2. **Policy:** Prevent adding features to Windows 10
3. **Policy Setting: Enabled**

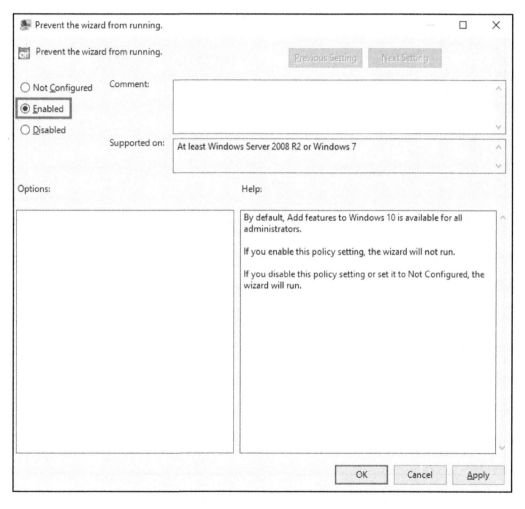

Figure C.14. Prevent adding features to Windows 10

Denying access to all removable media drives

To deny access to all removable media drives, perform the following steps:

1. **Path:** `User Configuration\Policies\Administrative Templates\System\Removable Storage Access`
2. **Policy: All Removable Storage Classes: Deny all access**
3. **Policy Setting: Enabled**

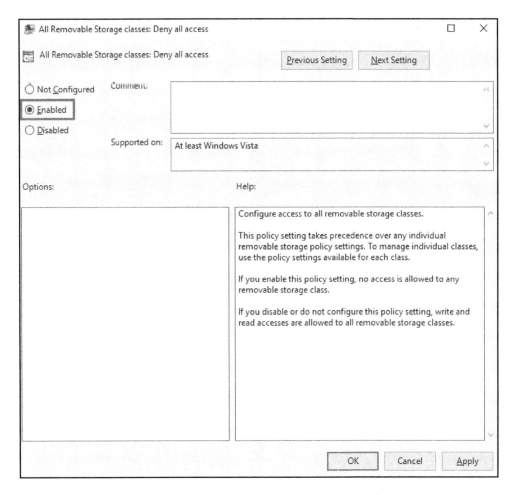

Figure C.15. Deny access to all removable media drives

Turning off Windows Installer

To turn off Windows Installer, perform the following steps:

1. **Path:** Computer Configurations\Policies\Administrative Templates\Windows Components\Windows Installer
2. **Policy: Turn off Windows Installer**
3. **Policy Setting: Enabled**

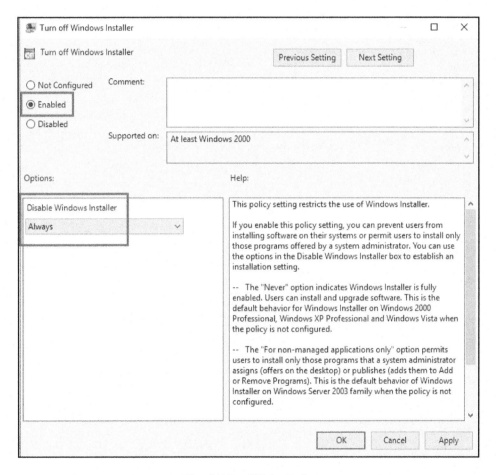

Figure C.16. Turn off Windows Installer

Preventing the usage of OneDrive for file storage

To prevent usage of OneDrive, we perform the following steps:

1. **Path:** Computer Configuration\Policies\Administrative Templates\Windows Components\OneDrive
2. **Policy: Prevent the usage of OneDrive for file storage**
3. **Policy Setting: Enabled**

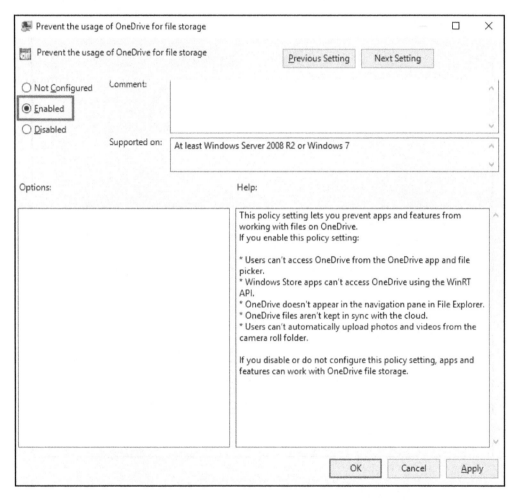

Figure C.17. Prevent the usage of OneDrive for file storage

Removing access to use all Windows Update features

For removing access to use all Windows update features, perform the following:

1. **Path:** `User Configuration\Policies\Administrative Templates\Windows Components`
2. **Policy: Remove access to use all Windows Update features**
3. **Policy Setting: Enabled**

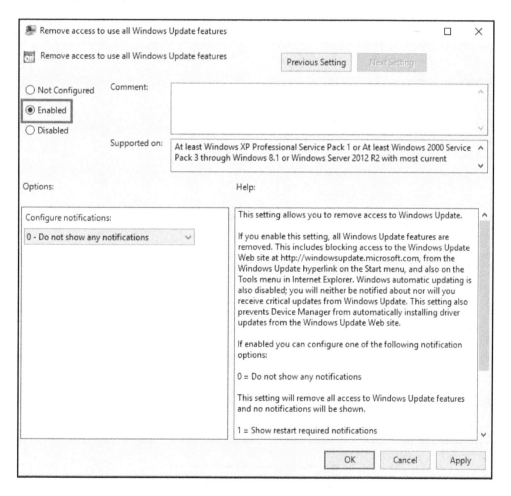

Figure C.18. Remove access to use all Windows Update features

Turning off Windows Defender

To turn off Windows Defender, do the following:

1. **Path:** `Computer Configuration\Policies\Administrative Templates\Windows Components\Windows Defender`
2. **Policy: Turn off Windows Defender**
3. **Policy Setting: Enabled**

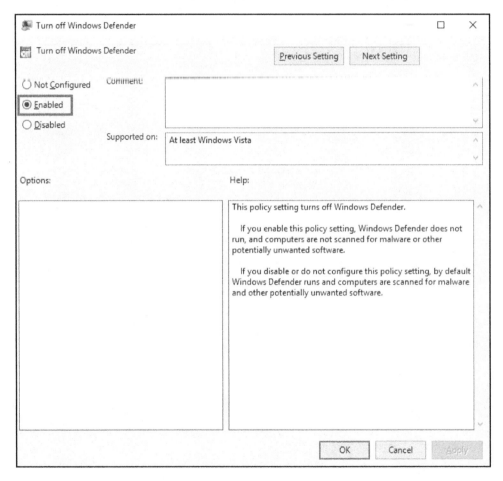

Figure C.19. Turn off Windows Defender

Preventing installation of devices not described by other policy settings

To prevent installation of devices, we do the following steps:

1. **Path:** `Computer Configuration\Policies\Administrative Templates\System\Device Installation\Device Installation Restrictions`

2. **Policy: Prevent installation of devices not described by other policy settings**

3. **Policy Setting: Enabled**

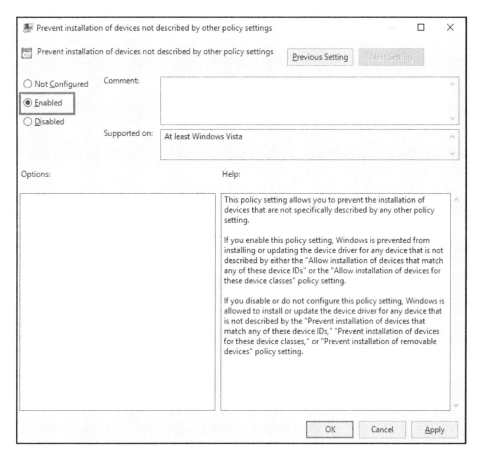

Figure C.20. Prevent installation of devices not described by other policy settings

C

Keyboard Shortcuts in Windows Server

In Windows OSes, besides working with the mouse, there is also the alternative of using a single key or keyboard keystrokes to do something that you would typically do with a mouse.

Windows key combinations in Windows Server 2016

As you might have noticed, here and there throughout the book, keyboard shortcuts are used to accomplish certain actions in Windows Server 2016 without using the mouse. The most common Windows key combinations in Windows Server 2016 are as follows:

- Open or close Start:

  Windows key

- Open Action center:

  Windows key + *A*

- Set focus on the notification area:

  Windows key + *B*

- Display and hide the desktop:

    Windows key + *D*

- Display and hide the date and time on the desktop:

    Windows key + *Alt* + *D*

- Open File Explorer:

    Windows key + *E*

- Open Game bar:

    Windows key + *G*

- Open Share:

    Windows key + *H*

- Open Windows Settings:

    Windows key + *I*

- Open the Connect quick action:

    Windows key + *K*

- Lock your PC or switch accounts:

    Windows key + *L*

- Minimize all windows:

    Windows key + *M*

- Choose a presentation display mode:

    Windows key + *P*

- Open the Run dialog box:

    Windows key + *R*

- Open Search

  Windows key + *S*

- Cycle through apps on the taskbar:

  Windows key + *T*

- Open Ease of Access Center:

  Windows key + *U*

- Open the Quick Link menu:

  Windows key + *X*

- Display the System Properties dialog box:

  Windows key + *Pause*

- Search for Computers:

  Windows key + *Ctrl* + *F*

- Restore minimized windows on the desktop:

  Windows key + *Shift* + *M*

- Open the desktop and start the app pinned to the taskbar in the position indicated by the number:

  Windows key along with the numbers present on the symbol keys

- Open the desktop and start a new instance of the app pinned to the taskbar in the position indicated by the number:

  Windows key + *Shift* + number

- Open the desktop and switch to the last active window of the app pinned to the taskbar in the position indicated by the number:

  Windows key + *Ctrl* + number

- Open the desktop and open the Jump List for the app pinned to the taskbar in the position indicated by the number:

  Windows key + *Alt* + number

- Open the desktop and open a new instance of the app located at the given position on the taskbar as an administrator:

  Windows key + *Ctrl* + *Shift* + number

- Open Task view:

  Windows key + *Tab*

- Maximize the window:

  Windows key + *Up arrow*

- Remove the current app from the screen, or minimize the desktop window:

  Windows key + *Down arrow*

- Maximize the app or desktop window to the left-hand side of the screen:

  Windows key + *Left arrow*

- Maximize the app or desktop window to the right-hand side of the screen:

  Windows key + *Right arrow*

- Minimize all except the active desktop window (restores all windows on the second stroke):

  Windows key + *Home*

- Switch the input language and keyboard layout:

  Windows key + Spacebar

- Change to a previously selected input:

    Windows key + *Ctrl* + Spacebar

- Add a virtual desktop:

    Windows key + *Ctrl* + *D*

- Switch between virtual desktops you have created on the right:

    Windows key + *Ctrl* + Right arrow

- Switch between virtual desktops you have created on the left:

    Windows key + *Ctrl* + Left arrow

- Close the virtual desktop you are using:

    Windows key + *Ctrl* + *F4*

Answers to Chapter Questions

As you have noticed, each chapter is accompanied by a considerable number of questions to help you reinforce the concepts and definitions gained from the book. That said, in the following sections, you can find the answers to chapter questions so you can compare your answers with the answers in the book.

Chapter 1 — Answers

1. False
2. Computer network:
3.
    1. Computers
    2. Servers
4. True:
5.
    1. Windows Server 2016 Essentials
    2. Windows Server 2016 Standard
    3. Windows Server 2016 Datacenter
6. TechNet Evaluation Center:
7.
    1. Blade servers
    2. Tower servers
8. True

9. Node:
10.
    1. Processor
    2. RAM
11. False
12. Peer to Peer (P2P)

Chapter 2—Answers

1. **GUID Partition Table (GPT)**
2. False
3. Nano Server:
4.
    1. **Windows Assessment and Deployment Kit (Windows ADK)**
    2. **Microsoft Deployment Toolkit (MDT)**
5. False
6. A migration
7.
    1. Desktop Experience
    2. Server Core
    3. Nano Server
8. Windows Server 2016 installation files are required to be on DVD media and should be bootable. Same as DVD media, USB flash drive is required to contain the Windows Server 2016 installation and be bootable. Network boot requires setting up a WDS server so that Windows Server 2016 is installed over the network.
9. The clean installation overwrites the existing operating system on a hard disk. The WDS server enables installation over the network. An unattended installation has little or no interactivity with the operating system installation. Tools like the Windows ADK and MDT, provide a unique platform to automate desktop and server deployments. An upgrade replaces your existing OS with a new one. Migration takes place when you bring in a new machine (physical or virtual) and you want to move the roles, features, apps, and settings into it.

Chapter 3—Answers

1. True
2. Plug and Play:
3.
    1. **Interrupt Request (IRQ)**
    2. **Direct Memory Access (DMA)**

4. True
5. Windows Registry
6.
    1. Devices
    2. Device Manager

7.
    1. Services Control Manager
    2. Registry Editor

8. Service account
9. Any changes made to your server are stored in the registry. That said, the *Windows Registry* is a hierarchical database that stores the hardware/software configuration and system security information. After you access the registry, you will notice that its console tree (left-hand side) consists of five registry keys known as hives (that is HKEYs): HKEY_CLASSES_ROOT (HKCR), HKEY_CURRENT_USER (HKCU), HKEY_LOCAL_MACHINE (HKLM), HKEY_USERS (HKU), and HKEY_CURRENT_CONFIG (HKCC).

10. Services are background services that *keep alive* the OS. When accessing services through the Services Control Manager, you will notice that for each service there is a description which helps us understand its purpose. Each service has the following start-up types: Automatic, Automatic (Delayed start), Manual, and Disable.

Chapter 4—Answers

1. True
2. Group nesting:
3.
    1. Roaming Profile
    2. Mandatory Profile

4. False
5. Replication topology:
    1. Global group
    2. Universal group

6.
    1. Global group
    2. Universal group

7. True

8. Domain Controller:
    1. Active Directory Administrative Center
    2. Active Directory Users and Computers

9.
    1. Active Directory Administrative Center
    2. Active Directory Users and Computers

10. True
11. Primary Zone:
12.
    1. Master schema
    2. Domain naming master

13. **Active Directory (AD)**, a Microsoft technology, is a distributed database that stores objects in a hierarchical, structured, and secure format. AD's objects typically represent users, computers, peripheral devices, and network services. Each object is uniquely identified by its name and attributes. DNS has a tree structure (hierarchical) where each branch represents the root zone and each leaf has zero or more resource records. Each zone represents a root domain or multiple domains, and subdomains. A domain name consists of one or more parts, called labels, and these are separated by points (for example, `packtpub.com`). DNS is maintained by a database that uses distributed clients/server architecture where network nodes represent the servers' names.

14. Both **Accounts, Global, Domain Local, Permissions (AGDLP)** and **Accounts, Global, Universal, Domain Local, Permissions (AGUDLP)** are Microsoft's recommendations for effectively using group nesting when assigning permissions.

Chapter 5—Answers

1. True
2. **File Transfer Protocol (FTP)**
3.
    1. Modify
    2. Write
    3. Read
4. False
5. Software port
6.
    1. **Simple Mail Transfer Protocol (SMTP)**
    2. **Post Office Protocol (POP)**

7. True
8. **Secure Sockets Layer (SSL)**
9. 3389
10. False
11. Share permissions
12.
    1. Change
    2. Read
13. Remote Access role in Windows Server 2016 enables remote access to resources inside an organization's network. **Remote Desktop Services (RDS)** enables GUI remote access to computers within an organization's network and over the internet.
14. Users can be allowed or denied access to the objects and this can be said to be related to user rights. Each allowance or denial has certain permissions that determine the type of access to the objects. Share permissions have to do with user access to the shared folders and drives on the network.

Chapter 6—Answers

1. True
2. Hyper-V architecture
3.
    1. Fully Virtualized mode
    2. Paravirtualized mode
4. True
5. **Virtualization Service Providers** (VSP) and **Virtualization Service Consumers** (**VSC**)
6.
    1. Production Checkpoints
    2. Standard Checkpoints
7. True
8. Hyper-V Manager

9.
    1. Hypervisor
    2. Root

10. Nowadays, when virtualization has become the major network service driver, organizations are migrating their **Active Directory Users and Computers** (P2V) for reasons such as cost, ease of management, and future expansion. Thus, knowing that VMs are using VHDs, Microsoft engineers have developed the Disk2vhd app (see *Figure 6.14*) to make the **physical disk drive** (PHD) conversion to the **virtual hard disk** (VHD).

11. Despite the reasons that may stand behind the decision to do **virtual to physical** (V2P) conversion, it is good to remind ourselves, in the technological era that we live in, that the trend is for **physical to virtual** (P2V) conversion. Other than that, it can be said that the hypervisor manufacturers, including Microsoft, will not encourage you to conduct V2P conversions.

Chapter 7—Answers

1. True
2. **Group Policy Management Console (GPMC):**
3.
    1. Enabled
    2. Disabled
4. True
5. **Group Policies (GPs)**
6. Local, Site, Domain, **Organizational Units (OUs)**
7. False
8. Not configured
9. gpupdate /force
10. Computer configuration policies are bound to computers, regardless of the users that are logged on to the computers. User configuration policies are the opposite of computer configuration policies.

Chapter 8 — Answers

1. True
2. **Storage Area Network (SAN):**
3.
    1. **Direct-Attached Storage (DAS)**
    2. **Network-Attached Storage (NAS)**
4. False
5. Disk controller:
6.
    1. **Small Computer System Interface (SCSI)**
    2. **Fiber Channel (FC)**
7. True
8. High Availability (HA):
9.
    1. RAID 1
    2. RAID 5

10. True
11. **Advanced Technology Attachment (ATA)**, also known as **Integrated Drive Electronics (IDE)**:
12.
    1. CD-ROM
    2. DVD-RAM
13. The idea behind the concept of **data deduplication (dedup)** is to provide disk space savings.
14. **Storage Spaces Direct (S2D)** is a new Microsoft feature in Windows Server 2016 that enables you to group disks into storage pools, thus creating software-defined storage called storage spaces.
15. **Distributed File Systems (DFS)** enable the sharing of data from your server in an authorized and controlled way.

Chapter 9 — Answers

1. True
2. Server baseline:
3.
    1. Cache
    2. Cores

4. True
5. Processors and HDDs:
6.
    1. **Network Load Balancing (NLB)**
    2. Network separation
7. False
8. Word size:
9.
    1. Performance Monitor
    2. Resource Monitor

10. True
11. Performance monitoring:
12.
     1. **Random Access Memory (RAM)**
     2. **Read-Only Memory (ROM)**
13. Performance Monitor is a Windows MMC that monitors server performance. Resource Monitor is at your disposal to view the real-time usage of both hardware and software resources.
14. Logs are useful for detailed analysis and the archiving records. Alerts enable you to be vigilant about the performance and configuration of servers.

Chapter 10 — Answers

1. False
2. Event Viewer:
     1. Systematic approach
     2. Specific approach
3. False
4. UPS
     1. Application
     2. Security
5. True
6. POST:
     1. NTLDR
     2. BOOTMGR

7. True
8. Clustering:
     1. Incremental
     2. Differential

9. The **Basic Input/Output System (BIOS)**, is a program that controls the functionality of the server hardware components. Bootsector is the sector on the server's disk that contains the information to boot your server. The bootloader is a program that loads the OS kernel into RAM. The bootloader is located in MBR. In Windows OSes there are two types of bootloaders: NTLDR and BOOTMGR. MBR is created when disk partitions are created too, however, MBR resides outside disk partitions. Multi boot: every time you turn on your computer you will notice a boot menu that lists multiple OSes. **Boot Configuration Data (BCD)** and represents a store consisting of a specific file that enables control of what should happen when an OS boots. POST is a diagnostic test that verifies that the server hardware is working correctly. Safe Mode is a Windows diagnostic mode that uses a minimal set of drivers and services.

10. Among the dozens of available methodologies, a six step troubleshooting model known as "detect method" is used by Microsoft Product Support Services engineers. The steps are: discover the problem, evaluate system configuration, list or track possible solutions, execute a plan, check results, and take a proactive approach.

11. The Event Viewer generates an enormous number of logs; thus, in finding the right information that would help in overcoming the issues, event filtering is used. Setting the wrong filtering criteria will result in getting filtered results that will not help find the right information to overcome the issues. The problems with event logs is that they consume storage space. Thus changing the default logs' locations helps in overcoming the lack of storage space for storing logs. That enables writing event messages to any of the log files due to a lack of storage space.

Index

Made in the USA
Middletown, DE
05 January 2019